News 2.0

News 2.0

Journalists, Audiences, and
News on Social Media

Ahmed Al-Rawi

WILEY Blackwell

Registered Office
John Wiley & Sons, Inc., 111 River Street, Hoboken, NJ 07030, USA

Editorial Office
111 River Street, Hoboken, NJ 07030, USA

For details of our global editorial offices, customer services, and more information about Wiley products visit us at www.wiley.com.

Wiley also publishes its books in a variety of electronic formats and by print-on-demand. Some content that appears in standard print versions of this book may not be available in other formats.

Library of Congress Cataloging-in-Publication Data

Names: Al-Rawi, Ahmed K., author.
Title: News 2.0 : journalists, audiences, and news on social media / Ahmed
   Al-Rawi.
Description: Hoboken, NJ : Wiley-Blackwell, 2020. | Includes
   bibliographical references and index.
Identifiers: LCCN 2020001719 (print) | LCCN 2020001720 (ebook) | ISBN
   9781119569664 (paperback) | ISBN 9781119569640 (adobe pdf) | ISBN
   9781119569626 (epub)
Subjects: LCSH: Social media and journalism. | Mass media–Audiences. |
   Journalism–Technological innovations. | Journalists–Effect of
   technological innovations on.
Classification: LCC PN4766 .A4 2020 (print) | LCC PN4766 (ebook) | DDC
   302.23–dc23
LC record available at https://lccn.loc.gov/2020001719
LC ebook record available at https://lccn.loc.gov/2020001720

Cover Design: Wiley
Cover Images: Social Network © Ani_Ka/Getty Images, Media concept © Vertigo3d/Getty Images

Set in 9.5/12.5pt STIXTwoText by SPi Global, Pondicherry, India

Printed and bound in Singapore by Markono Print Media Pte Ltd

10 9 8 7 6 5 4 3 2 1

To Nawal Namuq with my love and gratitude

Contents

About the Author

Ahmed Al-Rawi is Assistant Professor in News, Social Media, and Public Communication at the School of Communication at Simon Fraser University, Canada. He is the Director of the Disinformation Project, which empirically examines fake news discourses in Canada on social media and in mainstream media. His research expertise is related to global communication, news, social media, and the Middle East, with emphasis on critical theory. He has authored three books and over 50 peer-reviewed book chapters and articles, published in journals like *Information, Communication & Society*, *Online Information Review*, *Social Science Computer Review*, *Social Media + Society*, *Journalism*, *Journalism Practice*, *Digital Journalism*, *International Journal of Communication*, *International Communication Gazette*, and *Public Relations Review*.

Preface

This book provides an analytical assessment of recent developments, debates, and research on news, social media, and 2.0 news organizations. The main argument, which is drawn from empirical evidence, is that news production is largely biased, while news consumers are now mostly confined to their filter bubbles despite the widespread proliferation of news on social media. From the news-consumers side, this often leads to the dissemination of disinformation as well as misinformation, phenomena related to the term "fake news": a phrase deployed with divergent meanings and intentions. This is an important field of research due to its direct impact on democracy and politics, especially with the increasing popularity of clickbait and the influence of bots on Social Networking Sites (SNS).

The book focuses on three main areas, with emphasis on non-Western media outlets: content (news), audiences or "prosumers" (networked audiences), and producers (news organizations and journalists). Prosumers are not only consumers of news but also producers of data (posts and comments) and metadata (clicks) who exhibit their engagement with news organizations and their news productions in different ways. Chapter 1 provides an introduction to the meaning of News 2.0 and the advent of new technologies that are shaping the way news is produced and packaged, while Chapter 8 discusses mobile news: the future of news consumption.

I would like to acknowledge the generous assistance of Simon Fraser University's Rapid Response Fund, which provided the financial means to cover the costs of the copy editor. I would also like to thank Derrick O'Keefe, a graduate student at SFU, for his editorial assistance. Finally, versions of most of this book's materials have been previously published as journal articles, as indicated in each relevant chapter. What motivated me to produce this book is the thematic nature of the previous studies that I conducted using, primarily, computational journalism methods and cross-national comparative research with emphasis on news values theory. This combination of quantitative and qualitative analysis, with a focus on media produced and consumed outside of Europe and North America, remains all too rare. It is my hope that this humble contribution will encourage other research-ers, especially from the global south, to pursue similar projects in the study of international news flows and journalism. Finally, this book is dedicated to my mother as a way to express my gratitude for her love, generosity, and tremendous sacrifices.

1

News 2.0 and New Technologies

"News 2.0" is no longer a new term. It has been in common usage for over a decade (Meikle 2008), but it is more relevant than ever in today's world. I define it as news made, disseminated, and consumed on Web 2.0 outlets, for social media platforms have become so popular for news organizations that they are now indispensable in the news business (Newman et al. 2012; Phillips 2012). Some scholars consider social networking sites (SNS) like Twitter as news media themselves, because of the opportunities they provide for sharing news (André et al. 2012; Hermida 2013; Al-Rawi 2016a,b) and understanding the nature of "quantified audience" (Anderson 2011). In addition, many Internet users find SNS to be far more practical than visiting each news organization's individual website, because it allows them to find their news in one place, largely filtered based on their personalized and unique preferences.

Due to fierce competition and the changing news consumption behavior of people around the world, news organizations realized the need to change their traditional one-way communication strategy by allowing viewers to interact with the news on their websites, which included creating comments sections, allowing users to customize the online platforms according to their own preferences (Chung 2008; Chung and Yoo 2008), and sometimes even publishing readers' online comments in their print versions (McElroy 2013). These were some of the first steps taken by media outlets to broaden their readership, before the meteoric rise of SNS. Later, they created multimedia platforms, in which the news experience is characterized by three main features: portability, personalization, and participation (Project for Excellence in Journalism 2010). Interactive features provided by news organizations include discussion groups, blogs, and forums (Boczkowski 1999; Schultz 2000), which have been described as "demassified forms of feedback" (Lievrouw 2001, p. 21). All of these tools have, on the one hand, enabled journalists to interact with their readers and, on the other, allowed readers to exchange their opinions among themselves (Constantinescu and

News 2.0: Journalists, Audiences, and News on Social Media, First Edition. Ahmed Al-Rawi.
© 2020 John Wiley & Sons, Inc. Published 2020 by John Wiley & Sons, Inc.

Tedesco 2007, p. 449). Many newspapers and TV stations also provide hyperlinks to other topics and stories, enabling journalists to change the news frame in a way that "emphasizes broader social and political themes," since the "[e]xpanded framing may prove central to re-engaging an increasingly distrusting and alienated citizenry in a 21st Century democracy" (Pavlik 2001, p. 320).

What is important here is that news is read and shared much more than before; it has become a social experience (Redden and Witschge 2010, p. 181). Hermida calls this phenomenon "ambient journalism," which refers to "social information networks that provide an asynchronous, lightweight and always-on communication system … enabling citizens to maintain a mental model of news and events around them" (2010, p. 301). Goode notes that, in the world of ambient journalism, news stories are being "amplified, sustained and potentially morphed as they are re-circulated, reworked, and reframed by online networks" (2009, p. 1293). Most commonly, news organizations share hyperlinks to stories posted online in order to direct traffic from SNS to their own websites, where users can comment using their Facebook and Google+ accounts (Goodman 2013, p. 48; Ju et al. 2013, p. 1). In this way, news content can be disseminated "virally" (Stelter 2007, para. 11). Further, SNS offer solutions to news organizations that are less problematic and costly than comments sections, which have become notorious for containing a great deal of incivility (Howell 2007). Braun and Gillespie (2011) call SNS "digital intermediaries," because of their practical functions.

The interactive nature of social media has revolutionized the dissemination of news. The *New York Times*, as early as 2010, recorded people tweeting its articles 17 times per minute, equivalent to one tweet every four seconds (Harris 2010). Around that same time, the Associated Press was believed to attract more audiences to its YouTube channel than its website (May 2010). As for Facebook, in February 2012 it was found to attract higher traffic to the *Guardian*'s website than arrived via online search engines such as Google (Phillips 2012, p. 669). Data on the frequency of readers' visits, the time they spend on a site, their gender and age distribution, as well as the most shared, liked, and commented-on news stories are always important to news organizations (MacGregor 2007). Phillips believes this data "is now increasingly considered necessary to ensure that news is produced in a form that is capable of spreading virally" (2012, p. 669). As a result, many news organizations implement social media guidelines for their employees and hire social media specialists in order to maintain their image and identity and enhance their public relations efforts (Morton 2010; Steyn et al. 2010; Muralidharan et al. 2011, p. 228). Among the first TV stations to use Facebook to enhance its news dissemination was ABC News, which officially partnered with the site in 2007 to allow its users to "electronically follow ABC reporters, view reports and video and participate in polls and debates, all within a new 'U.S. Politics' category" (Stelter 2007). By 2018, CNN, for example, employed around 150 people to tweet the news (Garrison-Sprenger 2008) and used its "Facebook Connect" service to increase its online audiences and make them more connected (Emmett 2009). A study by Messner, Linke, and Eford found that by 2009, 81% of US TV stations had Facebook pages; by 2010, it was 100% (2011, pp. 14–15).

Social media sites themselves have been fiercely competing to attract as many readers as possible in order to guarantee the flow of money from advertisers. Indeed, this advertising revenue has been drained from the news organizations themselves, especially local and small news outlets, which have been greatly impacted by the emergence of social media outlets, forcing many to shut down or downsize. According to a report by the Pew Research Center (2018), newspaper advertising revenues reached their climax in 2005 at over $49.4 billion, but declined precipitously coinciding with the advent of social media to an estimated $11.2 billion in 2017. In other words, social media platforms have indirectly played a major role in downsizing the news industry. Facebook realized early on the importance of news consumption on its platform. In 2015, the company signed a deal with nine famous news organizations, including the *New York Times*, the BBC, and the *Guardian*, in return for a share of the advertising revenues. This deal allows Facebook to host instant news stories on its platform, so users won't need to browse to other websites in order to discover them (Evans 2015). One survey shows that online users consume news on Facebook-recommended pages more than they do pages recommended on Twitter, especially following the introduction of the Facebook Social Reader (Mitchell and Rosenstiel 2012), though this was shut down shortly after launching. While this survey deals with the US audience, it is important to mention the results of a Pew study here, which can provide a general insight into audiences' media habits in other regions. According to this study, about 30% of Facebook users get news onsite; this is higher than for any other SNS, including YouTube (10%) and Twitter (8%) (Pew Research – Journalism Project 2013).

Despite the financial and practical advantages of knowing the demographics and reading habits of online audiences, some communication scholars warn that the increasing obsession with what readers want to read or view can force news outlets into tailoring their stories and reports to fit their audiences' informational needs. In this regard, Shoemaker and Vos assert that "hard data about what readers want to read butts up against the social responsibility canon to give readers what they need to read" (2009, p. 7). Bright and Nicholls agree, and emphasize that while statistics on stories' popularity can be useful, they have also "created worries about the potential for populism online: that editorial judgment [will] be overridden by traffic statistics" (2014, p. 178). This view is bolstered by previous studies on how audience news clicks and online preferences can affect the placement of news stories and other vital editorial decisions in relation to news production and dissemination (Thurman 2011; Lee et al. 2014).

SNS news readers are not always engaged with or interested in everything posted by a news organization, even if they follow its Twitter or Facebook page, and there's no guarantee they will engage with a particular story beyond skimming the headline on SNS. For example, when NPR posted a story titled "Why Doesn't America Read Anymore?" to its Facebook page on April Fool's Day 2014, many online readers commented on it after reading just the headline, not the full story – which of course was the joke (Dickson 2014; NPR 2014). This example sheds light on the kind of weak involvement some online readers have with news, mostly due to time constraints. Yet, this phenomenon is not confined to news stories posted on SNS outlets. Earlier studies showed similar tendencies when it came to print and online media (Garcia et al. 1991; Holmqvist et al. 2003).

The other problematic issue with News 2.0 is that some indicators of popularity may be deceiving because of the use of bots, troll armies, and paid users. In addition, relying on one indicator may not always be a good option when studying News 2.0. For example, the public Facebook pages of news organizations show their number of likes or followers. This can be an important indicator of the popularity of some pages or outlets, but it does not necessarily reflect real engagement with news. To provide a clearer picture, I used Netvizz, a social media mining tool, in mid-2017 to extract data from 26 Facebook pages belonging to different Arabic and English news media outlets. In total, I retrieved the metadata of 157 844 Facebook posts made between January 20, 2010 and April 13, 2017, which generated 326 257 464 reactions. The digital tool has a 10 000-news-stories limitation, and it is not clear whether all or most of the stories were retrieved, so there is a clear research limitation here. Regarding the more than 300 million Facebook reactions, they refer to the total number of likes and emotional reactions (wow, anger, haha, awe, and sad) but do not include the number of comments and shares. A whopping 91 out of 100 of the top posts belonged to Fox News (Table 1.1), despite the fact that its Facebook page has far fewer likes than CNN and the BBC. These top 100 posts got 31 893 875 reactions, which is a useful reminder that researchers have to analyze several indictors before judging the popularity of, and audience engagement with, news organizations and their content.

In this book, I examine News 2.0 on different platforms, approaching the phenomenon from different angles using a variety of digital methods and computational journalism approaches. From the side of content and its producers, I mostly use news values theory to examine differences and similarities in news coverage, providing important insight into the nature of global and regional news flow. There are several studies that examine the comments sections of news sites using, for example, content analysis (Abdul-Mageed 2008; McCluskey and Hmielowski 2012), but there are few empirical studies that have investigated the content of news stories posted on news organizations' SNS channels, especially from a cross-national comparative perspective. Sonia Livingstone outlines the challenges of

Table 1.1 Facebook news pages and frequency of total reactions.

No.	Page	No. of posts	Total reactions
1)	CNN Arabic	9993	739 369
2)	The *Guardian*	3241	1 963 470
3)	The *Independent*	6663	5 737 015
4)	Youm 7 (اليوم السابع)	9995	3 547 479
5)	Al Arabi	7081	1 328 947
6)	*Hufftington Post-Arabi*	8366	2 022 548
7)	RT Arabic	9888	9 198 863
8)	DW Arabic	9965	8 263 656
9)	Fox News	7070	164 201 316
10)	Al Jazeera Arabic	9740	36 529 076
11)	The *Daily Mail*	4195	5 128 176
12)	SkyNews	2166	1 299 939
13)	SkyNews Arabia	9936	10 936 313
14)	France24	1657	107 467
15)	BBC News	3846	7 914 869
16)	DW	7956	827 397
17)	France24 Arabic	856	942 889
18)	RT	537	633 818
19)	XinhuaNewsAgency	9983	1 805 994
20)	The *New York Times*	3128	10 005 958
21)	CNN	5675	20 063 233
22)	CBC News	9981	3 519 474
23)	The *Washington Post*	2283	953 095
24)	Al Jazeera English	3363	2 743 514
25)	BBC Arabic	6755	6 152 507
26)	The *Hufftington Post*	3525	19 691 082
-	**Total**	**157 844**	**326 257 464**

this type of research, but also highlights its many benefits, including "improving understanding of one's own country; improving understanding of other countries; testing a theory across diverse settings; examining transnational processes across different contexts ... etc." (2003, p. 479). This book purposefully uses many non-English and non-Western case studies. For decades, many scholars have been calling for a de-Westernization of journalism, media, and communication research (Park and Curran 2000). Waisbord and Mellado define de-Westernization as follows: "It is grounded in the belief that the study of communication has been long dominated by ideas imported from the West .... Underlying this position is the argument that 'Western' theories and arguments are inadequate to understand local and regional communication processes and phenomena" (2014, p. 362). The main premise behind the de-Westernization trend is not a wholesale rejection of Western theories or media studies, but rather the "enrichment" of the available theories and methods (Wang 2010, p. 3). According to Shelton Gunaratne, de-Westernization should refer to "the addition of multiple approaches to investigate problems in their proper context, so that factors such as culture, environment, ideology and power are not omitted from the theoretical framework or held to be constant (ceteris paribus)" (2010, p. 474). This is an issue on which Wasserman and de Beer principally agree, calling for in-depth theoretical research rather than the mere provision of "descriptive comparative studies of journalism" (2009, pp. 428–429). One of the main problems of mainstream, Western media studies is its limited, Eurocentric and Anglo-American coverage. For example, in their review of previous research done on news sharing, Kümpel, Karnowski, and Keyling surveyed a total of 461 research papers published between 2004 and 2014, and found that there was an obvious focus on studies that dealt with the United States (about 79%), with "only a few that addressed other countries and almost none that discussed possible cultural differences or actually made cross-country comparisons" (2015, p. 10). Kümpel et al. recommend expanding news sharing studies "to multiple countries and cultural settings" (2015, p. 10). This suggestion was echoed by Wilkinson and Thelwall, who recommended examining "international differences in news interests through large-scale investigations of Twitter" (2012, p. 1634). Hanitzsch, among others, has noticed obvious Western bias in the selection of academic research topics, which "giv[es] scholars from the Global North a considerable advantage" (2019, p. 214). Instead of relying on social media data in the English language alone, this book attempts to fill a major gap in the literature by examining data in the Arabic language as posted by a variety of news organizations, allowing a closer examination of international news.

From the perspective of news consumers, I examine a variety of metrics, such as YouTube video views, number of Facebook comments, likes, and retweets. Here, the fact that some stories get viewed, commented on, liked, or retweeted more than others signifies that they are important, since online audiences not only select news articles to read but also disseminate them by liking or commenting on them. This activity can be linked to the concept of produsage (Bruns 2007; Horan 2013) because of its dual nature. According to Facebook, clicking like is an indication that someone is interested in a post or a story, which will also "be posted on [his or her] Timeline" (Facebook 2019), so liking a news story shows engagement and reflects a certain degree of interactivity with the online material. Indeed, human beings may have a variety of motives for viewing, liking, and commenting on social media posts, such as indexing materials in order to consume them at a later stage or showing engagement with certain types of materials in order to express certain political ideas or stances. Facebook likes and comments are similar to retweeting a story or sharing a YouTube video, since a user's preferences can be seen and read by their friends or followers on the site. In this way, the shared, liked, or commented-on news story is more likely to appear on the user's social media timeline, allowing their friends and followers to further engage with the story.

In view of the rapid developments in the news industry and new technologies, I argue here that we have in fact entered the era of "News 3.0," part of "Web 3.0," a term coined by Manuel Castells to refer to "the cluster of technologies, devices, and applications that support the proliferation of social spaces on the Internet thanks to increased broadband capacity, open source software, and enhanced computer graphics and interface, including avatar interaction in three-dimensional virtual spaces" (2011, p. xxvii). Many news organizations have recently employed new technologies in producing and disseminating news, taking advantage of advances in algorithmic, automated, and robo-journalism that often involve the "use of computer software (*Natural Language Generation* [NLG]) to transform data and other material into a story that resembles a piece of human journalism, by following a pre-programmed structure and formula" (Harcup 2014). The *Los Angeles Times*, for instance, was the first newspaper to publish an automated story about an earthquake in 2014 with the help of a robot "journalist." China's Xinhua news agency introduced artificial intelligence (AI) anchors in 2018 that report news non-stop to interested audiences (Kuo 2018). *ProPublica* became the first mainstream media (MSM) organization to create a website on the Dark Web in an effort to diversify its audiences. The *New York Times* later followed its example. Accessing the Dark Web requires installing a browser like Tor, so it is not as straightforward as accessing the Open Web. The author examined *ProPublica*'s website on the Dark Web and found that it looks exactly the same as the one available on the Open Web, but it seems to be for those users who want to maintain their online privacy. Other new methods have been employed, like using 3D technologies in making and disseminating news (e.g. Sky 3D in the United Kingdom), 360-degrees news, and Snapchat (Lichterman 2015). Outlets such as RT Arabic and CNN have developed virtual reality (VR) news to micro-target specific audiences. These and other news organizations have embraced the potential of Web 3.0: innovation fueled by a variety of new technologies, including mobile apps.

Despite all this, news organizations' new practices, as well as the algorithms used by many SNS, do not seem to assist news consumers in being more informed.

Instead, consumers and users are increasingly becoming insulated by focusing on personalized content and sensational entertainment. Another drawback is that some of these new technologies can be used against the interests of the public, such as the phenomenon of "deep fakes," which utilize AI techniques to make fake images and videos look real (Shwartz 2018). The use of online bots or automated accounts can also enhance the problems that exist in spreading fake news on social media (Al-Rawi et al. 2019). The disinformation problem is exacerbated by the reluctance of social media platforms to act effectively and promptly. For example, Facebook promised after the 2016 US election to act fast to end the spread of conspiracy theories by working closely with fact checkers; however, the results were not satisfactory, prompting many fact checkers to quit when the platform did not implement real changes (Levin 2018). Also, these platforms have themselves become a favorite venue from which to launch attacks against the news media by trolls, political parties, and public figures. For instance, the database of Google's Transparency Report, which includes details on political advertising on Google and YouTube, shows hundreds of content items attacking MSM. As of July 2019, almost all such ads in the United States are paid for by US President Donald Trump and his official political campaign. Facebook Ads Archive, which provides details on paid political ads in several countries around the world, turns up the same issue when searching for ads referencing "fake news" in the United States: the highest number of paid ads associating MSM with fake news are posted by Trump and his official campaign, bringing in millions of dollars for Facebook. Unfortunately, this is another way in which social media outlets are assisting in undermining the credibility of MSM, by providing a venue for attacking journalists and news outlets.

In terms of future news research, there are promising opportunities. Mobile news apps are still highly under-researched, especially the means by which audiences interact among themselves in a high-tech version of the comments section. Also, there are many digital tools and online platforms that can be better utilized by researchers for the future study of news. For instance, Facebook Ads Manager is an interesting platform that can be employed to understand the demographics of Facebook news production and dissemination. It can provide detail on international audiences' consumption of news along different variables, including gender, age, geographical location, educational level, ethnicity, interests, and so forth. This tool has recently been employed in many different studies to identify audiences' interests regarding a variety of issues, such as news bias, disease surveillance, migrant monitoring, gender gaps, and schizophrenia awareness, among other things (Araujo et al. 2017; Saha et al. 2017; Zagheni et al. 2017; Fatehkia et al. 2018; Ribeiro et al. 2018). For example, there are 6.7 million users on Facebook, aged from 18 to over 65, who show interest or engagement with the following media outlets: the *Globe and Mail*, ABC News, CNBC, the *New York*

Times, the *Washington Post*, the Canadian Broadcasting Corporation, BBC News, CTV Television Network, CBS News, the *Washington Times*, CNN, Fox Broadcasting Company, NBC, and the *Wall Street Journal*. To give another example, there are over 13 million people worldwide interested in the Fox News channel, including 6.8 million males and 6.8 million females aged between 18 and over 65. Geographically, there are 110 000 users in the United Kingdom, 67 000 in Australia, and 140 000 in Canada interested in this news channel.

There are many other avenues opening up for future research. The GDELT Project, a global media-monitoring database associated with Google Jigsaw, offers some interesting areas of news research, though there are limitations in terms of its thematic and visual classification of news stories. It can be used to examine and test several theories and concepts related to news values, biases, agenda setting, and intermedia agenda setting.

References

Abdul-Mageed, M. (2008). Online news sites and journalism 2.0: reader comments on Al-Jazeera Arabic. *tripleC: Communication, Capitalism & Critique* 6: 59–76.

Al-Rawi, A. (2016a). Assessing public sentiments and news preferences on Al Jazeera and Al Arabiya. *International Communication Gazette* 79 (1): 26–44.

Al-Rawi, A. (2016b). Understanding the social media audiences of radio stations. *Journal of Radio & Audio Media* 23 (1): 50–67.

Al-Rawi, A., Groshek, J., and Zhang, L. (2019). What the fake? Assessing the extent of networked political spamming and bots in the propagation of #fakenews on Twitter. *Online Information Review* 43 (1): 53–71.

Anderson, C.W. (2011). Between creative and quantified audiences: Web metrics and changing patterns of newswork in local US newsrooms. *Journalism* 12 (5): 550–566.

André, P., Bernstein, M., and Luther, K. (2012). Who gives a tweet?: Evaluating microblog content value. In: *Proceedings of the ACM 2012 Conference on Computer Supported Cooperative Work*. ACM.

Araujo, M., Mejova, Y., Weber, I., and Benevenuto, F. (2017). Using Facebook ads audiences for global lifestyle disease surveillance: promises and limitations. In: *Proceedings of the 2017 ACM on Web Science Conference*, pp. 253–257. ACM, June.

Boczkowski, P. (1999). Understanding the development of online newspapers. *New Media & Society* 1 (1): 101–126.

Braun, J. and Gillespie, T. (2011). Hosting the public discourse, hosting the public: when online news and social media converge. *Journalism Practice* 5 (4): 383–398.

Bright, J. and Nicholls, T. (2014). The life and death of political news: measuring the impact of the audience agenda using online data. *Social Science Computer Review* 32 (2): 170–181.

Bruns, A. (2007). Produsage: towards a broader framework for user-led content creation. In: *Proceedings of the 6th SIGCHI Conference on Creativity & Cognition*. ACM, Washington, DC, June 13–15.

Castells, M. (2011). *The Rise of the Network Society*, vol. 12. New York: Wiley.

Chung, D.S. (2008). Interactive features of online newspapers: identifying patterns and predicting use of engaged readers. *Journal of Computer-Mediated Communication* 13 (3): 658–679.

Chung, D.S. and Yoo, C.Y. (2008). Audience motivations for using interactive features: distinguishing use of different types of interactivity on an online newspaper. *Mass Communication and Society* 11 (4): 375–397.

Constantinescu, A.R. and Tedesco, J.C. (2007). Framing a kidnapping: frame convergence between online newspaper coverage and reader discussion posts about three kidnapped Romanian journalists. *Journalism Studies* 8 (3): 444–464.

Dickson, E. (2014). Here's proof that nobody reads stories you post on Facebook. Available from: http://www.dailydot.com/lol/npr-april-fools (accessed November 28, 2019).

Emmett, A. (2009). Networking news: traditional news outlets turn to social networking Web sites in an effort to build their online audiences. *American Journalism Review* 30 (6).

Evans, P. (2015). Facebook's Instant Articles service launches with 9 major Web publishers. *CBC News*. Available from: https://www.cbc.ca/news/business/facebook-s-instant-articles-service-launches-with-9-major-web-publishers-1.3072156 (accessed November 28, 2019).

Facebook (2019). Help Center: how news feed works. Available from: https://www.facebook.com/help/327131014036297 (accessed November 28, 2019).

Fatehkia, M., Kashyap, R., and Weber, I. (2018). Using Facebook ad data to track the global digital gender gap. *World Development* 107: 189–209.

Garcia, M.R., Stark, M.M., and Miller, E. (1991). Eyes on the news. Poyter Institute. Available from: http://www.poynter.org/tag/eyes-on-the-news/ (accessed November 28, 2019).

Garrison-Sprenger, N. (2008). Twittery-do-dah, twittering pays. *Quill* 96: 12–15.

Goode, L. (2009). Social news, citizen journalism and democracy. *New Media & Society* 11 (8): 1287–1305.

Goodman, E. (2013). Online comment moderation: emerging best practices; a guide to promoting robust and civil online conversation. *World Editors Forum*. Available from: http://wan-ifra.org/online_commenting_report (accessed November 28, 2019).

Gunaratne, S.A. (2010). De-Westernizing communication/social science research: opportunities and limitations. *Media, Culture & Society* 32 (3): 473–500.

Hanitzsch, T. (2019). Journalism studies still needs to fix Western bias. *Journalism* 20 (1): 214–217.

Harcup, T. (2014). *A Dictionary of Journalism*. Oxford: Oxford University Press.

Harris, J. (2010). How often is the *Times* tweeted? *New York Times*. Available from: http://open.blogs.nytimes.com/2010/04/15/how-often-is-the-times-tweeted/?_r=0 (accessed November 28. 2019).

Hermida, A. (2010). Twittering the news: the emergence of ambient journalism. *Journalism Practice* 4 (3): 297–308.

Hermida, A. (2013). #Journalism: reconfiguring journalism research about Twitter, one tweet at a time. *Digital Journalism* 1 (3): 295–313.

Horan, T.J. (2013). "Soft" versus "hard" news on microblogging networks: semantic analysis of Twitter produsage. *Information, Communication & Society* 16 (1): 43–60.

Holmqvist, K., Holsanova, J., Barthelson, M., and Lundqvist, D. (2003). Reading or scanning? A study of newspaper and net paper reading. *Mind* 2 (4): 1–17.

Howell, D. (2007). Online venom or vibrant speech *Washington Post*. Available from: http://www.washingtonpost.com/wp-dyn/content/article/2007/05/04/AR2007050401904.html (accessed November 28, 2019).

Ju, A., Jeong, S.H., and Chyi, H.I. (2013). Will social media save newspapers? Examining the effectiveness of Facebook and Twitter as news platforms. *Journalism Practice* 8 (1): 1–17.

Kümpel, A.S., Karnowski, V., and Keyling, T. (2015). News sharing in social media: a review of current research on news sharing users, content, and networks. *Social Media+ Society* https://doi.org/10.1177/2056305115610141.

Kuo, L. (2018). World's first AI news anchor unveiled in China. *Guardian*. Available from: https://www.theguardian.com/world/2018/nov/09/worlds-first-ai-news-anchor-unveiled-in-china (accessed November 28, 2019).

Lee, A.M., Lewis, S.C., and Powers, M. (2014). Audience clicks and news placement: a study of time-lagged influence in online journalism. *Communication Research* 41 (4): 505–530.

Levin, S. (2018) "They don't care": Facebook fact-checking in disarray as journalists push to cut ties. *Guardian*. Available from: https://www.theguardian.com/technology/2018/dec/13/they-dont-care-facebook-fact-checking-in-disarray-as-journalists-push-to-cut-ties (accessed November 28, 2019).

Lichterman, J. (2015). Snapchat wants to slip a little news into teens' social smartphone time. *NiemanLab*. Available from: https://www.niemanlab.org/2015/09/snapchat-wants-to-slip-a-little-news-into-teens-social-smartphone-time (accessed November 28, 2019).

Lievrouw, L. (2001). New media and the "pluralisation of life-worlds". *New Media and Society* 3: 7–28.

Livingstone, S. (2003). On the challenges of cross-national comparative media research. *European Journal of Communication* 18 (4): 477–500.

MacGregor, P. (2007). Tracking the online audience: metric data start a subtle revolution. *Journalism Studies* 8 (2): 280–298.

May, A. (2010). Who tube? How YouTube's news and politics space is going mainstream. *International Journal of Press/Politics* 15 (4): 499–511.

McCluskey, M. and Hmielowski, J. (2012). Opinion expression during social conflict. *Journalism* 13 (3): 303–319.

McElroy, K. (2013). Where old (gatekeepers) meets new (media): herding reader comments into print. *Journalism Practice* 7 (6): 755–771.

Meikle, G. (2008). *Interpreting News*. Hampshire: Macmillan International Higher Education.

Messner, M., Linke, M., and Eford, A. (2011). Shoveling tweets: an analysis of the microblogging engagement of traditional news organizations. Paper presented at the 12th International Symposium for Online Journalism, Austin, TX.

Mitchell, A. and Rosenstiel, T. (2012). The state of the news media 2012: an annual report on American journalism. The Pew Research Center's Project for Excellence in Journalism. Available from: https://www.pewresearch.org/wp-content/uploads/sites/8/2017/05/State-of-the-News-Media-Report-2012-FINAL.pdf (accessed November 28, 2019).

Morton, J. (2010). Staying neutral. *American Journalism Review*. Available from: https://ajrarchive.org/article.asp?id=4837&id=4837 (accessed November 28, 2019).

Muralidharan, S., Dillistone, K., and Shin, J.-H. (2011). The Gulf Coast oil spill: extending the theory of image restoration discourse to the realm of social media and beyond petroleum. *Public Relations Review* 37 (3): 226–232.

Newman, N., Dutton, W., and Blank, G. (2012). Social media in the changing ecology of news: the fourth and fifth estates in Britain. *International Journal of Internet Science* 7 (1): 6–22.

NPR (2014). Why doesn't America read anymore? Available from: http://www.npr.org/2014/04/01/297690717/why-doesnt-america-read-anymore (accessed November 28, 2019).

Park, M.J. and Curran, J. (eds.) (2000). *De-Westernizing Media Studies*. London: Psychology Press.

Pavlik, J. (2001). News framing and new media: digital tools to re-engage an alienated citizenry. In: *Framing Public Life: Perspectives on Media and Our Understanding of the Social World* (eds. S. Reese, O. Gandy and A. Grant), 311–321. London: Routledge.

Pew Research Center (2018). Estimated advertising and circulation revenue of the newspaper industry. Available from: https://www.journalism.org/chart/sotnm-newspapers-newspaper-industry-estimated-advertising-and-circulation-revenue (accessed November 28, 2019).

Pew Research – Journalism Project (2013). News use across social media platforms: social media as a pathway to news: Facebook leads the way. Available from: http://www.journalism.org/2013/11/14/news-use-across-social-media-platforms/2_social-media-as-a-pathway-to-news (accessed November 28, 2019).

Phillips, A. (2012). Sociability, speed and quality in the changing news environment. *Journalism Practice* 6.5 (6): 669–679.

Project for Excellence in Journalism (2010). Understanding the participatory news consumer. Available from: https://www.pewresearch.org/internet/2010/03/01/understanding-the-participatory-news-consumer/ (accessed November 28, 2019).

Redden, J. and Witschge, T. (2010). A new news order? Online news content examined. In: *New Media, Old Media: Journalism and Democracy in the Digital Age* (ed. N. Fenton), 171–186. Thousand Oaks, CA: Sage.

Ribeiro, F.N., Henrique, L., Benevenuto, F., Chakraborty, A., Kulshrestha, J., Babaei, M., and Gummadi, K.P. (2018). Media bias monitor: quantifying biases of social media news outlets at large-scale. In: ICWSM, pp. 290–299.

Saha, K., Weber, I., Birnbaum, M.L., and De Choudhury, M. (2017). Characterizing awareness of schizophrenia among Facebook users by leveraging Facebook advertisement estimates. *Journal of Medical Internet Research* 19 (5): e156.

Schultz, T. (2000). Mass media and the concept of interactivity: an exploratory study of online forums and reader email. *Media, Culture and Society* 22 (2): 205–221.

Shoemaker, P. and Vos, T. (2009). *Gatekeeping Theory*. New York: Routledge.

Shwartz, O. (2018). You thought fake news was bad? Deep fakes are where truth goes to die.*Guardian*. Available from: https://www.theguardian.com/technology/2018/nov/12/deep-fakes-fake-news-truth (accessed November 28, 2019).

Stelter, B. (2007). ABC News and Facebook in joint effort to bring viewers closer to political coverage. *New York Times*. Available from: http://www.nytimes.com/2007/11/26/technology/26abc.html?_r=0 (accessed November 28, 2019).

Steyn, P., Salehi-Sangari, E., Pitt, L. et al. (2010). The social media release as a public relations tool: intentions to use among B2B bloggers. *Public Relations Review* 36 (1): 87–89.

Thurman, N. (2011). Making "The Daily Me": technology, economics and habit in the mainstream assimilation of personalized news. *Journalism* 12 (4): 395–415.

Waisbord, S. and Mellado, C. (2014). De-Westernizing communication studies: a reassessment. *Communication Theory* 24 (4): 361–372.

Wang, G. (2010). Beyond de-Westernizing communication research: an introduction. In: *De-Westernizing Communication Research: Altering Questions and Changing Frameworks* (ed. G. Wang), 1–18. London: Routledge.

Wasserman, H. and de Beer, A.S. (2009). Towards de-Westernizing journalism studies. In: *The Handbook of Journalism Studies* (eds. K. Wahl-Jorgensen and T. Hanitzsch), 448–458. London: Routledge.

Wilkinson, D. and Thelwall, M. (2012). Trending Twitter topics in English: an international comparison. *Journal of the American Society for Information Science and Technology* 63 (8): 1631–1646.

Zagheni, E., Weber, I., and Gummadi, K. (2017). Leveraging Facebook's advertising platform to monitor stocks of migrants. *Population and Development Review* 43 (4): 721–734.

Part I

Content

2

Social Networking Sites and News

Introduction

This chapter deals with news dissemination practice on social networking sites (SNS) and empirically tests the news selection process, examining references to countries and political actors that are linked to newsworthiness, such as the relevance of ideology, social significance, and proximity. In this regard, the criteria followed in news selection are all part of news values theory. References to countries and political actors provide an indication of the general tendencies toward political coverage followed by ideologically diverse news organizations.

Arabic- and English-language stories are examined here because they provide an interesting cross-national comparative perspective. Esser and Hanitzsch argue that the comparative research approach in communication offers "a valuable tool for advancing our understanding of communication processes, and that it opens up new avenues of systematic research" (2012, pp. 3–4). Also, the majority of previous studies on news sharing have dealt with English-language Twitter data, and "tweets or Facebook postings in other languages than English were usually not included in the final sample of content analysis studies" (Kümpel et al. 2015, p. 3); hence, it is recommended to expand such studies "to multiple countries and cultural settings" (Kümpel et al. 2015, p. 10). Wilkinson and Thelwall echo this recommendation to study "international differences in news interests through large-scale investigations of Twitter" (2012, p. 1634).

This chapter is adapted from two previously published papers: Al-Rawi, A. (2017). News values on social media: news organizations' Facebook use. *Journalism*, 18 (7), pp. 871–889, available at: https://doi.org/10.1177/1464884916636142; and Al-Rawi, A. (2017). News organizations 2.0: a comparative study of Twitter news. *Journalism Practice*, 11 (6), pp. 705–720, available at: https://doi.org/10.1080/17512786.2016.1195239.

In the following literature review, an account is provided of the use of social media by news organizations. This is related to the main goal of the chapter, which is focused on examining news posted by outlets on Facebook and Twitter. The chapter empirically investigates online journalism practices by using a large Twitter data set (n = 360 448 news headlines) taken from 12 Arabic and English news organizations. By incorporating a large data set and analyzing headlines from different countries, it offers researchers a method of studying news headlines posted on various outlets' social media that can hopefully be of use in further studies. Despite the international focus of major English-language news organizations like CNN and SkyNews, my research suggests there is evidence that preference in news attention is given to the countries in which these organizations are originally based. The same applies to state-owned media outlets like France24 and Russia Today (RT). Arabic-language outlets show a clear preference for covering events in the Arab world, a not unexpected result that reflects language use that limits the nature of their audiences.

Regarding news on Facebook, the chapter also provides a cross-national comparative perspective of news articles posted by the Iranian Al-Alam TV, the Russian RT, the German Deutsche Welle (DW), and the British BBC. It is important here to provide some background information on each outlet. First, Al-Alam (The World) TV is a 24-hour Arabic channel that is financed and run by the Republic of Iran Broadcasting (IRIB). The channel airs 36 newscasts, both extended and brief, compiled by 50 correspondents stationed in 40 countries. It has four main bureaus – in Tehran, Baghdad, Beirut, and Damascus – and it started broadcasting in February 2003, coinciding nearly precisely with the onset of the US-led invasion of Iraq (Al-Alam 2012). The timing of the channel's launch seems to suggest Iran's need to influence public opinion in the Arab world and to communicate the official Iranian government outlook toward events in the region. Al-Alam's website is in two languages, Persian and Arabic, and it allows readers to post comments. The channel admits that it gives special attention to some important issues in the Islamic world, especially news from Iraq, Iran, Palestine, Lebanon, and certain African states (Al-Alam 2012). According to its goals as published on the website, the channel aims to air "fast, credible, and precise" news, and it claims to seek to provide "solutions to the problems that the Islamic and Arab world is suffering from after investigating their deep roots" (Al-Alam 2012). From the beginning, Iranian authorities installed TV transmitters near the Iraqi border to guarantee that Al-Alam's airwaves would reach a large segment of the Iraqi public. During the US-led invasion of Iraq, the channel played an important role in emphasizing the number of Iraqi civilian causalities, calling the conflict a "war of domination" and routinely referring to coalition forces as "occupiers" (BBC Monitoring 2003). Al-Alam's Facebook page had over 673 k likes and 354 k people talking about it (facebook.com/alalamarabic) as of March 27, 2014.

BBC Arabic television started broadcasting in March 2008, though an earlier iteration of the channel broadcast for about two years in cooperation with Orbit Network beginning in 1994. BBC Arabic TV is part of the BBC public broadcaster organization in the United Kingdom, but it is not as old as the BBC Arabic radio service, which began transmission in 1938. On its website (bbcarabic.com), readers cannot post any comments on news reports; instead, there is the option to "share your opinion" in a special section. In contrast, the news organization seems to freely allow online readers to post their views on Facebook, because it apparently takes no time and effort for staff to moderate the comments on this platform. According to the BBC Arabic website, the news organization is regarded as among the "most credible and objective outlets in the Arab world" (BBC Arabic 2014). Over 21 million people visit it, including about 1.5 million unique visitors. As for its Facebook page, as of 2014 it had over 2.3 million likes and 107 k people talking about it (facebook.com/bbcarabic).

RT Arabic (arabic.rt.com), or Rusiya Al-Yaum, started broadcasting on May 4, 2007. The name of the channel has since officially changed to RT, and it is run by TV-Novosti, which is affiliated with the Russian government. On its website, the channel claims to be "non-commercial and independent," and about 350 million people can view it in the Middle East, North Africa, and Europe (RT Arabic 2014). Unlike BBC Arabic, RT Arabic allows online readers to post comments on its website. As of 2014, its Facebook page had over 2.5 million likes and 242 k people talking about it (facebook.com/rtarabic.ru).

Finally, DW Arabic (dw.de/الرئيسية/s-9106) is part of Germany's public international broadcaster. It was established in 2002. Initially, it aired programs for just two hours per day, extending to six hours in 2011 (DW 2011). The TV channel is not as old as the DW Arabic radio station, which began transmission in 1959. Comments posted on DW Arabic are moderated and controlled. For example, online readers have to fill in and submit a special form in order to be able to post. Since 2011, airtime hours have been further extended. Currently, DW Arabic airs 10 hours of Arabic programs per day in addition to 14 hours in English, reaching viewers in the Middle East and North Africa. According to the DW website, two programs are especially popular in the Arab world, Shababtalk (Youth Talk) and The New Arab Debates, because they involve young Arabs debating politics and social issues (DW 2014). As of March 2014, its Facebook page had over 601 k likes and 31 k people talking about it (facebook.com/dw.arabic).

All of these channels are very different in nature, yet they share one thing in common: the use of Arabic language. Since the 9/11 attacks in the United States, there has been a growing interest among many foreign governments in disseminating media messages to the Arab masses, especially through the use of national cultural industries like television (Straubhaar 1991). Taylor and Snow assert that the "war on terror is essentially a global struggle for hearts and minds, and the media are the principal channels for winning the argument" (2006, p. 400). As a result, many satellite TV channels have emerged that target the Arab world with long hours of Arabic-language programs (Lahlali 2011). It is estimated that the US government spent over 1 billion dollars up to mid-2013 on running a single Arabic-language channel, Al-Hurra TV (Seib 2013, p. 11). It seems that the majority of such channels gained popularity because they offered news insights into events taking place around the world while also covering important issues and topics in the Arab region, competing with other Pan-Arab channels like Al Jazeera and Al Arabiya (El-Nawawy 2006). Most of these channels, including BBC Arabic, provided platforms for participation and debate among Arab audiences (Hill and Alshaer 2010), and many of them have gained credibility due to the timely and professional manner in which their news is produced (Elareshi and Gunter 2012; Al-Jaber and Gunter 2013). Indeed, these channels are used as tools for public diplomacy "as part of the ongoing political rivalry in the region" by serving the various economic, cultural, and political interests, as well as the foreign policies, of the non-Arab governments that run them (Hill and Alshaer 2010; Mellor et al. 2011, p. 96).

Facebook has been chosen for this news investigation because of its great importance as an SNS tool for reading and commenting on news. When SNS users like a Facebook page that belongs to a news organization, they begin receiving its news feeds. This is regarded as a new kind of news subscription (Ju et al. 2013, p. 4). The following section includes a discussion of news values and ideology and of news organizations' SNS use, because these are directly linked to the focus of this chapter: the news selection process on SNS, which is another under-researched area in journalism and media studies.

News Values and Social Media News

Since this chapter deals with the concept of news values, it is important to begin the discussion with one of the first studies in this field. This research relied on the pioneering work of Galtung and Ruge's (1965) classic taxonomy of news, in which Harcup and O'Neill proposed a set of 10 news values criteria: the power elite, celebrity, entertainment, surprise, bad news, good news, magnitude, relevance, follow-up, and newspaper agenda (2001, p. 279; see also Brighton and Foy 2007). The political and cultural dimensions of this taxonomy can both be linked to ideology that is relevant to this chapter.

In their hierarchical model of news values, Shoemaker and Reese (1996) explained that news is influenced by several factors, including routine newsroom practices and the ideological values adhered to by journalists and their news organization. In their more developed theory, Shoemaker and Cohen (2006) focused on the elements of deviance intensity and social significance to explain newsworthiness. The former is classified into three main types: statistical, social change, and normative; while the latter is defined as "relevance for the social system" in relation to four dimensions: political, economic, cultural, and public (Shoemaker and Cohen 2006, pp. 7, 15, and 49). In these two models, there is a clear focus on the impact of the relevant context and ideological values on newsworthiness as they apparently encompass political and religious attitudes and stances that can explain the newsworthiness measures followed by some news organizations. Indeed, ideology largely influences and shapes the way news organizations and journalists function; this is described as news ideology (Jensen 1987). In this regard, Schudson discusses ideology by emphasizing that it involves "the cultural knowledge that constitutes news judgment" (2002). In other words, ideology largely determines the ways in which news organizations pay attention to, or ignore, certain countries, people, and events.

Adams (1986) examined how proximity in the news can be an important indicator of newsworthiness, especially in terms of the economic, political, and cultural ties that connect nations together. This seems to be related to people's beliefs and general interests. Cohen et al. (1990) refer to a similar concept called psychological proximity, where people have "zones of relevance" that they use to determine the relative importance of news to their lives. This, of course, applies to journalists' decisions in the news selection process as well. These zones of relevance can be of various kinds, including sharing certain political, religious, or cultural beliefs and values. In other words, countries and nations tend to be newsworthy for those countries and nations that share similar ideologies or cultural values.

Indeed, news organizations cannot escape the influence of certain ideologies. Thompson emphasizes that ideology is a "meaning in the service of power" (1990, p. 7), which can explain how news organizations sometimes become tools used by their owners to convey certain messages. This is in line with Herman and Chomsky's (2008) propaganda model, in which one of the main news filters is media ownership. On the other hand, journalists themselves must be influenced by their own ideology, even if they have not noticed it. Stuart Hall affirms that journalists are "inscribed by an ideology to which they do not consciously commit themselves, and which, instead, 'writes them'" (1985, p. 101).

Finally, and in relation to international news differences, Cohen et al. argue that studying foreign or international news is very important given the increasing role of globalization in our modern world (2013, p. xix). Global broadcasters like CCTV, France24, the BBC, and CNN "all send their signals around the globe" and are "gaining in popularity, mostly among young adults in some countries" (Cohen et al. 2013, p. xx). Further, Cohen et al. (2013) discuss how foreign news is becoming an increasingly important field of comparative communication research. They suggest that studying foreign news is important as it is one way of distinguishing foreign from domestic news based on the location of events – yet, such a distinction is always dependent on the audience receiving the news (Cohen et al. 2013, pp. 3 and 6). They classify news into four types, based on location (foreign or domestic) and involvement (foreign or domestic) (Cohen et al. 2013, p. 8). Wu, in his study of systematic determinants of international news coverage in 38 countries, found that the United States is the most reported-on country and that "traits of nations, magnitude of interaction and relatedness between nations, and logistics of news gathering" largely determine the news selection process (2000, p. 110).

Researching News on Facebook and Twitter

In terms of method, a webometric tool called NVivo 10 – N-Capture was used to mine the Facebook posts of the Arabic-language TV channels Al-Alam TV (Iranian), RT (Russian), DW (German), and the BBC (British) in late February 2014. These channels were chosen because they represent a broad spectrum of foreign channels broadcasting to the Arab world in the Arabic language, so it is relevant to compare them, especially given that the journalists working at these stations presumably have diverse ideological backgrounds due to the different political and media systems in which they live. For example, Al-Alam TV is run by a government characterized by its totalitarian rule, which maintains a tight control over the media (Semati 2007, p. 144); hence, Al-Alam is used as a state instrument to influence the opinions of Arab masses. Similarly, RT is regarded as a propaganda tool serving the foreign-policy interests of Putin's government (Ioffe 2010). In contrast, the BBC and DW are both regarded as public broadcasting services, seen as more independent from their respective governments, and originate from well-established Western democracies.

In most cases, the Facebook page administrator posts the news headline, a hyperlink that leads to the online article on the news organization's website, and a blurb containing a brief description of the article. In some cases, a video link or photo accompanies them. Based on a cross examination of a random sample of over 160 news stories posted on the four Facebook pages, it appears that all the headlines and blurbs are typical of what is found on the websites themselves, since the Facebook page administrators copy and paste the original materials without altering them. If any online reader feels interested in a news report, he or she can click the hyperlink leading to the complete version posted on the website.

This chapter examines all the news articles posted on Facebook from mid-December 2013 until mid-February 2014. The news stories that are studied include 822 by DW, 1040 by the BBC, 5741 by RT, and 7986 by Al-Alam; the total number of news stories investigated in this chapter is 15 589, all in Arabic language. The

US State Department's Arabic channel, Al-Hurra TV, was initially chosen, but its Facebook page contained mostly questions for its online audience, so it was excluded from the chapter.

The collected posts were analyzed using QDA Miner 4 – WordStat, with the most recurrent words being identified (Al-Rawi 2014, 2015). Stephen studied concept analysis by "identifying key concepts and clusters of concepts" and examining "the analysis of the distribution and interconnection of pivotal ideas appearing in a textual database" (2000, p. 197). In some of his framing studies, Entman used QDA Miner, which he mentioned was useful due to its "improved efficiency in carrying our more complex content analyses" (2010, p. 334). This quantitative method is useful in identifying the most dominant words used by posters, which "minimizes problems of research judgment" (Miller 1997, p. 376).

In this chapter, two main news selections were made. First, I examined the most recurrent words based on a repetition of three times or more; all references to countries, their capitals, and any derivation of the countries' name like their different adjectives were counted. This was part of the news values study, used to determine which countries were most prominent in the news reports. The names of countries' capitals were incorporated because in some cases the reference to the capital was used as a metonym, standing for the government or state as a whole. In the end, the top 10 most-referenced countries were identified, as shown in Table 2.1. Second, I examined the number of references to politicians or political actors. As a great number were mentioned, I limited my selection to those who had a total of 100 references or more (see Table 2.2 and Figure 2.1). All prepositions and articles were removed in order to focus on proper nouns.

In relation to Twitter news, data was collected through an academic partnership with the commercial data analytics company Crimson Hexagon via its social impact program. In leveraging access to the full Twitter firehose, which provides old tweets dating back to December 2013, a complete population of Twitter data was gathered from 12 leading global and Arabic news outlets that have been shown in previous studies to be important international and regional outlets that set national agendas (Seib 2005; Volkmer 2007). Previous studies on Twitter focused on news recommendations and identification of live news events (Phelan et al. 2009; Abel et al. 2011; Jackoway et al. 2011), but none of them, to this researcher's knowledge, used Twitter for news analysis of large data sets in order to examine the theory of news values.

These news organizations cover a diverse geographical base of national origins (set in parentheses), and include the following, with language of content collection identified after the slash: Al Jazeera/English and Al Jazeera/Arabic (Qatari), BBC/English and BBC/Arabic (British), CNN/English and CNN/Arabic (American), France 24/English and France 24/Arabic (French), RT/English and RT/Arabic (Russian), and SkyNews/English and SkyNews/Arabic (UAE- and

Table 2.1 Frequency of references (and average percentages) to countries by the four channels on their Facebook pages.

	DW		BBC		Al-Alam		RT		Total
Country	Perc.	Freq.	Perc.	Freq.	Perc.	Freq.	Perc.	Freq.	Freq.
1) Syria	13.4	129	13.9	142	23.9	2231	25.2	1106	3608
2) Iran	1.5	15	1.2	13	16.3	1528	4.9	216	1772
3) Iraq	12.5	121	5.9	60	11.7	1098	4.3	191	1470
4) Egypt	16.5	159	18.3	186	7.5	703	7	311	1359
5) Russia	—	0	1.1	12	1.6	151	22.3	980	1143
6) Switzerland	5.6	54	2.8	29	6.4	600	7.7	340	1023
7) Saudi Arabia	3.5	34	2.4	25	8.4	785	1.3	60	904
8) Bahrain	—	0	1.7	0	9.1	854	0.4	18	872
9) USA	4.3	42	3.7	38	2	188	7.5	333	601
10) Lebanon	1.9	19	2	21	4.6	431	2.2	99	570
11) UK	—	0	23.8	242	0.5	49	1.5	67	358
12) Germany	29.6	285	—	0	—	0	0.5	24	309

Table 2.2 Frequency of references (and average percentages) to political actors by the four channels on their Facebook pages.

	DW		BBC		Al-Alam		RT		Total
Topic	Perc.	Freq.	Perc.	Freq.	Perc.	Freq.	Perc.	Freq.	Freq.
1) Sergei Lavrov	—	0	—	0	11.5	109	21.9	179	288
2) John Kerry	17.2	14	22.4	13	12.2	115	14.9	102	244
3) Bashar Assad	18.5	15	—	0	14.4	136	6.2	43	194
4) Vladimir Putin	—	0	—	0	3.6	34	21.9	150	184
5) Abdulfatah Al-Sisi	29.6	24	34.4	20	6.9	65	8	55	164
6) Nouri Maliki	16	13	—	0	12	113	4	28	154
7) Walid Al-Mu'lam	—	0	—	0	10.4	98	7.7	53	151
8) Mohammed Mursi	18.5	15	43.1	25	5.9	56	6.4	44	140
9) Hasan Rouhani	—	0	—	0	14.7	139	—	0	139
10) Ban Ki Moon	—	0	—	0	8	76	8.6	59	135

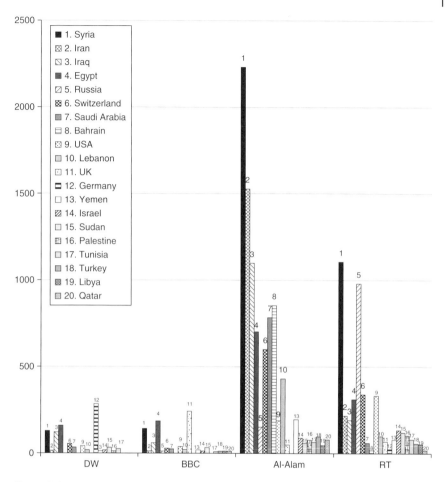

Figure 2.1 Frequency of references to countries by the four channels on their Facebook pages. (The numbers above the columns correspond to the unique countries' numbers on the right side of the figure.)

UK-based). The total combined number of followers for the official Twitter accounts studied here is over 53.9 million, with an average of 4.1 million apiece as of June 2015 (Table 2.3). Some news organizations have other Twitter accounts for their other outlets, such as Al Jazeera Documentary. For the purpose of this chapter, the choice was to select only the main and official Twitter account of each organization.

Given the technical specifications of the Crimson Hexagon platform and the goals of this chapter, all historical Twitter data for each news outlet under consideration was collected from a start date of December 19, 2013 until February 7,

Table 2.3 Number of news stories and retweets by the 12 news organizations.

Channel	Total account followers[a]	Total no. of news stories included in the study	No. of retweets for all news stories	Average no. of retweets for each news story
CNN	17.4 M	18 896	2 113 494	111.8
CNN Ar.	3.3 M	23 487	519 850	22.1
Al Jazeera	2.4 M	25 784	749 773	29
Al Jazeera Ar.	5 M	36 010	1 111 926	30.8
RT	924 K	36 167	2 508 374	69.3
RT Ar.	1.3 M	43 571	288 004	6.6
SkyNews	2.1 M	32 711	1 049 324	32
SkyNews Ar.	1.5 M	37 351	155 546	4.1
BBC	10.1 M	34 385	2 509 756	72.9
BBC Ar.	1.6 M	18 791	288 802	15.3
France24	99.6 K	27 005	103 148	3.8
France24 Ar.	2.3 M	26 290	163 787	6.2
Total for all channels	48 M	360 448	11 561 784	403.9
Average for all channels	4 M	30 037	963 482	33.6

[a] Figures for total Twitter accounts followers were collected on June 2, 2015.

2015, which was the day data analysis began. Altogether, with just over one year of complete Twitter content to consider, this approach yielded 360 448 tweets of news stories' headlines. Almost all news tweets contain only headlines because it is not possible to put full articles on Twitter due to its 280-character (originally 140-character) limitation. The general practice is to include a headline and hyperlink that leads to the original story on the news organization's website, in case the reader is interested in knowing more. The unit of analysis for this chapter is the news headline. Numerous s previous research studies have relied on headlines (Yang 2003; Groshek 2008; Dalton et al. 2015) or on the words used in headlines (Kiousis 2004) in order to collect sample or model features in the coverage of different issues by various outlets.

As with the Facebook news analysis already described, the collected Twitter data was analyzed using the text analysis software program QDA Miner 4 – WordStat. References to the names of capitals, cities, and countries and derivations thereof, in Arabic and in English, were identified. As mentioned, understanding which countries are more recurrent in news coverage helps in identifying specific organizational news values, as this gives an indication of proximity and the prominence placed on certain areas over others. Cohen et al. note that "nations offer a convenient shorthand for comparative analysis" in news coverage (2013, p. 5). For the sake of parsimony and due to the fact that many countries are mentioned in the headlines, analyses are limited to the most recurrent 400 words in the headlines of each news channel, and the 10 most-referenced countries in tweeted news stories' headlines are identified, the summary of which can be seen in Table 2.4. In the next analytic step, the number of references to figures and actors, namely politicians, celebrities, and political bodies such as the United Nations and European Union, is also examined. The top 10 references are then selected, similarly to how references to countries were selected (see Table 2.5).

Facebook News Analysis

As already described, this chapter examines the Arabic-language posts of four TV channels' Facebook pages. The results show that there are stark variations in the kind of attention and emphasis given to countries and political actors. It is important to note, however, that some of these differences are due to the vast variations in the news volume or number of news reports posted on Facebook, as previously indicated. For example, Al-Alam posted 7986 stories during the period under study, while DW Arabic posted only 822. So, there is a need to examine the percentage of coverage in relation to countries and political actors. The figures cited in Tables 2.1 and 2.2 are taken from raw data, while the percentages are calculated based on the total number of references to countries and political figures made by each news organization.

In relation to the countries cited in the headlines and leads, Table 2.1 shows the frequency of attention and average percentage by the four channels. By examining all the TV channels' raw data, we find that the top five countries cited are: (i) Syria ($n = 3608$), (ii) Iran ($n = 1772$), (iii) Iraq ($n - 1470$), (iv) Egypt ($n = 1359$), and (v) Russia ($n = 1143$). Due to the disparity in the number of news stories posted on the four Facebook pages, it is also important to examine the average percentage of each country mentioned among them, which are as follows: (i) Syria 19.1%, (ii) Egypt 12.3%, (iii) Iraq 8.6%, (iv) Russia 6.2%, and (v) Iran 5.9%. (For a more complete overview of the countries' frequencies, see Figure 2.1).

As for the references and average percentage of political actors by the four channels, Table 2.2 illustrates the results. The raw data from the TV channels in relation to references to political figures reveal that the top five actors are: (i) Sergei Lavrov ($n = 288$), (ii) John Kerry ($n = 244$), (iii) Bashar Assad ($n = 194$), (iv) Vladimir Putin ($n = 184$), and (v) Abdulfatah Al-Sisi ($n = 164$) (see Table 2.6 for another overview of the political actors highlighted by the four channels). Similar

Table 2.4 Frequency of references (and average percentages) to countries on different channels' Twitter accounts.

	BBC Arabic		CNN Arabic		France24 Arabic		Al Jazeera Arabic		RT Arabic		SkyNews Arabia	
Country	Country	Frq. and perc.	Country	Frq. and perc.	Country	Frq. and perc.	Country	Frq. and perc.	Country	Frq. and perc.	Country	Frq. and perc.
Egypt	Egypt	1444 (16.6%)	Egypt	3791 (21.8%)	France	4355 (29.5%)	Palestine	3480 (19.2%)	Russia	9231 (22.7%)	Egypt	3593 (18.3%)
UK	UK	1347 (15.5%)	Iraq	2282 (13.1%)	Syria	1724 (11.6%)	Syria	2945 (16.3%)	Ukraine	7192 (17.7%)	Syria	3111 (15.8%)
Syria	Syria	1247 (14.3%)	USA	2230 (12.8%)	Egypt	1407 (9.5%)	Egypt	2871 (15.9%)	Syria	5198 (12.8%)	Iraq	2369 (12%)
Iraq	Iraq	1068 (12.3%)	Saudi Arabia	2145 (12.3%)	Palestine	1272 (8.6%)	Israel	2201 (12.1%)	Egypt	4576 (11.2%)	Libya	2342 (11.9%)
USA	USA	841 (9.6%)	Syria	2119 (12.2%)	Iraq	1218 (8.2%)	Iraq	1830 (10.1%)	USA	3831 (9.4%)	USA	2082 (10.6%)
Palestine	Palestine	736 (8.4%)	UAE	1557 (8.9%)	Algeria	1154 (7.8%)	USA	1606 (8.8%)	Palestine	3451 (8.5%)	Palestine	1862 (9.5%)
Ukraine	Ukraine	654 (7.5%)	Palestine	1176 (6.7%)	Tunisia	1086 (7.3%)	Yemen	1067 (5.9%)	Iraq	2653 (6.5%)	UAE	1349 (6.8%)
Israel	Israel	565 (6.5%)	Israel	738 (4.2%)	Libya	1077 (7.2%)	Libya	783 (4.3%)	Israel	2352 (5.8%)	Yemen	1204 (6.1%)
Libya	Libya	400 (4.6%)	Qatar	645 (3.7%)	USA	797 (5.3%)	Ukraine	742 (4.1%)	Iran	1169 (2.8%)	Saudi Arabia	949 (4.8%)
Saudi Arabia	Saudi Arabia	378 (4.3%)	Lebanon	630 (3.6%)	Israel	672 (4.5%)	Tunisia	523 (2.8%)	Tunisia	845 (2%)	Ukraine	734 (3.7%)

BBC Country	BBC Frq. and perc.	CNN Frq. and perc.	CNN Country	France24 Frq. and perc.	France24 Country	Al Jazeera Frq. and perc.	Al Jazeera Country	RT Frq. and perc.	RT Country	SkyNews Country	SkyNews Frq. and perc.
USA	3280 (23.9%)	1835 (56.2%)	USA	5741 (39.8%)	France	1474 (15.7%)	USA	7441 (27.1%)	USA	UK	2697 (45.7%)
Ukraine	2225 (16.2%)	264 (8%)	Ukraine	1808 (12.5%)	USA	1425 (15.2%)	Palestine	6989 (25.5%)	Ukraine	USA	1022 (17.3%)
Russia	1541 (11.2%)	254 (7.7%)	Russia	1807 (12.5%)	Ukraine	1100 (11.7%)	India	5131 (18.7%)	Russia	France	450 (7.6%)
China	1398 (10.2%)	225 (6.8%)	France	992 (6.8%)	Russia	1035 (11%)	Israel	2578 (9.4%)	UK	Ukraine	414 (7%)
India	1061 (7.7%)	197 (6%)	Iraq	988 (6.8%)	Syria	906 (9.6%)	Ukraine	1021 (3.7%)	France	Russia	365 (6.1%)
UK	1004 (7.3%)	147 (4.5%)	Korea	739 (5.1%)	China	893 (9.5%)	Syria	1101 (4%)	Israel	China	239 (4%)
Syria	952 (6.9%)	131 (4%)	Syria	649 (4.5%)	Iraq	756 (8%)	Palestine	921 (3.3%)	Iraq	Iraq	238 (4%)
France	860 (6.2%)	108 (3.3%)	Israel	599 (4.1%)	Egypt	636 (6.8%)	Syria	883 (3.2%)	Syria	Syria	216 (3.6%)
Australia	748 (5.4%)	100 (3%)	UK	569 (3.9%)	Russia	614 (6.5%)	Iraq	735 (2.6%)	Korea	Korea	136 (2.3%)
Iraq	618 (4.5%)	—	Palestine	508 (3.5%)	Afghanistan	506 (5.4%)	Germany	562 (2%)	Palestine	Palestine	123 (2%)

Table 2.5 Frequency of references (and average percentages) to political actors on different channels' Twitter accounts.

	BBC Arabic		CNN Arabic		France24 Arabic		Al Jazeera Arabic		RT Arabic		SkyNews Arabia	
Actor	Actor	Frq. and perc.	Actor	Frq. and perc.	Actor	Frq. and perc.	Actor	Frq. and perc.	Actor	Frq. and perc.	Actor	Frq. and perc.
ISIS	ISIS	1078 (53.7%)	ISIS	2382 (47%)	ISIS	1220 (41.2%)	ISIS	1107 (31.4%)	ISIS	2004 (22.9%)	ISIS	1101 (31.3%)
Obama	Obama	180 (8.9%)	Sisi	706 (13.9%)	Sisi	327 (11%)	Houthis	402 (11.4%)	Putin	1388 (15.9%)	Sisi	522 (14.8%)
Sisi	Sisi	154 (7.6%)	Obama	358 (7%)	Hollande	320 (10.8%)	Sisi	394 (11.1%)	Lavrov	1299 (14.9%)	Obama	450 (12.7%)
Kerry	Kerry	111 (5.5%)	Assad	316 (6.2%)	EU	263 (8.8%)	Obama	347 (9.8%)	EU	1114 (12.7%)	Kerry	247 (7%)
Hamas	Hamas	105 (5.2%)	brothers	310 (6.1%)	Obama	192 (6.4%)	Hamas	284 (8%)	Obama	813 (9.3%)	[Muslim] Brothers	241 (6.8%)
Maliki	Maliki	83 (4.1%)	Morsi	235 (4.6%)	Hamas	135 (4.5%)	Kerry	255 (7.2%)	Sisi	582 (6.6%)	Erdogan	237 (6.7%)
Brothers	Brothers	75 (3.7%)	Hamas	233 (4.6%)	Qaida	134 (4.5%)	Erdogan	209 (5.9%)	Kerry	500 (5.7%)	Houthis	207 (5.8%)
Netanyahu	Netanyahu	74 (3.6%)	Qaida	223 (4.4%)	Putin	133 (3.4%)	EU	184 (5.2%)	[Muslim] Brothers	413 (4.7%)	EU	175 (4.9%)
Houthis	Houthis	73 (3.6%)	Putin	169 (3.3%)	Boko [Haram]	130 (4.3%)	Netanyahu	176 (4.9%)	NATO	302 (3.4%)	Qaida	169 (4.8%)
Abbas	Abbas	71 (3.5%)	Kerry	131 (2.5%)	Kerry	105 (3.5%)	Morsi	167 (4.7%)	Hamas	299 (3.4%)	Maliki	167 (4.7%)

BBC		CNN		France24		Al Jazeera		RT		SkyNews	
Actor	Frq. and perc.	Actor	Frq. and perc.	Actor	Frq. and perc.	Actor	Frq. and perc.	Actor	Frq. and perc.	Actor	Frq. and perc.
EU	667 (25.2%)	Obama	788 (47%)	EU	894 (31.6%)	ISIS	459 (24.3%)	ISIS	1562 (23.2%)	Cameron	377 (21%)
UN	596 (22.5%)	ISIS	632 (37.7%)	Hollande	535 (18.9%)	UN	382 (20.2%)	EU	1166 (17.3%)	Obama	256 (14.3%)
Obama	590 (22.3%)	Clinton	147 (8.7%)	Obama	371 (13.1%)	EU	366 (19.3%)	Putin	1083 (16.1%)	[Ed] Miliband	226 (12.6%)
ISIS	457 (17.2%)	Brown	107 (6.3%)	Putin	295 (10.4%)	Obama	201 (10.6%)	Obama	842 (12.5%)	EU	211 (11.7%)
Putin	334 (12.6%)	—	—	Sarkozy	130 (4.6%)	Taliban	149 (7.8%)	NSA	514 (7.6%)	[George] Osborne	156 (8.7%)
—	—	—	—	Kerry	127 (4.5%)	Putin	119 (6.3%)	Lavrov	445 (6.6%)	Putin	153 (8.5%)
—	—	—	—	Hamas	121 (4.2%)	Modi	106 (5.6%)	Snowden	434 (6.4%)	ISIS	143 (7.9%)
—	—	—	—	Pope	120 (4.2%)	Qaida	105 (5.5%)	CIA	270 (4%)	[Nigel] Farage	140 (7.8%)
—	—	—	—	Erdogan	116 (4.1%)	—	—	Poroshenko	202 (3%)	[Andy] Murray	127 (7%)
—	—	—	—	Boko [Haram]	113 (4%)	—	—	Pentagon	200 (2.9%)	—	—

Table 2.6 Total frequency and percentage of the top 10 most referenced figures and actors.[a]

Arabic channels		English channels		All channels	
Actor	Freq. and perc.	Actor	Freq. and perc.	Actor	Freq. and perc.
ISIS	8892 (39%)	EU	3304 (18.8%)	ISIS	21 667 (36.4%)
Sisi	2685 (11.7%)	ISIS	3253 (18.5%)	Obama	8247 (13.8%)
Obama	2340 (10.2%)	Obama	3048 (17.3%)	EU	6776 (11.3%)
EU	1736 (7.6%)	Putin	1984 (11.3%)	Sisi	5735 (9.6%)
Putin	1690 (7.4%)	UN	978 (5.5%)	Putin	5364 (9%)
Kerry	1349 (5.9%)	Hollande	535 (3%)	Kerry	3209 (5.3%)
Lavrov	1299 (5.6%)	NSA	514 (2.9%)	Lavrov	3043 (5.1%)
Hamas	1056 (4.6%)	Lavrov	445 (2.5%)	Hamas	2376 (3.9%)
Brothers	1039 (4.5%)	Snowden	434 (2.4%)	Brothers	2078 (3.4%)
Qaida	708 (3.1%)	Cameron	377 (2.1%)	UN	978 (1.6%)

[a] Spearman correlation coefficient R 0.700, significance (2-tailed) P = 0.188 (correlation is significant at the 0.05 level [2-tailed]).

to the procedure followed with respect to countries, the average percentages of each political actor mentioned among the four Facebook pages are as follows: (i) Abdulfatah Al-Sisi 19.7%, (ii) Mohammed Mursi 18.4%, (iii) John Kerry 16.6%, (iv) Bashar Assad 9.7%, and (v) Nouri Maliki 8%.

As discussed, news production is affected by different factors, such as the ideological values of the journalists and their news organizations, as well as media ownership. Shoemaker and Cohen refer to social significance as one of the important elements of newsworthiness, defined as news "relevance for the social system" along four dimensions: political, economic, cultural, and public (2006, pp. 7 and 15). Further, Adams (1986) and Cohen et al. (1990) emphasize the importance of psychological proximity in the news as another indicator of newsworthiness. In general, a news organization gives more prominence to an issue by devoting more coverage to it (Hofstetter 1976; Siune et al. 1984), which is evident either by the volume of coverage or by ongoing reporting on the issue.

In relation to the dominance of news stories in relation to references to countries, there seems to be great variation in the number of news stories and their focus among the four channels – but it is important to note that most of these have special sections for language teaching (Farsi, German, Russian, and English) and general information about the countries that run or host them. This clearly indicates that the news organizations function as public diplomacy tools, especially RT Arabic and Al-Alam, which are managed by their respective governments (though other purposes like promoting tourism might be involved).

For RT Arabic, Syria is the country that attracted most of the attention, 25.2% (n = 1106), which is clearly due to the ongoing conflict there. References to Russia came second, 22.3% (n = 980), which is also understandable because of the need to add relevance and proximity to the news. Switzerland came third at 7.7% (n = 340), mostly in relation to the UN-organized Geneva meeting in which officials from the Syrian government met with opposition groups and parties. The United States came fourth at 7.5% (n = 333), followed by Egypt at 7% (n = 311).

Regarding Al-Alam TV, we find the same editorial tendency. There is a clear emphasis on highlighting Iran and its role in the region. There is also the social significance or cultural relevance of sectarian proximity. For example, Al-Alam made 50 references to the Houthis, the Shiite opposition group in Yemen; no other channel referred to them at all. Syria comes first again because of the conflict, at 23.9% (n = 2231), followed by Iran at 16.3% (n = 1528), Iraq at 11.7% (n = 1098), and Bahrain at 9.1% (n = 854). Again, religious proximity seems to play a role here, as Bahrain is not regarded as a newsworthy topic by the other news organizations, but Al-Alam emphasizes the Shiite protests against the Sunni monarchy in its news reports. In fact, the channel devotes a special section to Bahraini news in order to thoroughly cover events taking place there. Also noteworthy is the fact that Al-Alam put a great deal of emphasis on airing the Shiite protests in Saudi Arabia, as well as the fighting between the Shiite Houthis and government troops in Yemen. At the same time, the channel downplayed the events taking place in Syria and Iraq between Sunni rebels and Shiite government forces. As Sebastian Usher (2006) claims, Iran used Al-Alam to "influence and stir up opinion in the Arab world and beyond – just as it tries to control the information available to its own people within the country." As a result, Al-Alam news coverage created anger and distrust among policy makers in the Arab world, which led to the jamming of its signals (Press TV 2011) and the decision to stop its transmission on Nilesat and Arabsat on November 3, 2010. Arabsat did allow the channel to resume broadcasting, before blocking its transmission again two months later (Al-Alam 2010). It is assumed that the limitations on the channel's viewership in the Arab world via the two popular Arab satellites led Al-Alam to enhance its social media activity, especially on Facebook. The result is that it maintained and possibly increased its audience engagement. This partly explains the high number of stories posted on Al-Alam's Facebook page in comparison to the other channels examined in this chapter. According to Socialbakers (2014), Al-Alam's Facebook page fan distribution is as follows: 21.6% Iraq, 17.5% Syria, 9.5% Egypt, 4.8% Yemen, 4.7% Russia, 4.7% Saudi Arabia, 3.3% Lebanon, and 2.7% Bahrain. There seems to be some level of correlation between Al-Alam's Facebook fans and the demographic specificities of some of these countries.

As for BBC Arabic, the United Kingdom was mentioned more than any other country (23.8%, n = 242), followed by Egypt (18.3%, n = 186), Syria (13.9%, n = 142), and Iraq (5.9%, n = 60). Again, there is emphasis on the country of origin that runs or sponsors the news organization. Finally, and as expected, DW Arabic highlighted Germany more than any other country (29.6%, n = 285), followed by Egypt (n = 159), Syria (n = 129), and Iraq (n = 121). From these results, we can see that the BBC and DW highlighted the events and political changes in Egypt more than the conflict in Syria. This can be explained by the political dimension of social significance as well as the social change deviance in news values, which focuses on "threats to the status quo" in connection to covering "civil demonstrations that bring about a new presidential election" (Shoemaker and Cohen 2006, p. 49).

When examining all four TV channels' average percentages, we find that Syria comes first at 19.1%, followed by Egypt at 12.3%, Iraq at 8.6%, Russia at 6.2%, and Iran at 5.9%. The magnitude of events taking place in Syria, the follow-up factor, and the fact that it deals with bad news all explain why this country ranks first, as these are all basic elements of news values (Harcup and O'Neill 2001). Based on the number of references to countries, it becomes clear that Al-Alam pays great attention to Bahrain and the Shiite protests in the Gulf region even though their news significance cannot be compared to other important events taking place in the Arab region. Aside from the ideological influence already mentioned, other elements like social significance and proximity are involved in explaining the prominence given to certain countries, such as Russia on RT Arabic, Germany on DW Arabic, and the United Kingdom on BBC Arabic.

As for the dominance of news stories in relation to references to political actors, we find that RT Arabic focused on Russian politicians much more than other actors. The Russian foreign minister, Sergei Lavrov, came first with 150 references (21.9%), followed by the Russian president, Vladimir Putin, with 150 (21.9%), John Kerry with 102 (14.9%), and Ban Ki Moon with 59 (8.6%). The latter was mostly mentioned in connection to the Geneva meeting already cited. As for the attention given to political actors by Al-Alam, Iranian President Hasan Rouhani came first with 139 references (14.7%), followed by Bashar Assad with 136 (14.4%), John Kerry with 115 (12.2%), and Nouri Maliki with 113 (12%). Ideological affinity and psychological proximity seem to play a role here, as Assad, an Alawite whose government is strongly backed by the Iranian regime, was highlighted in Al-Alam's news reports far more than on the other channels. Al-Alam and RT Arabic are also the only two channels that highlighted the activities of Walid Al-Mu'lam, the Syrian foreign minister. Much like Iran, Russia is a staunch ally of Assad's regime for various reasons, including some shared interests as well as Putin's alleged fear that the popular sentiment toward overthrowing totalitarian regimes in the Middle East might spread to Russia (Allison 2013, pp. 815–818).

According to a qualitative study examining the Russian media coverage of the Syrian conflict, more blame for the prevailing violence is directed at Islamist radicals than at Assad's regime. One blatant example included accusing the Syrian opposition of being behind a significant chemical attack on the outskirts of Damascus (Brown 2014, p. 57). This kind of coverage is understandable if one takes into account that the media in Russia is largely polarized, especially in relation to "nationally distributed TV channels," which includes the state-funded RT; these channels are "increasingly used by the state as tools to support the vertical power system" (Vartanova 2012, p. 134).

Regarding the main political actors mentioned by BBC Arabic, we find Mohammed Mursi, the former Egyptian president, coming first with 25 references (43.1%), followed by Abdulfatah Al-Sisi with 20 (34.4%), and John Kerry with 13 (22.4%). As for DW Arabic, Abdulfatah Al-Sisi comes first with 24 references (29.6%), followed by Mohammed Mursi with 15 (18.5%), Bashar Assad with 15 (18.5%), and John Kerry with 14 (17.2%) (see Table 2.2 and Figure 2.2).

Again, the more attention given to a country or political actor, the more importance is attached to them. In other words, each news organization gave special emphasis to its own country and national politicians except the BBC and DW, though the latter did make 21 references to Chancellor Angela Merkel. One of the main possible explanations for such a difference in coverage is that the Iranian and Russian channels are directly supported and influenced by their respective governments, as already mentioned, and this ultimately affects their news values choices. The BBC and DW show a different emphasis because, in contrast, they are more independent from their governments, especially in terms of funding, due to their mandates as public broadcasting services.

Since SNS use has become an integral part of the news consumption experience in today's world, it is important to thoroughly study news organizations' social media use. Social media offers new opportunities for news organizations to reach more audiences, in what Hermida (2010) has called "ambient journalism," or a non-moderated arena for online readers. Social media platforms have become magnets for interested readers to consume, share, like, and disseminate news and interact with others on a variety of issues and in a very timely, thorough, and engaging manner.

Twitter News Analysis

Twitter is a microblogging service that allows its users to send short text messages of up to 280 characters, known as tweets. (Twitter famously used to limit tweets to 140 characters, but recently doubled this.) When a user follows a news organization's Twitter account, he or she will begin receiving its news updates. This is another version of the diffuse modern equivalent to subscribing to a newspaper

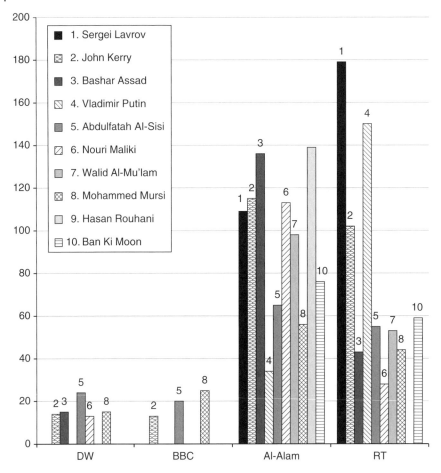

Figure 2.2 Frequency of references to political actors by the four channels on their Facebook pages. (The numbers above the columns correspond to the unique political figures' numbers on the right side of the figure.)

(Ju et al. 2013, p. 4). One study revealed that an "average Twitter user is two to three times more likely to visit a leading news Web site than the average person" (Farhi 2009, para. 23) since most Twitter trends (the hottest topics at a given time) are related to news (Kwak et al. 2010; Thelwall et al. 2011; Wilkinson and Thelwall 2012). Among Internet users in the United States, about 37% of them has done at least one of the following online activities: "commenting on a news story (25%); posting a link on a social networking site (17%); tagging content (11%), creating their own original news material or opinion piece (9%), or Tweeting about news (3%)" (Pew Research Center 2010, p. 4).

As already mentioned, references to countries and to national figures and political actors are regarded as important elements in determining the differences in international news coverage among the 12 news outlets under discussion. This chapter examines the results of the analysis of over 360 000 tweets (consisting of a headline and a hyperlink to the relevant story) that generated over 12.1 million retweets from the online audience. On average, each news organization's Twitter page posted 30 037 news headlines for the period under discussion, and this content generated an aggregate average of 963 482 retweets overall, or 33.6 retweets per news story posted.

Broadly speaking, CNN/English has the most active Twitter page in terms of explicit audience sharing with 111.8 retweets per story, followed by the BBC/English (72.9), RT/English (69.3), Al Jazeera/Arabic (30.8), and Al Jazeera/English (29). These baseline findings are also shown in Table 2.3.

The findings show that there are clear variations between the Arabic channels and the English ones in terms of the attention given to figures and political actors and to countries. The results for the most referenced figures and actors on the Arabic channels show that news about the power elite, one of the news values elements, is always significant. The most prominent actor highlighted in the news was the Islamic State of Iraq and the Levant (ISIS), which was mentioned far more than any other actor (39%) due to the long-running conflict in Syria and Iraq. This is expected, as events involving ISIS have been newsworthy for several reasons, including the horror inflicted on the civilian population and the shocking and graphic footage and images (including of beheadings) disseminated by this terrorist group. The attention given to ISIS can be understood as part of the bad news and magnitude elements of news values. More importantly, Adams (1986) and Cohen et al. (1990) discuss the importance of (psychological) proximity as an indicator of newsworthiness. Aside from economic and security interests, as well as Western countries' military and humanitarian involvement in the crisis, ISIS has recruited many foreigners from Western countries, a factor that has increased the newsworthiness of the group and its activities. Among the Arabic channels, the BBC highlighted ISIS more than the other five channels at 53.7%, followed by CNN at 47%, France24 at 41.2%, and Al Jazeera at 31.4% (Table 2.5).

The second most referenced political actor based on the total frequencies of all channels was the Egyptian President Al-Sisi (11.7%), who ranked second on three of them: SkyNews (14.8%), CNN (13.9%), and France24 (11%). This is also expected, since Egypt plays an important role in the Middle East (power elite) due to its large population and its proximity to Europe. Besides this, the ongoing political tension in the country, mostly due to the removal of its former elected president, Mohammed Mursi, adds to Al-Sisi's newsworthiness (follow-up and magnitude).

Former US President Barack Obama comes in third place among all the Arabic channels, at 10.2%. This is mostly related to the important role the US government plays in the Middle East region and its direct military and diplomatic involvement in some of the conflicts taking place there. In fact, Obama came in second on one Arabic channel, BBC Arabic (8.9%), and third on two more, SkyNews Arabia (12.7%) and CNN Arabic (7%) (see Table 2.5).

Other prominent figures and political actors highlighted by the Arabic channels include the European Union, which ranked fourth at 7.6%, followed by the Russia's Putin at 7.4%, the United States' Kerry at 5.9%, Russia's Lavrov at 5.6%, the Palestinian Islamic organization Hamas at 4.6%, the Egyptian Muslim Brotherhood at 4.5%, and the Al Qaida group at 3.1%. As already discussed, news channels and journalists tend to generally reflect an ideology that either supports or shapes them. Ideology, in other words, is disseminated via media channels, which are used as tools by the political and corporate elites. As Shoemaker and Reese (2013) emphasize, newsroom practices and ideological beliefs cannot be avoided in the news production process. This theoretical framework provides the best explanation for the results shown here. For example, the Russian state-run station, RT, highlighted news on Vladimir Putin, who ranked second at 15.9%, and Sergey Lavrov, who came in third with nearly as much coverage at 14.9%. No other channel covered these two Russian politicians as much; in fact, Lavrov did not make the top 10 for any other channel analyzed except RT English, where he ranked sixth at 6.6%. Putin, meanwhile, only squeezed in at the ninth rank on CNN Arabic, with 3.3%, and at the seventh rank on France24 Arabic, with 4.4%. On RT English, Putin came third following ISIS and the European Union with 16.1%. This clearly shows the importance given by RT Arabic and English to Russian political leaders at the expense of other world leaders (news agenda and ideology). Similarly, the French state-run France24 emphasized news on then French President Francois Hollande, who ranked third at 10.8% and who is not in the top 10 of any other channel examined in this chapter except France24 English, on which he came second at 18.9% (see Table 2.5).

Another interesting aspect of these findings is that all the figures and political actors are in some way connected to the Middle East. This can be attributed to the zones of relevance (Cohen et al. 1990) or "relevance for the social system" in connection to the political dimension (Shoemaker and Cohen 2006, p. 49), which explains the newsworthiness of these stories. For example, Kerry and Lavrov are connected to the Syrian conflict as both were directly involved in the Geneva negotiations with Syrian political factions. This is no surprise, again, since the Arabic-language channels are targeting audiences living in Arab countries, so the news scope must be carefully selected to meet their information needs.

As for the English-language channels, the results show that Europe and the European Union came first among all six at 18.8%. This is likely due to the fact that the majority of the English news organizations examined in this chapter are based in Europe, and to the growing political and economic importance of the

European Union. Europe and the European Union came first on France24 with 31.6% and on the BBC with 25.2%, and second on RT with 17.3%. Overall, the European Union is closely followed at 18.5% by ISIS, which came first on Al Jazeera (24.3%) and RT (23.2%). As discussed earlier, ISIS was one of the most important news actors in 2014 (see Table 2.5).

The third most cited figure on the English-language channels was President Obama (17.3%), who unsurprisingly came first on CNN (47%), mostly due to proximity and zones of relevance. CNN only referred to four political figures and actors in total, with Hillary Clinton in the third rank at 8.7% and Michael Brown in fourth at 6.3%; Brown's killing by a policeman caused massive protests in Ferguson, Missouri starting in August 2014. Following the pattern of CNN, SkyNews highlighted British politicians in its reports more than any other Arabic or English news channel. On this UK-based channel, then Prime Minister David Cameron came first (21%), followed in the third rank by then Labour Party leader Ed Miliband (12.6%), ahead of other political figures like George Osborne in fifth (8.7%) and Nigel Farage in eighth (7.8%), and the tennis player Andy Murray in ninth (7%) (see Table 2.5). In fact, SkyNews reports were more focused on UK national news than on international events, a news focus feature they shared with CNN. Yet, the coverage by CNN Arabic and SkyNews Arabia was exclusively focused on the Middle East, with no references to US and British politicians or other political figures and actors except Barack Obama.

Finally, in terms of total frequencies across all the channels included in this chapter, ISIS came first with 36.4%, followed by Obama with 13.8%, the European Union with 11.3%, Sisi with 9.6%, and Putin with 9% (see Table 2.6). RT Arabic and English highlighted news on the Russian president as well as on Lavrov, the foreign minister, which explains their prominence in the final list. As for the statistical differences between Arabic- and English-language media channels, Spearman correlation coefficient test of ranking R 0.177, P = 0.431, indicated no significant differences between the two language outlets.

Regarding the frequency of countries covered by Arabic channels, Egypt came first among all the channels (17.6%) (Table 2.7). Egypt plays an important role in the Middle East region, and Egyptian TV viewers are regarded as the most numerous in the whole Arab world. Three channels had Egypt as their most frequently mentioned country: CNN (21.8%), SkyNews (18.3%), and the BBC (16.6%).

In second place was Syria (15.8%), highlighted on all channels due to the severity of the humanitarian and security situation there. In fact, the Syrian conflict is regarded by the United Nations as the worst international humanitarian crisis of recent decades (Euronews 2013). Therefore, it is surprising that Syria was not the most cited country in Arabic news headlines. Three channels had Syria in the second rank: Al Jazeera (16.3%), SkyNews (15.8%), and France24 (11.6%). In general, the prominence given to it can be interpreted in terms of reporting bad news, follow-up, and magnitude.

Table 2.7 Total frequency and percentage of the top 10 most referenced countries.[a]

Arabic channels		English channels		All channels	
Country	Freq. and perc.	Country	Freq. and perc.	Country	Freq. and perc.
Egypt	18197 (17.6%)	USA	16860 (22.7%)	USA	39119 (14.8%)
Syria	16344 (15.8%)	Ukraine	12605 (17%)	Ukraine	38082 (14.4%)
Palestine	11977 (11.6%)	Russia	8897 (12%)	Syria	37864 (14.3%)
Iraq	11420 (11.1%)	France	8297 (11.2%)	Egypt	31249 (11.8%)
USA	10872 (10.5%)	UK	6848 (9.2%)	Russia	28163 (10.6%)
Ukraine	9322 (9%)	Syria	4063 (5.4%)	Palestine	27583 (10.4%)
Russia	9231 (8.9%)	Iraq	3193 (4.3%)	Iraq	27359 (10.3%)
Israel	6528 (6.3%)	Palestine	3077 (4.1%)	France	17007 (6.4%)
Libya	4602 (4.4%)	Israel	2843 (3.8%)	Israel	9371 (3.5%)
France	4355 (4.2%)	China	2376 (3.2%)	UK	8195 (3.1%)

[a] Spearman correlation coefficient R 0.119, Significance (2-tailed) P = 0.779 (Correlation is significant at the 0.05 level [2-tailed]).

The third most referenced "country" among the Arabic channels was Palestine (11.6%), especially Gaza, due to the 2014 Israel–Gaza conflict that resulted in the deaths of over 2000 people (Alexander 2014). Indeed, the Arab–Israeli conflict is an important issue for many Arab viewers, so it is understandable that there is such emphasis on Palestine, especially in view of the high number of casualties (bad news). In fact, Al Jazeera had Palestine as the most cited "country" (19.2%) in its coverage, while its English-language channel had it in second place (15.2%). Two further news values elements, magnitude and follow-up, can explain the attention given to Palestine.

The fourth most referenced country was Iraq (11.1%), due to the ongoing conflict there involving ISIS and Western governments. CNN, for example, had Iraq in second place (13.1%).

Finally, a clear link can be seen on some channels between news values decisions and the influence of the country of origin. For example, the most referenced country in the news on France24 was France (29.5%), which was mentioned over twice as many times as the following country, Syria (11.6%). Similarly, Russia (22.7%), closely followed by Ukraine (17.7%), was the top country repeatedly reported on by RT (see Table 2.4). These examples clearly show the impact of the channels' sponsors or supporters in determining the nature of news focus.

As for the English-language channels, the results indicate that the United States came first in the total frequency for all channels (22.7%) – a predictable result given it is a military and economic global superpower. In fact, the United States came first on four of the six channels. France24 and SkyNews were the exceptions, preferring to highlight the countries from which they air their programs. It is important to note here that CNN paid far more attention to the United States (56.2%) than any of the other channels. For CNN, the second most referenced country was Ukraine, mentioned in 8% of its coverage (Table 2.4).

The second most referenced country among all English channels was Ukraine (17%), mostly due to Russia's annexation of Crimea. Ukraine scored second on three channels other than France24 and SkyNews: RT (25.5%), the BBC (16.2%), and CNN (8%). Russia came in third place (12%) on three channels, RT (18.7%), the BBC (11.2%), and CNN (7.7%), mostly because of its connection to the Ukraine crisis. The attention given to Ukraine can be explained in part by the news values elements of bad news and magnitude.

France came fourth (11.2%) among all the English channels, though it scored first on France24 (39.8%). The United Kingdom came fifth (9.2%) overall, though it scored first on SkyNews (45.7%), due to proximity and zone of relevance. It's clear that these news values factors help determine news focus, as illustrated by CNN's emphasis on the United States, SkyNews' on the United Kingdom, France24's on France, and RT's on Russia and Ukraine. Finally, the total frequencies for all 12 channels reveal that the United States was the most cited country in the news (14.8%), followed by Ukraine (14.4%), Syria (14.3%), Egypt (11.8%), and Russia (10.6%) (see Table 2.7). As for the statistical differences between Arabic and English media outlets, Spearman correlation coefficient test of ranking R 0.119, P = 0.779, indicated no significant differences between the two language outlets (see Table 2.7).

Conclusion

This chapter examined large data sets of news on Facebook and Twitter. Regarding Facebook, it analyzed news posted on the Facebook pages of four foreign Arabic-language TV stations: the Iranian Al-Alam TV, the Russian RT, the German DW, and the British BBC. From a total of 15 589 news stories, it revealed that social significance and proximity, as well as the news organizations' ideological agendas, are among the elements that explain the news selection process. These results correspond with Galtung and Ruge's (1965) and Harcup and O'Neill's (2001) theory on the taxonomy of news, particularly in relation to social significance and proximity as well as a news organization's ideological agenda (Thompson 1990).

In relation to Twitter, the chapter empirically examined a large data set of news posted on the official Twitter accounts of 12 news organizations. The headlines of over 360 000 news stories showed that a number of news values such as bad news, magnitude, proximity, and zones of relevance mostly determine news selection decisions. For example, state-sponsored channels like France24 and RT in Arabic and English pay far more attention to their own countries and politicians than does any other channel examined, which can be explained based on their ideological preferences and agendas. In terms of the general differences between English- and Arabic-language channels, the results indicate that Arabic channels are highly focused on the Middle East (proximity), while a number of English-language channels show obvious preference for the countries from which they originate, especially CNN, SkyNews, France24, and RT. This is perhaps somewhat unexpected because most of these news outlets claim to be global in their outreach and scope, yet we still see that they exhibit clear limitations in their news coverage. In this regard, Cohen et al. assert that "news production is still strongly geared toward news agendas that prioritize domestic news, media coverage that champions national actors, and journalists who speak to national or local audiences" (2013, p. 5). Furthermore, some countries like Ukraine and Syria are highly prominent in the news due to conflicts taking place there (bad news), while the United States remains the most cited country on all channels due to its political, military, and diplomatic importance in the world (power elite).

The advantage of analyzing large data sets like the ones featured in this chapter is that they give communication scholars a better understanding and clearer insight into the overall nature of the news coverage of news organizations than could be gained by examining a small sample. Further, cross-national comparative studies can be useful in contrasting different types of news coverage. Hence, other studies are needed to examine more channels in other languages as well as other social media platforms in order to further test the theory of news values and understand newsworthiness. Finally, news-related data extracted from social media such as Facebook and Twitter can be particularly useful for researchers not only in examining news but also in exploring audience reactions to that news. In future research, other news organizations should be selected in order to find differences and similarities in the news stories posted on SNS. Also, other social media platforms like Instagram and YouTube should be chosen to determine whether differences exist in the quantity and type of news stories posted to them by the same and different news organizations. Finally, semi-structured interviews with journalists and news organization staff responsible for managing their various SNS platforms could shed light on important aspects that were not covered in this chapter.

References

Abel, F., Gao, Q., Houben, G.-J., and Tao, K. (2011). Analyzing user modeling on twitter for personalized news recommendations. In: *User Modeling, Adaption and Personalization* (eds. J.A. Conejo, K. Ricardo, J.L. Marzo and N. Oliver), 1–12. Berlin, Heidelberg: Springer.

Adams, W. (1986). Whose lives count? TV coverage of natural disasters. *Journal of Communication* 36: 113–122.

Al-Alam (2010). For the second time within two months … Al-Alam channel is barred from transmission on Arabsat. Available from: https://www.alalamtv.net/news/10527/عربسات-تمنع-قناة-العالم-من-البث-إيقاف-شهرين-خلال-الثانية-للمرة (accessed November 28, 2019).

Al-Alam (2012). About us. Available from: http://www.alalam.ir/aboutus (accessed November 28, 2019).

Alexander, D. (2014). Israel tried to limit civilian casualties in Gaza: US military chief. *Reuters*. Available from: http://www.reuters.com/article/2014/11/06/us-israel-usa-gaza-idUSKBN0IQ2LH20141106 (accessed November 28, 2019).

Al-Jaber, K. and Gunter, B. (2013). News developments and changes to news consumption patterns in the Arab world. In: *News Media in the Arab World: A Study of 10 Arab and Muslim Countries* (eds. B. Gunter and R. Dickinson), 135–152. New York: Bloomsbury.

Allison, R. (2013). Russia and Syria: explaining alignment with a regime in crisis. *International Affairs* 89 (4): 795–823.

Al-Rawi, A. (2014). Framing the online women's movements in the Arab world. *Information, Communication & Society* 19 (9): 1147–1161.

Al-Rawi, A. (2015). Sectarianism and the Arab Spring: framing the popular protests in Bahrain. *Global Media and Communication* 11 (1): 25–42.

BBC Arabic (2014). BBC Arabic: information about us. Available from: https://www.bbc.com/arabic/institutional/2011/01/000000_aboutus.shtml (accessed November 28, 2019).

BBC Monitoring (2003). Iran TV channel targets Iraq. Available from: http://news.bbc.co.uk/2/hi/middle_east/2913593.stm (accessed November 28, 2019).

Brighton, P. and Foy, D. (2007). *News Values*. Thousand Oak, CA: Sage.

Brown, J.D. (2014). "Better one tiger than ten thousand rabid rats": Russian media coverage of the Syrian conflict. *International Politics* 51 (1): 45–66.

Cohen, A.A., Adoni, H., Bantz, C.R. et al. (1990). *Social Conflict and Television News*. Newbury Park, CA: Sage.

Cohen, A., Hanitzsch, T., Stfpinska, A. et al. (2013). Rationale, design, and methodologies. In: *Foreign News on Television: Where in the World Is the Global Village?* (ed. A. Cohen), 23–40. New York: Peter Lang.

Dalton, B., Jung, K., Willis, J., and Bell, M. (2015). Framing and dominant metaphors in the coverage of North Korea in the Australian media. *Pacific Review* 1 (4): 1–25.

DW (2011). Deutsche Welle presents new television services in Arabic. Available from: http://www.dw.de/deutsche-welle-presents-new-television-services-in-arabic/a-6616014-1 (accessed November 28, 2019).

DW (2014). Multimedia content in 30 languages. Available from: http://www.dw.de/multimedia-content-in-30-languages/a-15703976 (accessed November 28, 2019).

Elareshi, M. and Gunter, B. (2012). Credibility of televised news in Libya: are international news services trusted more than local news services? *Journal of Middle East Media* 8 (1): 1–24.

El-Nawawy, M. (2006). US public diplomacy in the Arab world the news credibility of Radio Sawa and Television Alhurra in five countries. *Global Media and Communication* 2: 183–203.

Entman, R. (2010). Framing media power. In: *Doing News Framing Analysis: Empirical and Theoretical Perspectives* (eds. P. D'Angelo and J. Kuypers), 331–355. London: Routledge.

Esser, F. and Hanitzsch, T. (2012). On the why and how of comparative inquiry in communication studies. In: *The Handbook of Comparative Communication Research* (eds. F. Esser and T. Hanitzsch), 3–22. London: Routledge.

Euronews (2013). UN: Syrian conflict is the worst humanitarian crisis in nearly 20 years. Available from: https://www.euronews.com/2013/07/16/un-syrian-conflict-is-worst-humanitarian-crisis-in-nearly-20-years- (accessed November 28, 2019).

Farhi, P. (2009). The Twitter explosion. *American Journalism Review*. Available from: https://ajrarchive.org/article.asp?id=4756&id=4756 (accessed November 28, 2019).

Galtung, J. and Ruge, M.H. (1965). The structure of foreign news the presentation of the Congo, Cuba and Cyprus crises in four Norwegian newspapers. *Journal of Peace Research* 2 (1): 64–90.

Groshek, J. (2008). Homogenous agendas, disparate frames: CNN and CNN International coverage online. *Journal of Broadcasting & Electronic Media* 52 (1): 52–68.

Hall, S. (1985). Signification, representation, ideology: Althusser and the post-structuralist debates. *Critical Studies in Mass Communication* 2 (2): 91–114.

Harcup, T. and O'Neill, D. (2001). What is news? Galtung and Ruge revisited. *Journalism Studies* 2 (2): 261–280.

Herman, E.S. and Chomsky, N. (2008). *Manufacturing Consent: The Political Economy of the Mass Media*. New York: Random House.

Hermida, A. (2010). Twittering the news: the emergence of ambient journalism. *Journalism Practice* 4 (3): 297–308.

Hill, A. and Alshaer, A. (2010). BBC Arabic TV: participation and the question of public diplomacy. *Middle East Journal of Culture and Communication* 3 (2): 152–170.

Hofstetter, C.R. (1976). *Bias in the News: Network Television Coverage of the 1972 Election Campaign*. Columbus, OH: Ohio State University Press.

Ioffe, J. (2010). What is Russia Today? A Kremlin propaganda outlet has an identity crisis. *Columbia Journalism Review*. Available from: https://archives.cjr.org/feature/what_is_russia_today.php (accessed November 28, 2019).

Jackoway, A., Samet, H., and Sankaranarayanan, J. (2011). Identification of live news events using Twitter. In: *Proceedings of the 3rd ACM SIGSPATIAL International Workshop on Location-Based Social Networks* (LBSN'11). ACM, pp. 25–32.

Jensen, K.B. (1987). News as ideology: economic statistics and political ritual in television network news. *Journal of Communication* 37 (1): 8–27.

Ju, A., Jeong, S.H., and Chyi, H.I. (2013). Will social media save newspapers? Examining the effectiveness of Facebook and Twitter as news platforms. *Journalism Practice* 8 (1): 1–17.

Kiousis, S. (2004). Explicating media salience: a factor analysis of *New York Times* issue coverage during the 2000 US presidential election. *Journal of Communication* 54 (1): 71–87.

Kümpel, A.S., Karnowski, V., and Keyling, T. (2015). News sharing in social media: a review of current research on news sharing users, content, and networks. *Social Media+ Society* https://doi.org/10.1177/2056305115610141.

Kwak, H., Lee, C., Park, H., and Moon, S. (2010). What is Twitter, a social network or a news media? In: *Proceedings of the 19th International Conference on World Wide Web*. ACM, pp. 591–600.

Lahlali, E.M. (2011). *Contemporary Arab Broadcast Media*. Edinburgh: Edinburgh University Press.

Miller, M. (1997). Frame mapping and analysis of news coverage of contentious issues. *Social Science Computer Review* 15: 367–378.

Mellor, N., Rinnawi, K., Dajani, N., and Ayish, M. (2011). *Arab Media: Globalization and Emerging Media Industries*. Cambridge: Polity.

Pew Research Center (2010). Understanding the participatory news consumer: how Internet and cell phone users have turned news into a social experience. Available from: https://www.pewresearch.org/internet/2010/03/01/understanding-the-participatory-news-consumer/ (accessed November 28, 2019).

Phelan, O., McCarthy, K. and Smyth, B. (2009). Using Twitter to recommend real-time topical news. In: *Proceedings of the Third ACM Conference on Recommender Systems* (RecSys' 09). ACM, pp. 385–388.

Press TV (2011). Al-Alam signal plagued by jamming. Available from: http://edition.presstv.ir/detail/170209.html (accessed November 28, 2019).

RT Arabic (2014). Information about the channel. Available from: http://arabic.rt.com/channel (accessed November 28, 2019).

Schudson, M. (2002). The news media as political institutions. *Annual Review of Political Science* 5 (1): 249–269.

Seib, P. (2005). Hegemonic no more: Western media, the rise of Al-Jazeera, and the influence of diverse voices. *International Studies Review* 7 (4): 601–615.

Seib, P. (2013). *Public Diplomacy and the Media in the Middle East*. Los Angeles, CA: Figueroa Press.

Semati, M. (2007). Media, the state, and the prodemocracy movement in Iran. In: *Negotiating Democracy: Media Transformations in Emerging Democracies* (eds. I. Blankson and P. Murphy), 143–159. New York: SUNY Press.

Shoemaker, P.J. and Cohen, A.A. (2006). *News Around the World: Content, Practitioners, and the Public*. New York: Routledge.

Shoemaker, P.J. and Reese, S.D. (1996). *Mediating the Message*. New York: Longman.

Shoemaker, P.J. and Reese, S.D. (2013). *Mediating the Message in the 21st century: A Media Sociology Perspective*. New York: Routledge.

Siune, K., McQuail, D., and Blumler, J.G. (1984). Broadcasting European elections. *Electoral Studies* 3: 256–263.

Socialbakers (2014). Alalam News: distribution of fans. Available from: http://www.socialbakers.com/facebook-pages/120435151326642-alalam-news (accessed November 28, 2019).

Stephen, T. (2000). Concept analysis of gender, feminist, and women's studies research in the communication literature. *Communications Monographs* 67 (2): 193–214.

Straubhaar, J. (1991). Beyond media imperialism: assymetrical interdependence and cultural proximity. *Critical Studies in Media Communication* 8 (1): 39–59.

Taylor, P. and Snow, N. (2006). The revival of the propaganda state. *International Communication Gazette* 68: 389–407.

Thelwall, M., Buckley, K., and Paltoglou, G. (2011). Sentiment in Twitter events. *Journal of the American Society for Information Science and Technology* 62 (2): 406–418.

Thompson, J. (1990). *Ideology and Modern Culture: Critical Theory in the Era of Mass Communication*. Palo Alto, CA: Stanford University Press.

Usher, S. (2006). Iran's leaders harness media power. BBC News. Available from: http://news.bbc.co.uk/2/hi/middle_east/4804328.stm (accessed November 28, 2019).

Vartanova, E. (2012). The Russian media model in the context of post-Soviet dynamics. In: *Comparing Media Systems Beyond the Western World* (eds. D. Hallin and P. Mancini), 119–142. Cambridge: Cambridge University Press.

Volkmer, I. (2007). Governing the "spatial reach"? Spheres of influence and challenges to global media policy. *International Journal of Communication* 1 (1): 18.

Wilkinson, D. and Thelwall, M. (2012). Trending Twitter topics in English: an international comparison. *Journal of the American Society for Information Science and Technology* 63 (8): 1631–1646.

Wu, D. (2000). Systemic determinants of international news coverage: a comparison of 38 countries. *Journal of Communication* 50 (2): 110–130.

Yang, J. (2003). Framing the NATO air strikes on Kosovo across countries: comparison of Chinese and US newspaper coverage. *International Communication Gazette* 65 (3): 231–249.

3

Fake News Discourses on SNS vs. MSM

Introduction

This chapter compares the coverage of fake news in mainstream news outlets and the discourse about fake news on social media. It offers an analysis of a large data set, constituting of over 8 million tweets and about 1350 news stories collected from different mainstream media (MSM) print outlets. Several computational approaches were used, especially topic modeling as this method is appropriate for the large data set examined. There is no doubt that the empirical study of fake news discourse is still under-researched, and this chapter aims to fill a gap in the literature on this area. Previous research on fake news seems to be more focused on the use of automated bots (Bessi and Ferrara 2016; Howard and Kollanyi 2016; Kollanyi et al. 2016; Gallacher et al. 2017; Howard et al. 2017) rather than on comparisons of what is being disseminated. Looking at the study of the discourse on fake news coverage and social media mentions provides insight into this significant phenomenon in our modern lives, since online news in general has a direct impact on democracy and political knowledge (Bimber 2003; Mossberger et al. 2007). "Fake news" was chosen by Collins Dictionary as its word of the year 2017 because it "saw an unprecedented usage increase (of) 365 per cent since 2016" (Roy 2017).

In the age of social media, fake news has become more pertinent because of its proliferation and expected impact on people's social and political beliefs (Allcott and Gentzkow 2017a; Vargo et al. 2017, p. 4). Facebook, for example, released a report detailing its own definition of the fake news phenomenon. This falls within the concept of "information operations," which are understood to be "actions

This chapter was previously published as Al-Rawi, A. (2019). Gatekeeping fake news discourses on mainstream media versus social media. *Social Science Computer Review*, 37 (6), pp. 687–704, available at: https://doi.org/10.1177/0894439318795849.

taken by organized actors (governments or non-state actors) to distort domestic or foreign political sentiment, most frequently to achieve a strategic and/or geopolitical outcome. These operations can use a combination of methods, such as false news, disinformation, or networks of fake accounts aimed at manipulating public opinion." According to Facebook, networks of fake accounts are called "false amplifiers" (Weedon et al. 2017). A review of 34 academic papers on fake news showed there are six main definitions, including: (i) news satire, (ii) news parody, (iii) fabrication, (iv) manipulation, (v) advertising, and (vi) propaganda (Tandoc et al. 2017). Martinson (2017), for example, believes that fake news constitutes "a deliberate, viral spreading of misinformation for commercial or political ends." Similarly, Allcott and Gentzkow (2017b) describe fake news stories as those that "have no factual basis but are presented as facts," while Benkler et al. (2017) think that "their power stems from a potent mix of verifiable facts (the leaked Podesta emails), familiar repeated falsehoods, paranoid logic, and consistent political orientation within a mutually-reinforcing network of like-minded sites."

More recently, fake news has come to be understood as a weaponized tool used by some political parties and individuals to undermine their opponents by associating them with the concept (Al-Rawi et al. 2018). In this sense, fake news has come to be defined by "those on the [political] right to mean anything they don't agree with," (Jamieson 2017), including, famously, the "mainstream media which the [US] President refers to as fake news" (Boland 2017). In fact, Donald Trump and his former aides like Steve Bannon and Sean Spicer repeatedly refer to CNN and other outlets like the *New York Times* and the BBC as "fake news organizations" that produce "garbage journalism" (Davis and Grynbaum 2017; Gambno 2017).

Fake News on Social Media

Due to the distortion of political reality caused by fake news, it can be considered a direct threat to democracy (Epstein and Robertson 2015; Cadwalladr 2016). One report, for example, found that "the more you consume fake news, the more likely you are to vote" (BBC Trending 2017), while another emphasized that conspiracy theories and fake news stories cannot easily be debunked or stopped on social media (Criss 2017). Of course, fake news is nearly as old as human civilization (McNair 2017), and it is especially popular during times of conflict such as the period that preceded the invasion of Iraq (Rampton and Stauber 2003; O'Shaughnessy 2004; Buncombe 2006). Social media, however, has enhanced its spread due to its integral shareability and connectivity features. A report released by Trend Micro, a cybersecurity firm, stated that spending as little as $400 000 on fake news and propaganda can sway the outcomes of an election. For example, "to maximize the reach of the content, campaigns can spend $6000 to gain about 40 000 'high quality' likes. Within these fake news services, it can also cost $5000 for 20 000 comments and $2700 for a false story" (Levin 2017). Many professional fake news companies and individuals have found effective means of making and spreading fake news and reaching audiences through the affordances of social media, and these efforts can surely undermine democracy. Jonathan Albright calls such websites "micro-propaganda machine[s]," which he describes as follows:

> Most are simple in design, and many appear to be made from the same web templates. These sites have created an *ecosystem of real-time propaganda*: they include viral hoax engines that can instantly shape public opinion through mass "reaction" to serious political topics and news events. This network is triggered on-demand to spread false, hyper-biased, and politically-loaded information. (Albright 2016)

In their propaganda model, Herman and Chomsky referred to five filters that shape news media, including flak, which is generally defined as the "negative responses to a media statement or program. It may take the form of letters, telegrams, phone calls, petitions, lawsuits, speeches and bills before Congress, and other modes of complaint, threat, and punitive action. It may be organized centrally or locally, or it may consist of the entirely independent actions of individuals" (1988, p. 26). The main goal behind the use of flak is related to "disciplining the media" (1988, p. 2), and it can cost media outlets considerable financial losses, especially if "produced on a large scale, or by individuals or groups with substantial resources" (1988, p. 2). This propaganda model will be expanded in order to connect it to the findings discussed in this chapter.

Networked Gatekeeping

Since this chapter deals with the discourse on fake news on MSM and social networking sites (SNS), it is also relevant to discuss the theoretical concept of networked gatekeeping. Inspired by the work of Kurt Lewin, David White (1950) was one of the first scholars to refer to the concept of gatekeeping in the context of journalism and communication. White stated that the "traveling of a news item through certain communication channels was dependent on the fact that certain areas within the channels functioned as 'gates' ... [These] gate sections are governed either by impartial rules or by 'gate keepers,' and in the latter case an individual or group is 'in power' for making the decision between 'in' and 'out'" (1950, p. 383). He argued that the gatekeeping discourse is often "subjective" since it is "based on the 'gate keeper's' own set of experiences, attitudes and expectations" (1950, p. 390). Similarly, Barzilai-Nahon (2009) defines gatekeeping as "the process of controlling information as it moves through a gate or filter ... and is associated with exercising different types of power (e.g., selecting news, enforcing the status quo in parliamentary committees, mediating between professional and ethnic groups, brokering expert information)." In these two definitions, the concept of gatekeeping involves a sort of information filtering process. Pamela Shoemaker (1991) asserts that gatekeeping is about cutting down billions of potential messages into the few hundred ones that reach us every single day. According to the gatekeeping framework, journalists follow certain standardized and centralized rules in order to make sense of the world and provide an overview of the "important" events they believe their readers seek and need. This plays a significant role in the overall news selection process and the ways by which traditional news organizations are shaped.

In relation to social media, there is a clear non-centralization in the way users post and share information. However, there are always "influencers," or popular figures, who often dominate the online chatter. Barzilai-Nahon (2008, 2009) explains in her theory of networked gatekeeping the importance of vertical communication flow, and Shaw (2012) refers to the centralized role of gatekeeping activity as most but not all online chatter is actually filtered by gatekeepers whose communication flows from top to bottom (Castells 2013, p. 71). In this regard, the new version of the two-step flow theory of communication of Katz and Lazarsfeld (1955) seems relevant. The original two-step flow theory focused on how "ideas often flow from radio and print to opinion leaders and from these to the less active sections of the population" (Katz 1957, p. 61). Katz and Lazarsfeld (1955, p. 3) originally defined "opinion leaders" as "the individuals who were likely to influence other persons in their immediate environment," and this definition remains in use, more or less unchanged (Grewal et al. 2000, p. 236). In the age of social media, some studies find this theory retains validity in the sense that opinion leaders can generate interest and communication flows among ordinary people (Hilbert et al. 2016). For example, Choi (2015) relied on Katz and Lazarsfeld's theory to explain the influence of opinion makers in South Korea who are more effective than online content creators. Also, Southgate et al. (2010) found that celebrity status or offline fame plays a crucial role in making viral content such as YouTube videos. Several other studies confirm that celebrities have a clear impact on making some online media content popular (Wu and Wang 2011; Nahon and Hemsley 2013, p. 78). In social network analysis, some scholars believe that examining the so-called focal structure is important as it is concerned with the influential group of individuals in a network. The focal structure comprises people who act together in order to achieve greater power in an online network (Şen et al. 2016).

To sum up, MSM often follows clear gatekeeping processes, and this plays a role in determining the way news is made, including discourse on fake news. This is based on a vertical type of communication flow. On the other hand, social media users also practice what is known as networked gatekeeping activity, in which influencers play a major role as part of a bottom-up communication flow (Bro and Wallberg 2014). This chapter attempts to explore the topics associated with the (networked) gatekeeping discourse of fake news on MSM and SNS.

Methodologically, two sets of large data were collected. The first consisted of 8 116 792 tweets covering a period of over seven months (from January to August 2017) (Borra and Rieder 2014; Groshek 2014). The tweets were posted to Twitter by 1 501 976 distinct users who mentioned #fakenews. The second set of data was retrieved from MSM using a subscribed journalism database called ProQuest-Newstream. All news articles referring to fake news were collected from 23 US and UK newspapers. The original search yielded a total of 1599 newspaper items, including news stories, features, and editorials; however, duplicates were removed and only full-text news articles were used for this analysis, for a total of 1353 news stories (794 US and 559 UK news items) (see Table 3.1). The reason for choosing all the available news stories within this timeframe is that they were limited in number, and a great deal of the news coverage of this topic was published in the years 2016 and 2017 due to its increasing popularity following Brexit and the 2016

Table 3.1 US and British MSM coverage of fake news.

No.	US newspapers	Items	No.	UK newspapers	Items
1)	*New York Times*	135	1)	*The Times*	269
2)	*Washington Post*	118	2)	telegraph.co.uk	133
3)	*Wall Street Journal*	88	3)	*Daily Telegraph*	104
4)	*Los Angeles Times*	76	4)	*Financial Times*	56
5)	*The Daily Beast*	75	5)	*Sunday Times*	55
6)	*New York Post*	66	6)	*Guardian*	50
7)	*Chicago Tribune*	57	7)	*Observer*	37
8)	*USA Today*	40	8)	*Herald*	32
9)	*New York Observer*	44	9)	*International Herald Tribune*	19
10)	*Boston Globe*	39	10)	*Independent*	15
11)	*Christian Science Monitor*	41	11)	*Sunday Telegraph*	13
12)	*USA Today*	37		Total	783
	Total	816			

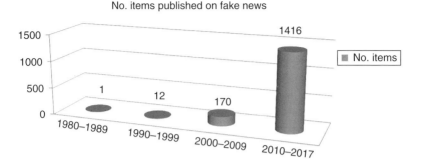

Figure 3.1 Timeline distribution of news items referencing fake news in US and British MSM.

US election (see Figure 3.1). This timeframe is appropriate for identifying the dominant topics in MSM coverage of fake news.

Topic modeling, a text mining tool that identifies topics in a given corpus, was employed for this analysis. Since a large amount of data was retrieved from Twitter, this method was used for "the application of natural language processing tasks commonly used with Twitter data," including "language identification, topic modelling, and sentiment analysis" (Brown and Soto-Corominas 2017, p. 136). Built on a statistical model and using a specific algorithm, topic modeling is part of machine learning based on calculating the most frequent words used and their associations with other terms and phrases in an unstructured body of text. There are usually two categories in topic modeling. The first is Probabilistic Latent Semantic Analysis (PLSA), while the second is Latent Dirichlet Allocation (LDA). The former is a "statistical technique for the analysis of two-mode and co-occurrence data" (Hofmann 1999), while the latter is regarded as "an unsupervised machine learning technique which identifies latent topic information in large document collections" (Hong and Davison 2010). Topic modeling often functions in two ways: first, by producing "each word on the basis of some number of preceding words or word classes," and, second, by generating "words based on latent topic variables inferred from word correlations independent of the order in which the words appear" (Wallach 2006). Many research studies employ topic modeling using different procedures and types of software, such as studies of big data on Twitter (Conover et al. 2013; Ghosh and Guha 2013), while others use or reference it in journalism-related issues (Berendt 2011; Boumans and Trilling 2016; Jacobi et al. 2016), especially in examining some case studies in media coverage (DiMaggio et al. 2013; Kang et al. 2013).

QDA Miner – WordStat 7, a new topic modeling tool using Factor Analysis (FA) that shares similarities with PLSA (Péladeau and Davoodi 2018), is also used in this analysis. FA has been used since the early 1960s for classifying documents and retrieving topics (Borko and Bernick 1963). The software program also provides Eigenvalue, which is a mathematical linear system (Marcus and Minc 1988, p. 145); the higher this value, the more dominant the topic found in the corpora, not because of its frequency but because of the amount of variance from the correlation matrix explained by the Eigen factor. This method of study, it is important to note, requires contextualization and interpretation from the researcher. Finally, the software provides accurate statistical measures to further investigate each topic through the use of a proximity plot and its Jaccard coefficient, which assesses the connections among various words and phrases. The coefficient ranges between 0.0 for no co-occurrence and 1.0 for complete co-occurrence (Tan et al. 2006).

As mentioned, this chapter investigates MSM coverage of fake news and compares it to online references to the same topic in order to understand the discourse on the two platforms. The findings show that the top five most dominant topics used in MSM were as follows: "advertising/ads" (Eigenvalue < 5.10), "intelligence" (Eigenvalue < 2.95), "Jon Stewart Show" (Eigenvalue < 2.19), "Hillary Clinton" (Eigenvalue < 2.11), and "Donald Trump" (Eigenvalue < 1.92) (see Table 3.2). For space considerations, only a selection of topics will be discussed here.

Table 3.3 provides a list of the top 100 words used in MSM, which helps in understanding some of the prominent topics. For example, the most recurrent topic is related to "advertising/ads," which is first connected to "sites" (Jaccard coefficient < 0.104) and "Google" (Jaccard coefficient < 0.093). In other words, the topic of "Sites for Google advertising" is the most recurrent one tackled by MSM, mostly in connection to the financial profits to be made off of fake news stories. The most recurrent phrases made up of three words in the corpus are "fake news sites" (n = 183), "fake news stories" (n = 148), "Comet Ping Pong" (n = 101), and "Facebook and Google" (n = 96). As part of its gatekeeping discourse, MSM is focused on highlighting the connection between Google ads and the spread of misinformation due to the proliferation of fake news sites (see Figure 3.2).

The second most recurrent topic is related to "intelligence," which is most associated with "Russian" (Jaccard coefficient < 0.116), "officials" (Jaccard coefficient < 0.086), and "Russia" (Jaccard coefficient < 0.078). As will be explained later, it seems that MSM is far more likely to highlight the Russian connections to Trump's electoral campaign than SNS networked gatekeeping discourse.

The third most recurrent topic is "Jon Stewart," a reference to *The Daily Show* TV program, which became popular long before the 2016 US election as a result of the numerous political commentaries made by host Jon Stewart on the subject of fake news. *The Daily Show* itself, known for its satire as well as its full-throated critique of mainstream outlets like Fox News, was known as "the Real Fake News" (Kothe 2007); that's why the word "real" is strongly associated with Stewart (Jaccard coefficient < 0.026). The "real fake news" moniker, of course, has no relation to news fabrication as the show is known for news parody and satire.

Table 3.2 Topic clustering in MSM.

No.	Topic	Keywords	Eigenvalue
1)	Ads; Advertising	Ads; Advertising; Sites; Ad; Google	5.10
2)	Intelligence	Intelligence; Agencies; Officials	2.95
3)	With Jon Stewart	Stewart; Show; Daily; Comedy	2.19
4)	Hillary Clinton	Clinton; Hillary; Child	2.11
5)	Donald Trump	Trump; President; Elect; Donald; Obama	1.92
6)	CEO Mark Zuckerberg	Zuckerberg; Mark; Facebook	1.85
7)	Fact-Checking	Checking; Fact; Organizations	1.82
8)	White House	House; White	1.76
9)	United States	United; States	1.75
10)	YORK TIMES	York; Times	1.68
11)	Social Media	Media; Social; Mainstream; Outlets	1.63
12)	Michael Flynn; National Security	Flynn; Security; Michael; National	1.56
13)	Hate Speech	Speech; Hate; Free; Germany	1.55
14)	Wall Street	Wall; Street; Journal	1.47
15)	University; School	University; School; Journalism; Director	1.44
16)	Presidential; Election Campaign	Presidential; Election; Campaign; Spread	1.40
17)	Buzzfeed Published; Website	Published; Website; Site; Story; Article; Buzzfeed; Page	1.38
18)	Facebook Users	Users; Facebook; Shared	1.36
19)	National Committee	Committee; Democratic; Republican; National	1.33
20)	Bush Administration; Foreign Policy	Administration; Bush; Policy; Foreign; Government	1.31
21)	Google Search	Search; Popular; Vote; Google	1.30
22)	Press Conference	Press; Conference; Secretary	1.28
23)	Chief Executive	Chief; Executive; Editor	1.26
24)	Tech Companies	Companies; Tech; Technology; Information	1.25
25)	Washington Post	Washington; Post	1.24
26)	TV Shows; Late-Night	Shows; TV; Night; Late; Young; Television	1.22
27)	Russia; Putin	Russia; Putin; Russian; Elections; Germany; Influence	1.22
28)	Fake News	Fake; News; Real	1.21

Table 3.3 Top 50 most recurrent words in MSM.

No.	Word	Frequency	No.	Word	Frequency
1)	News	9241	26)	Times	1016
2)	Fake	5880	27)	Campaign	984
3)	Trump	5296	28)	Make	983
4)	Media	3116	29)	Russia	973
5)	Facebook	3082	30)	Company	962
6)	Mr.	2956	31)	Fact	953
7)	People	2824	32)	Russian	946
8)	President	2293	33)	False	922
9)	Full	1578	34)	Twitter	916
10)	Election	1570	35)	Online	902
11)	Social	1459	36)	White	901
12)	Stories	1449	37)	House	897
13)	Text	1423	38)	Years	897
14)	Year	1358	39)	American	884
15)	AccountID	1353	40)	Sites	870
16)	Time	1349	41)	Week	869
17)	Story	1325	42)	Credit	865
18)	Show	1301	43)	Report	835
19)	Information	1154	44)	Google	833
20)	World	1117	45)	Day	822
21)	Political	1093	46)	Government	810
22)	Press	1044	47)	Content	792
23)	Real	1037	48)	Internet	777
24)	Donald	1030	49)	Clinton	773
25)	Public	1023	50)	Post	756

As for the fourth most recurrent topic, it is "Hillary Clinton," which unsurprisingly is closely linked to terms like "campaign," "Trump," and "election." However, this topic is also used in reference to "conspiracy" stories (Jaccard coefficient <0.056 with "Hillary" and <0.065 with "Clinton") such as the Pizzagate fake story, which involved an alleged child sex ring at a pizza restaurant. In fact, "Hillary Clinton" is first connected to "conspiracy theories" (Jaccard coefficient < 0.034); "Comet Ping Pong" (the name of the restaurant) ranks fifth (Jaccard coefficient < 0.024) (see also Table 3.4).

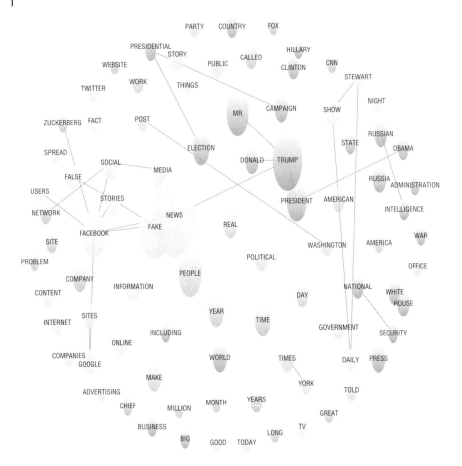

Figure 3.2 Top 100 words in MSM and their associations.

As for "Donald Trump," we find the term is associated with other common words like "President," "Mr.," and "news," but also "fake" (Jaccard coefficient < 0.103) and "Russia" (Jaccard coefficient < 0.070). It is important to mention here that the most recurrent phrase consisting of four words in MSM is "President Elect Donald Trump" (n = 75), followed by "spread of fake news" (n = 69), "President of the United" (n = 46), and "proliferation of fake news" (n = 40). These findings suggest MSM was clearly focused on covering Donald Trump and associating him with the fake news phenomenon, especially prior to his inauguration.

It is important to discuss a few more prominent topics, such as "Mark Zuckerberg." His name is most associated with other familiar terms like "CEO," "Facebook," "Chief," and "company," but also "misinformation"

Table 3.4 Top 50 phrases (two to three words) in MSM.

No.	Phrase	Frequency	No.	Phrase	Frequency
1)	Fake News	4773	26)	News Organizations	155
2)	Social Media	958	27)	Real News	153
3)	Donald Trump	795	28)	Fake News Stories	148
4)	White House	616	29)	Vice President	146
5)	Mr. Trump	479	30)	Mainstream Media	144
6)	United States	408	31)	President Obama	144
7)	President Elect	384	32)	False News	142
8)	Hillary Clinton	362	33)	News Feed	141
9)	York Times	341	34)	Comedy Central	140
10)	News Stories	304	35)	Hate Speech	137
11)	Daily Show	298	36)	Jon Stewart	135
12)	Presidential Election	273	37)	News Story	133
13)	President Trump	259	38)	Barack Obama	132
14)	News Media	247	39)	Vladimir Putin	130
15)	News Sites	241	40)	Conspiracy Theories	120
16)	Fact Checking	238	41)	Wall Street	120
17)	Fox News	238	42)	Prime Minister	119
18)	Chief Executive	201	43)	News Conference	117
19)	National Security	195	44)	Fact Checkers	114
20)	Social Network	184	45)	News Outlets	114
21)	Fake News Sites	183	46)	Intelligence Agencies	113
22)	Mark Zuckerberg	180	47)	Presidential Campaign	112
23)	Press Conference	179	48)	Fake Stories	109
24)	Washington Post	179	49)	American People	108
25)	Years Ago	157	50)	Ping Pong	105

(Jaccard coefficient < 0.061), "problem" (Jaccard coefficient < 0.048), and "fake" (Jaccard coefficient < 0.036). In relation to "Facebook," we find that the most associated word is "news" (Jaccard coefficient < 0.177), followed by "fake" (Jaccard coefficient < 0.175).

We also examined a number of opposite topics as covered by MSM, including "fake news" versus "real news." We found that "social media" is strongly connected with "fake news" (Jaccard coefficient < 0.037), followed by "Donald Trump" (Jaccard coefficient < 0.035) and "presidential election" (Jaccard coefficient < 0.022). On the other hand, the term second most associated with real news is "Jon Stewart" (Jaccard coefficient < 0.025), followed by "Daily Show" (Jaccard coefficient < 0.024). We also investigated "mainstream media" and "social media." We found that "fake news" is first associated with "social media" (Jaccard coefficient < 0.037), while "mainstream media" is first connected to "Comet Ping Pong" (Jaccard coefficient < 0.020), followed by "press conference" (Jaccard coefficient < 0.019).

Interestingly, when investigating the "social networks" topic, we found that the third most connected term is "false news" (Jaccard coefficient < 0.035), while the topic of "hate speech" is first connected to "social networks" (Jaccard coefficient < 0.034). In brief, it appears MSM outlets focused on covering Trump and linking him to fake news and Russia as part of their gatekeeping discourses, while the coverage on social media was mostly linked to the spread of fake news stories, conspiracy theories, misinformation, and hate speech.

As for the data analysis of Twitter, the most dominant topics are "pleased extremely" (Eigenvalue < 4.81), "producer admits" (Eigenvalue < 3.53), "beat social" (Eigenvalue < 2.76), "House opinion" (Eigenvalue < 2.52), and "changing thinking" (Eigenvalue < 2.38) (Table 3.5). In order to better understand the reasons for the prominence of these topics, we need to investigate the most frequent phrases consisting of four words. We find that "fakenews and garbage journalism" comes first (n = 39 923), followed by "report the great economic" (n = 22 082) and "fakenews CNN producer admits" (n = 19 692). The significance of these recurrent phrases will be discussed later.

In order to better understand these topics, we need to investigate the proximity plots of other terms. For example, examination shows that the topic of "fake news" or "fakenews" comes in the first three places in different formats, with a total of 1 345 014 occurrences (Table 3.6). This is directly followed by "fakenews CNN" (n = 136 599), which is linked to "changing thinking," part of a Trump tweet cited later. By closely investigating the term "CNN," we find that it is actually the most frequently used word on Twitter (n = 1 690 723), followed by "Trump" (n = 1 300 202), "realdonaldtrump" (n = 714 542), "media" (n = 686 885), and "news" (n = 580 203) (Table 3.7). Figure 3.3 provides a visual representation of these dominant words and their links to other ones. Here, it is relevant to examine the proximity plot of "CNN," especially since it is the most discussed and referenced topic in the online chatter. We can see that it is most connected with "Trump" (Jaccard coefficient < 0.094); other connected terms include "fake" (Jaccard coefficient < 0.044), "CNNBlackmail" (Jaccard coefficient < 0.033), "exposed" (Jaccard coefficient < 0.030), "garbage" (Jaccard coefficient < 0.030), and "lies" (Jaccard coefficient < 0.020).

Table 3.5 Topic clustering on Twitter.

No.	Topic	Keywords	Eigenvalue
1)	Pleased; Extremely	Pleased; Extremely; Garbage; Exposed; Finally; Journalism; Time	4.81
2)	Producer; Admits	Producer; Admits; Bullshit; Narrative; Ht; Breaking; AmericanPravda; Russia; Video; Ratings	3.53
3)	Beat; Social	Beat; Social; Continue; Election	2.76
4)	House; Opinion	House; Opinion; Leaks; White; Coming; Lies	2.52
5)	Changing; Thinking	Changing; Thinking; FraudnewsCNN	2.38
6)	CBS; NBC	CBS; NBC; ABC; AP; MSNBC	2.24
7)	Washington; Post	Washington; Post; Russians; WAPO	2.02
8)	Veritas; Project	Veritas; Project; Video	1.93
9)	AmericaFirst; Draintheswamp	AmericaFirst; Draintheswamp; Trumptrain; MAGA; Pizzagate; TCOT	1.82
10)	Bfraser; Telling	Bfraser; Telling; Proof; USA; Muslim; Presidenttrump	1.76
11)	Great; Day	Great; Day; Election; Report; MSM	1.67
12)	Clinton; Entire	Clinton; Entire; Hillary; Wikileaks; Scandal; Sethrich; DNC	1.63
13)	News; Fake	News; Fake; Enemy; Sources	1.56
14)	Terror; Protest	Terror; Protest; Muslim; Anti; Isis; Caught	1.54
15)	Americanpravda; Jamesokeefeiii	Americanpravda; Jamesokeefeiii; Words; Morning	1.52
16)	Hard; Care	Hard; Care; Outlets; Realjameswoods; Democrats	1.50
17)	Jim; Acosta	Jim; Acosta; Years; Donaldjtrumpjr	1.49
18)	Week; Sick	Week; Sick; Stand; People; President	1.47
19)	CBSnews; NBCnews	CBSnews; NBCnews; ABC; Gmoneyrainmaker; MSNBC	1.46
20)	Biggest; Today	Biggest; Today; Story; Report; Media	1.42
21)	Push; Create	Push; Create; HTT; Narrative	1.41
22)	Claims; Buzzfeed	Claims; Buzzfeed; Russia; Trump	1.38
23)	Speech; Seanhannity	Speech; Seanhannity; Free; Conspiracy; Foxnews	1.37
24)	Journalists; Face	Journalists; Face; Washingtonpost	1.36
25)	Retweet; Agree	Retweet; Agree	1.35
26)	American; Truth	American; Truth; People; Interview; Trust	1.34
27)	Collusion; Investigation	Collusion; Investigation; Trumprussia; Comey; FBI; Evidence	1.33
28)	Fraud; Guess	Fraud; Guess	1.32

Table 3.6 Top 50 most recurrent phrases (two to five words) on Twitter.

No.	Phrase	Frequency	Cases	No	Phrase	Frequency	Cases
1)	Fakenews Https	934 019	632 240	26)	CNN Producer	28 903	28 898
2)	Fakenews Media	211 623	192 807	27)	Russia Narrative	27 155	27 119
3)	Fake News	199 372	177 440	28)	Anti Trump	26 656	26 410
4)	Fakenews CNN	136 599	129 804	29)	Fakenews Outlets	25 819	25 517
5)	Project Veritas	87 743	86 112	30)	Fakenews Stories	24 274	24 053
6)	Fakenews MSM	69 412	65 981	31)	Trump Https	23 952	23 727
7)	MAGA Https	68 763	66 980	32)	Washington Post	23 531	23 224
8)	Fakenews Story	59 861	58 232	33)	MSM Doesn	22 825	22 803
9)	President Trump	56 485	55 208	34)	Election Day	22 427	22 410
10)	White House	51 957	50 818	35)	Fakenews MSM Doesn	22 228	22 218
11)	Donald Trump	49 227	47 883	36)	Economic News	22 167	22 163
12)	Garbage Journalism	40 080	40 055	37)	York Times	22 116	21 689
13)	Fakenews and Garbage	40 047	40 023	38)	Great Economic	22 109	22 105
14)	Finally Been Exposed	39 955	39 931	39)	Great Economic News	22 105	22 101
15)	Fakenews and Garbage Journalism	39 923	39 899	40)	Report The Great	22 103	22 097

No.	Phrase	Frequency	Cases	No.	Phrase	Frequency	Cases
16)	CNN Has Finally	39 870	39 846	41)	Report The Great Economic News	22 081	22 077
17)	CNN Has Finally Been Exposed	39 832	39 809	42)	News Since Election	21 865	21 861
18)	Extremely Pleased	39 674	39 655	43)	Russia Story	21 861	21 665
19)	CNN Https	39 593	38 974	44)	News Since Election Day	21 856	21 852
20)	Mainstream Media	38 868	38 168	45)	Economic News Since Election Day	21 840	21 836
21)	Social Media	37 565	36 943	46)	Great Economic News Since Election	21 837	21 833
22)	Real News	35 713	34 889	47)	Producer Admits	21 802	21 801
23)	American People	33 280	32 959	48)	Fox News	21 533	21 042
24)	Trump Russia	32 541	31 939	49)	CNN Producer Admits	21 297	21 296
25)	Thinking About Changing	30 708	30 697	50)	Trump Supporters	20 134	19 841

Table 3.7 Top 50 most recurrent words on Twitter.

No.	Word	Frequency	Cases	No.	Word	Frequency	Cases
1)	CNN	1 690 723	841 683	26)	Stop	123 992	114 335
2)	Trump	1 300 202	735 000	27)	Watch	119 047	112 109
3)	Realdonaldtrump	714 542	519 311	28)	Washingtonpost	116 741	110 326
4)	Media	686 885	505 880	29)	Election	114 462	106 013
5)	News	580 203	425 114	30)	Day	112 333	102 186
6)	MAGA	380 492	322 678	31)	Russian	103 529	94 538
7)	Fake	374 019	289 645	32)	Jamesokeefeiii	102 612	100 041
8)	MSM	356 311	299 616	33)	Narrative	99 856	95 761
9)	Potus	338 503	288 833	34)	Veritas	99 375	93 977
10)	Russia	320 803	260 631	35)	Left	96 605	91 794
11)	Story	248 456	220 105	36)	Press	95 484	89 353
12)	People	227 763	204 659	37)	Donaldjtrumpjr	94 833	93 231
13)	Time	199 888	178 600	38)	American	94 362	90 251
14)	Obama	190 153	171 012	39)	Lindasuhler	94 224	90 913
15)	Real	186 089	167 548	40)	ABC	93 166	87 124
16)	President	179 459	164 155	41)	Project	91 885	89 924

No.	Word	Frequency	Cases	No.	Word	Frequency	Cases
17)	Report	171 889	155 724	42)	Today	91 616	87 971
18)	Lies	170 323	153 671	43)	White	90 879	84 705
19)	Video	163 979	150 899	44)	Acosta	89 202	75 954
20)	Truth	159 074	145 801	45)	Reporting	88 032	83 986
21)	NYtimes	157 363	142 915	46)	Hillary	85 998	81 634
22)	Foxnews	150 753	137 034	47)	Make	85 916	81 904
23)	MSNBC	145 343	133 197	48)	Jaketapper	84 745	80 455
24)	America	129 798	121 758	49)	Democrats	84 577	80 465
25)	Propaganda	125 400	117 826	50)	Journalism	83 788	80 636

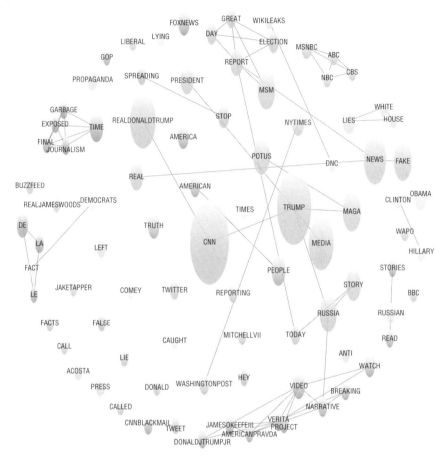

Figure 3.3 Top 100 most recurrent words in the text corpus on Twitter and their associations.

We also compared two opposite terms, "fake" and "real" news, in order to examine the differences between them. The proximity plot of the two topics indicates that Twitter users are far more likely to associate CNN with fake news (Jaccard coefficient < 0.044) than with real news (Jaccard coefficient < 0.018). Aside from their strong connection to news, we can see that "Trump" (Jaccard coefficient < 0.037) and "RealDonladTrump" (Jaccard coefficient < 0.034) are more associated with fake news. On the other hand, the word "people" is first connected to real news (Jaccard coefficient < 0.027), followed by a reference to a right-wing activist, "Jamesokeefeiii" (Jaccard coefficient < 0.023), and then "report" (Jaccard coefficient < 0.022). As a phrase, we examined the topic "fake news" and found similar results. It is first associated with "Fakenews CNN" (Jaccard coefficient

< 0.012), followed by "MAGA HTTPS" (Jaccard coefficient < 0.009), "Fakenews Trump" (Jaccard coefficient < 0.008), and "Donald Trump" (Jaccard coefficient < 0.007). Examination of "fake" and "fakenews" reveals similar results, as "CNN" (Jaccard coefficient < 0.044) and "FakenewsCNN" (Jaccard coefficient < 0.039) are closely connected to them. It is important to mention here that other terms are also associated with "fake" and "fakenews," including "Trump" (Jaccard coefficient < 0.037), "Realdonaldtrump" (Jaccard coefficient < 0.034), "Sean Hannity" (a Fox News presenter) (Jaccard coefficient < 0.035), and "MSNBC" (Jaccard coefficient < 0.012).

Finally, it is relevant to examine other prominent topics such as "propaganda," which is most likely to be associated with "liberals" (Jaccard coefficient < 0.031), "MSM" (Jaccard coefficient < 0.018), "Left" (Jaccard coefficient < 0.018), and "CNN" (Jaccard coefficient < 0.014). Other terms, such as "Foxnews" (Jaccard coefficient < 0.011) and "Russian" (Jaccard coefficient < 0.011), manifest weaker connections. In summary, Twitter users are more likely to associate fake news and CNN with conspiracy, lies, and propaganda, while real news is more connected to Trump supporter James O'Keefe. As part of its centralized networked gatekeeping activity, some influencers, especially Trump and a number of his superfans, are likely to dominate the online chatter, as will be explained later.

These findings indicate that there is an obvious disparity in the way fake news is presented on MSM and SNS, due to the differences in the (networked) gatekeeping discourses. On the one hand, MSM coverage of fake news is more focused on highlighting its connection with sites generating revenues from Google advertising, social media (especially Facebook), and Donald Trump. This is evident in the most dominant topics that are identified, as well as their connections to other terms. For example, fake news is highly linked to social media and Donald Trump's presidential campaign, while real news is related to Jon Stewart and *The Daily Show*. Also, "fake news sites" are more related to spreading conspiracy theories like the Pizzagate story, as well as to Facebook and Google. Mark Zuckerberg, for instance, is more likely to be mentioned on MSM in connection to spreading fake news or misinformation. Similar findings can be found by examining the topic of social networks, which are more likely to be connected to false news and hate speech than to other topics.

Due to its news filtering activity, which is connected to the gatekeeping discourse, MSM frequently highlights another significant topic: the alleged relation between the Russian government or its intelligence services and US officials, especially those linked to Trump's election campaign team. Numerous news reports covered the Russian efforts to undermine the 2016 US elections, including the hacking of some Democratic National Committee members' email accounts and contact with a number of US officials associated with Trump's administration. This is also evident in the topic of Hillary Clinton, which is often mentioned in relation to conspiracy theories such as Pizzagate. In other words, MSM clearly blames SNS, at least in part, for the spread of fake news and conspiracy theories like Pizzagate, while emphasizing the alleged connection between Trump, social media, and Russia and the way all this negatively impacted Clinton's campaign. The news outlets selected for this analysis, it is worth noting, are for the most past reputable newspapers that have often been directly criticized by Donald Trump. The president routinely calls many of the selected outlets fake news organizations, especially the *New York Times* and the *Washington Post*, largely because they are major publications that critically cover his administration and policies.

The impact of Trump's attacks on MSM, as well as those by other major influencers, can be seen in our data analysis. The majority of Twitter users discussing CNN and fake news present the cable news channel negatively, echoing Trump and his staffers by calling it a fake news organization. In MSM, references to CNN are very rare, whereas on Twitter many negative terms are strongly associated with it, including "CNNBlackmail," "garbage journalism," "exposed," "propaganda," "enemy," and "lies." The pervasiveness of this negative attitude toward CNN seems to be related to the number of times certain anti-CNN posts are retweeted. In fact, the most dominant topics and recurrent phrases in the corpus are actually fragments taken from larger statements that have become popular on Twitter, and they are all parts of tweets or retweets by famous figures, especially Trump himself. For instance, the most retweeted post was written by Trump on July 1, 2017: "I am extremely pleased to see that @CNN has finally been exposed as #FakeNews and garbage journalism. It's about time!" (n = 39 955). In second place is another tweet from Trump, posted that same day: "I am thinking about changing the name #FakeNews CNN to #FraudNewsCNN!" (n = 30 708). The third most retweeted post is also by Trump, and was written on June 11, 2017: "The #FakeNews MSM doesn't report the great economic news since Election Day" (n = 22 228). As for the fourth most retweeted post, it was written on June 26, 2017 by conservative provocateur and conspiracy theorist James O'Keefe, who has close ties with Breitbart News: "#FakeNews CNN Producer admits the CNN Russia narrative is 'bullshit.' #AmericanPravda" (n = 21 297). Another popular tweet by Trump reads as follows: "The FAKE NEWS media (failing @nytimes, @NBCNews, @ABC, @CBS, @CNN) is not my enemy, it is the enemy of the American People!" (n = 17 836). All of this provides a sense of the way partisan political views become prominent in the online public sphere. The views of a few popular Twitter users, the influencers and gatekeepers, play a major role in shaping the discussion on the platform.

When it comes to the topic of "fake news," it is strongly connected to "Trump" and "RealDonladTrump" because of the number of times the US president tweets about the topic. The discussion of "real news" on Twitter is heavily linked to James O'Keefe, suggesting that he is a credible and real news source. This stands in contrast to "fake news" coverage in MSM, wherein Jon Stewart and his *Daily Show* are strongly linked to the topic of "real news." Other topics investigated on Twitter, such as "propaganda," show a clear partisan stance, as the majority of associated terms are linked to the political left or liberals.

There appears to be an obvious ideological divide that separates MSM from SNS in relation to fake news due to the different gatekeeping discourses. While the MSM, for instance, has emphasized the role of Russia and its connection to Trump, this topic is not as prominent on Twitter, as Trump and his supporters have dominated the online discourse related to fake news. Additionally, MSM has highlighted the negative influence of fake news sites and their connection to Google advertising and the role of SNS – including, especially, Facebook and its CEO. These topics, again, are largely missing on Twitter in relation to fake news. Instead, on this topic, the majority of Twitter users have focused their attention on attacking CNN by retweeting posts written by Trump and many of his most popular supporters.

In summary, the gatekeeping discourses of MSM outlets show unfavorable coverage of Trump, fake news sites, Google, and Facebook. The networked and centralized gatekeeping activity of Trump on Twitter indicates that he holds significant power over the general topics discussed, and we can speculate that his use of the medium is aimed directly and indirectly at pressuring MSM outlets to change their tone and editorial stance. Based on the empirical findings of this chapter, and building on Herman and Chomsky's (1988) propaganda model, I argue that Twitter offers Trump a *networked flak* tool with which he attempts to continuously undermine the credibility of MSM and "discipline" it, especially those outlets that are most critical of his administration and policies (Reporters without Borders 2017). This networked flak activity is meant to undermine the general public's trust in MSM (Tavernise 2016; Marwick and Lewis 2017). This was made explicit by Trump's team during the 2016 election, when they openly suggested that mainstream "news cannot be trusted" (Faris et al. 2017, p. 21). There's evidence to suggest this type of strategy is working. A recent Gallup survey, for example, showed that while 53% of respondents in 1997 trusted MSM, as of 2016 only 32% hold that same belief (Swift 2016). This contributes to an explanation of how people allow "low-quality information" to become viral on SNS, since they often consider it more credible than MSM (Qiu et al. 2017). A BuzzFeed News analysis showed that "top fake [US] election news stories generated more total engagement on Facebook than top election stories from 19 major news outlets combined" (Silverman 2016). This networked flaking strategy also exerts additional collective pressure on MSM outlets to change their editorial stance. As part of his continuous efforts to undermine the credibility of MSM, Trump announced "Fake News Awards" on his Twitter account in January 2018, targeting outlets like the *New York Times*, ABC, CNN, the *Washington Post*, and *Newsweek* (CBC 2018). According

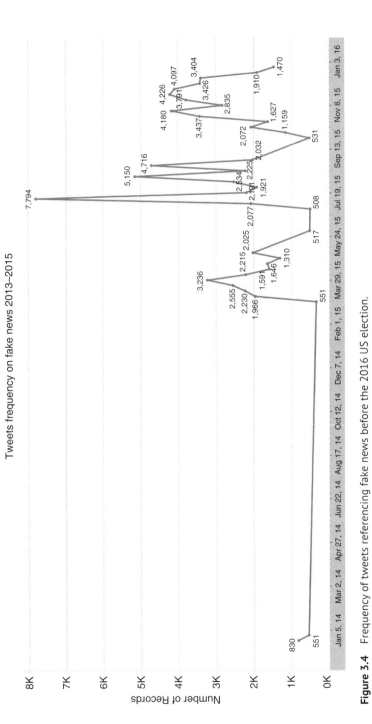

Figure 3.4 Frequency of tweets referencing fake news before the 2016 US election.

to the website www.trumptwitterarchive.com, which has archived all of Trump's tweets since he became president, Trump tweets mostly on fake news (n = 184), followed by Fox News and Sean Hannity (n = 182). Only time will reveal the longer-term impact of this strategy of relentlessly attacking the MSM.

Finally, it should be noted that this chapter is limited in many aspects, providing a holistic overview of this coverage. The investigation has focused on the discourse about fake news on social media and the role of influencers, rather than identifying all the original creators of fake news stories. Future studies can examine how MSM coverage of fake news has changed over time. Topic modeling, as a computational method, has its own limitations in terms of decontextualizing the data set, so using some qualitative approaches would be useful in complementing the findings presented here. Perhaps most importantly, there is an urgent need to study fake news discourse in non-Western contexts. In my examination of fake news discourses before the US presidential primary elections and caucuses, which began in early 2016, I collected a total of 90 332 tweets posted from December 25, 2013 to December 31, 2015 (Figure 3.4). The majority of these tweets and most of the discussion centered not on US politics, but on attacking Indian MSM by using the hashtag #Media420 and associating it with lies and fake news. An understanding of India's media and its geopolitical context, as well as other major media markets in the Global South, is required in order to gain a better understanding of global fake news discourses. The contest over fake news and its weaponization for political purposes will unfold worldwide, and it has only just begun.

References

Albright, J. (2016). The #election2016 micro-propaganda machine. *Medium*. Available from: https://medium.com/@d1gi/the-election2016-micro-propaganda-machine-383449cc1fba (accessed November 28, 2019).

Allcott, H. and Gentzkow, M. (2017a). Social media and fake news in the 2016 election. *Journal of Economic Perspectives* 31 (2): 211–236.

Allcott, H. and Gentzkow, M. (2017b). Social media and fake news in the 2016 election. Stanford University, New York University, National Bureau of Economic Research, January 5–6.

Al-Rawi, A., Groshek, J., and Zhang, L. (2018). What the fake? Assessing the extent of networked political spamming and bots in the propagation of #fakenews on Twitter. *Online Information Review* https://doi.org/10.1108/oir-02-2018-0065.

Barzilai-Nahon, K. (2008). Toward a theory of network gatekeeping: a framework for exploring information control. *Journal of the American Society for Information Science and Technology* 59: 1493–1512.

Barzilai-Nahon, K. (2009). Gatekeeping: a critical review. *Annual Review of Information Science and Technology* 43 (1): 1–79.

BBC Trending (2017). The rise of left-wing, anti-Trump fake news. Available from: http://www.bbc.com/news/blogs-trending-39592010 (accessed November 28, 2019).

Benkler, Y., Faris, R., Roberts, H., and Zuckerman, E. (2017). Study: Breitbart-led right-wing media ecosystem altered broader media agenda. *Columbia Journalism Review*. Available from: https://www.cjr.org/analysis/breitbart-media-trump-harvard-study.php (accessed November 28, 2019).

Berendt, B. (2011). Text mining for news and blogs analysis. In: *Encyclopedia of Machine Learning* (eds. C. Sammut and G.I. Webb), 968–972. Boston, MA: Springer.

Bessi, A. and Ferrara, E. (2016). Social bots distort the 2016 US presidential election online discussion. *First Monday* https://doi.org/10.5210/fm.v21i11.7090.

Bimber, B. (2003). *Information and American Democracy: Technology in the Evolution of Political Power*. Cambridge: Cambridge University Press.

Boland, H. (2017). Facebook shareholders reject fake news proposal. *Telegraph*. Available from https://www.telegraph.co.uk/technology/2017/06/01/facebook-shareholders-reject-fake-news-proposal/ (accessed November 28, 2019).

Borko, H. and Bernick, M. (1963). Automatic document classification. *Journal of the ACM* 10 (2): 151–162.

Borra, E. and Rieder, B. (2014). Programmed method: developing a toolset for capturing and analyzing tweets. *Aslib Journal of Information Management* 66 (3): 262–278.

Boumans, J.W. and Trilling, D. (2016). Taking stock of the toolkit: an overview of relevant automated content analysis approaches and techniques for digital journalism scholars. *Digital Journalism* 4 (1): 8–23.

Bro, P. and Wallberg, F. (2014). Digital gatekeeping: news media versus social media. *Digital Journalism* 2 (3): 1–9.

Brown, D.M. and Soto-Corominas, A. (2017). Overview – the social media data processing pipeline. In: *The SAGE Handbook of Social Media Research Methods* (eds. L. Sloan and A. Quan-Haase), 125–145. Thousand Oaks, CA: Sage.

Buncombe, A. (2006). Bush planted fake news stories on American TV. *Independent*. Available from http://www.independent.co.uk/news/world/americas/bush-planted-fake-news-stories-on-american-tv-480172.html (accessed November 28, 2019).

Cadwalladr, C. (2016). Google, democracy and the truth about internet search. *Guardian*. Available from: https://www.theguardian.com/technology/2016/dec/04/google-democracy-truth-internet-search-facebook (accessed November 28, 2019).

Castells, M. (2013). *Communication Power*. Oxford: Oxford University Press.

CBC (2018). Trump continues attacks on US media, releases "Fake News Awards." Available from: http://www.cbc.ca/news/world/trump-fake-news-awards-1.4492535 (accessed November 28, 2019).

Choi, S. (2015). The two-step flow of communication in Twitter-based public forums. *Social Science Computer Review* 33 (6): 696–711.

Conover, M.D., Ferrara, E., Menczer, F., and Flammini, A. (2013). The digital evolution of occupy wall street. *PLoS One* 8 (5): e64679.

Criss, D. (2017). 5 fake stories that just won't go away. CNN. Available from: http://www.cnn.com/2017/03/10/us/snopes-five-fake-stories-trnd/ (accessed November 28, 2019).

Davis, J. and Grynbaum, M. (2017). Trump intensifies his attacks on journalists and condemns FBI "leakers." *New York Times*. Available from: https://www.nytimes.com/2017/02/24/us/politics/white-house-sean-spicer-briefing.html?_r=0 (accessed November 28, 2019).

DiMaggio, P., Nag, M., and Blei, D. (2013). Exploiting affinities between topic modeling and the sociological perspective on culture: application to newspaper coverage of US government arts funding. *Poetics* 41 (6): 570–606.

Epstein, R. and Robertson, R.E. (2015). The search engine manipulation effect (SEME) and its possible impact on the outcomes of elections. *Proceedings of the National Academy of Sciences* 112 (33): E4512–E4521.

Faris, R., Roberts, H., Etling, B., Bourassa, N., Zuckerman, E., and Benkler, Y. (2017). Partisanship, propaganda, and disinformation: online media and the 2016 US presidential election. Berkman Klein Centre For Internet and Society at Harvard University. Available from: https://cyber.harvard.edu/publications/2017/08/mediacloud (accessed November 28, 2019).

Gallacher, J., Kaminska, M., Kollanyi, B., Yasseri, T., and Howard, P. N. (2017). Social media and news sources during the 2017 UK general election. Available from: http://comprop.oii.ox.ac.uk/wp-content/uploads/sites/89/2017/06/Social-Media-and-News-Sources-during-the-2017-UK-General-Election.pdf (accessed November 28, 2019).

Gambno, L. (2017). Trump aide Steve Bannon calls mainstream media "opposition party." *Guardian*. Available from: https://www.theguardian.com/us-news/2017/jan/26/steve-bannon-media-trump-fox (accessed November 28, 2019).

Ghosh, D. and Guha, R. (2013). What are we "tweeting" about obesity? Mapping tweets with topic modeling and geographic information system. *Cartography and Geographic Information Science* 40 (2): 90–102.

Grewal, R., Mehta, R., and Kardes, F.R. (2000). The role of the social-identity function of attitudes in consumer innovativeness and opinion leadership. *Journal of Economic Psychology* 21 (3): 233–252.

Groshek, J. (2014). Twitter Collection and Analysis Toolkit (TCAT) at Boston University. Available from: https://sites.bu.edu/cmcs/bu-tcat/ (accessed November 28, 2019).

Herman, E.S. and Chomsky, N. (1988). *Manufacturing Consent: The Political Economy of the Mass Media*. New York: Pantheon.

Hilbert, M., Vásquez, J., Halpern, D. et al. (2016). One step, two step, network step? Complementary perspectives on communication flows in Twittered citizen protests. *Social Science Computer Review* https://doi.org/10.1177/0894439316639561.

Hofmann, T. (1999). Probabilistic latent semantic analysis. In: *Proceedings of the Fifteenth Conference on Uncertainty in Artificial Intelligence*, pp. 289–296.

Hong, L. and Davison, B.D. (2010). Empirical study of topic modeling in Twitter. In: *Proceedings of the First Workshop on Social Media Analytics*. ACM, pp. 80–88.

Howard, P.N. and Kollanyi, B. (2016). Bots, #StrongerIn, and #Brexit: computational propaganda during the UK–EU referendum. Cornell University. Available from: http://arxiv.org/abs/1606.06356 (accessed November 28, 2019).

Howard, P.N., Bolsover, G., Kollanyi, B., Bradshaw, S., and Neudert, L.M. (2017). Junk news and bots during the US election: what were Michigan voters sharing over Twitter? Data Memo 2017.1. Oxford: Project on Computational Propaganda. Available from: https://comprop.oii.ox.ac.uk/research/working-papers/junk-news-and-bots-during-the-u-s-election-what-were-michigan-voters-sharing-over-twitter/ (accessed November 28, 2019).

Jacobi, C., van Atteveldt, W., and Welbers, K. (2016). Quantitative analysis of large amounts of journalistic texts using topic modelling. *Digital Journalism* 4 (1): 89–106.

Jamieson, A. (2017). *New Yorker* editor: Trump is seeking to divide Americans by making press an enemy. *Guardian*. Available from: https://www.theguardian.com/media/2017/mar/03/covering-trump-media-columbia-journalism-conference-the-guardian (accessed November 28, 2019).

Kang, B., Song, M., and Jho, W. (2013). A study on opinion mining of newspaper texts based on topic modeling. *Journal of the Korean Society for Library and Information Science* 47 (4): 315–334.

Katz, E. (1957). The two-step flow of communication: an up-to-date report on an hypothesis. *Public Opinion Quarterly* 21 (1): 61–78.

Katz, E. and Lazarsfeld, P. (1955). *Personal Influence: The Part Played by People in the Flow of Mass Communications*. Glencoe, IL: The Free Press.

Kollanyi, B., Howard, P.N., and Woolley, S.C. (2016). Bots and automation over Twitter during the first US presidential debate. *COMPROP Data Memo*. Available from: https://assets.documentcloud.org/documents/3144967/Trump-Clinton-Bots-Data.pdf (accessed November 28, 2019).

Kothe, A. (2007). When fake is more real: of fools, parody, and *The Daily Show with Jon Stewart*. *Americana: The Journal of American Popular Culture, 1900 to Present* 6 (2).

Levin, S. (2017). Pay to sway: report reveals how easy it is to manipulate elections with fake news. *Guardian* Available from: https://www.theguardian.com/

media/2017/jun/13/fake-news-manipulate-elections-paid-propaganda (accessed November 28, 2019).

Marcus, M. and Minc, H. (1988). *Introduction to Linear Algebra*. New York: Dover.

Martinson, J. (2017). A question for a dystopian age: what counts as fake news? *Guardian*. Available from: https://www.theguardian.com/media/2017/jun/18/a-question-for-a-dystopian-age-what-counts-as-fake-news (accessed November 28, 2019).

Marwick, A. and Lewis, R. (2017). Media manipulation and disinformation online. Data & Society Research Institute. Available from: https://datasociety.net/pubs/oh/DataAndSociety_MediaManipulationAndDisinformationOnline.pdf (accessed November 28, 2019).

McNair, B. (2017). *Fake News: Falsehood, Fabrication and Fantasy in Journalism*. London: Routledge.

Mossberger, K., Tolbert, C.J., and McNeal, R.S. (2007). *Digital Citizenship: The Internet, Society, and Participation*. Cambridge, MA: MIT Press.

Nahon, K. and Hemsley, J. (2013). *Going Viral*. Oxford: Polity.

O'Shaughnessy, N.J. (2004). *Politics and Propaganda: Weapons of Mass Seduction*. Manchester: Manchester University Press.

Péladeau, N. and Davoodi, E. (2018). Comparison of latent dirichlet modeling and factor analysis for topic extraction: a lesson of history. In: *Conference Proceedings, The Hawaii International Conference on System Sciences (HICSS)*, January 3–6, pp. 1–9.

Qiu, X., Oliveira, D.F., Shirazi, A.S., Flammini, A., and Menczer, F. (2017). Limited individual attention and online virality of low-quality information. Available from: https://arxiv.org/abs/1701.02694 (accessed November 28, 2019).

Rampton, S. and Stauber, J.C. (2003). *Weapons of Mass Deception: The Uses of Propaganda in Bush's War on Iraq*. London: Penguin.

Reporters without Borders (2017). Does Donald Trump see himself as a media mogul? Available from: https://rsf.org/en/news/does-donald-trump-see-himself-media-mogul (accessed November 28, 2019).

Roy, A. (2017). Fake news in real news. *Telegraph*. Available from: https://www.telegraphindia.com/india/fake-news-in-real-news-183083 (accessed November 28, 2019).

Şen, F., Wigand, R., Agarwal, N. et al. (2016). Focal structures analysis: identifying influential sets of individuals in a social network. *Social Network Analysis and Mining* 6 (1): 1–22.

Shaw, A. (2012). Centralized and decentralized gatekeeping in an open online collective. *Politics & Society* 40 (3): 349–388.

Shoemaker, P. (1991). *Gatekeeping*. Newbury Park, CA: Sage.

Silverman, C. (2016). This analysis shows how viral fake election news stories outperformed real news on Facebook. *BuzzFeed*. Available from: https://www.buzzfeed.com/craigsilverman/viral-fake-election-news-outperformed-real-news-on-facebook?utm_term=.labzXAO7X#.eoemDr6wD (accessed November 28, 2019).

Southgate, D., Westoby, N., and Page, G. (2010). Creative determinants of viral video viewing. *International Journal of Advertising* 29 (3): 349–368.

Swift, A. (2016). Americans' trust in mass media sinks to new low. *Gallup*. Available from: http://www.gallup.com/poll/195542/americans-trust-mass-media-sinks-new-low.aspx (accessed November 28, 2019).

Tan, P., Steinbach, M., and Kumar, V. (2006). *Introduction to Data Mining*. New York: Pearson.

Tandoc, E.C. Jr., Lim, Z.W., and Ling, R. (2017). Defining "fake news": a typology of scholarly definitions. *Digital Journalism* 6 (2): 1–17.

Tavernise, S. (2016). As fake news spreads lies, more readers shrug at the truth. *New York Times*. Available from: http://www.nytimes.com/2016/12/06/us/fake-news-partisan-republican-democrat.html?_r=0 (accessed November 28, 2019).

Vargo, C.J., Guo, L., and Amazeen, M.A. (2017). The agenda-setting power of fake news: a big data analysis of the online media landscape from 2014 to 2016. *New Media & Society* 20 (5): 2028–2049.

Wallach, H.M. (2006). Topic modeling: beyond bag-of-words. In: *Proceedings of the 23rd International Conference on Machine learning*. ACM, pp. 977–984.

Weedon, J., Nuland, W., and Stamos, A. (2017). Information operations and Facebook. Facebook Security. Available from: https://fbnewsroomus.files.wordpress.com/2017/04/facebook-and-information-operations-v1.pdf (accessed November 28, 2019).

White, D.M. (1950). The "gate keeper": a case study in the selection of news. *Journalism Bulletin* 27 (4): 383–390.

Wu, P.C. and Wang, Y.C. (2011). The influences of electronic word-of-mouth message appeal and message source credibility on brand attitude. *Asia Pacific Journal of Marketing and Logistics* 23 (4): 448–472.

Part II

Audiences

4

Social Media News Audiences

Introduction

This chapter investigates the online public comments posted on the Facebook pages of a variety of news organizations. Since it is part of the news consumption experience, it is important to thoroughly study the social networking sites (SNS) of news organizations; they have become a facet of the daily online routine in today's world.

Regarding radio news organizations, two famous Arabic-language channels are examined. Both are foreign-run, and both are popular in the Arab world due to their credibility and long history. It is important to note here that I was not able to locate a Facebook page for BBC Arabic, another popular radio station, while the US State Department's Arabic-language radio station, Sawa, was not included because its Facebook page mostly consisted of posts in the form of questions addressed to its social media audience during the period in which research for the chapter was conducted.

In relation to Radio Netherlands Worldwide (RNW) (www.rnw.org), its slogan is translated from Arabic as "Here Is Your Voice: A Voice for the Voiceless." It is run by the Dutch government and airs from the Netherlands. Though it can be traced back to 1927, RNW was officially established in 1947 as the Dutch international public broadcaster. It used to broadcast in four languages: Dutch, Indonesian, English, and Spanish. Its Arabic and Afrikaans service started in 1949

This chapter is adapted from two previously published papers: Al-Rawi, A. (2017). Assessing public sentiments and news preferences on Al Jazeera and Al Arabiya. *International Communication Gazette*, 79 (1), pp. 26–44, available at: https://doi.org/10.1177/1748048516642732; and Al-Rawi, A. (2016). Understanding the social media audiences of radio stations. *Journal of Radio & Audio Media*, 23 (1), pp. 50–67, available at: https://doi.org/10.1080/19376529.2016.1155298.

(RNW n.d. b). The radio station's Arabic website allows users to comment only by registering to create an account, or by logging on through Facebook. Most of its programs are focused on three areas: human rights, freedom of speech, and sexual rights (translated from Arabic as "love matters"). In 2013, the radio station changed to a Web-based operation because "it was no longer tasked with plugging information gaps around the world or portraying a realistic image of the Netherlands abroad" (RNW n.d. a). As part of its mission, RNW targets people aged 15–30 years in order to create change (RNW n.d. a). According to its website, RNW "reached more than 15 million people [in 2014] through its websites, an increase of almost 50 percent on the previous year. In the same period, our social media community doubled to more than three million" (RNW n.d. b). Its focus in the Arab world is on three countries, Syria, Libya, and Yemen, all of which witnessed the Arab Spring events. The articles posted about these countries tend to be long and to include in-depth features revolving around the three topics previously mentioned (human rights, freedom of speech, and sexual rights). RNW is also involved in training journalists, and sometimes relies on partners that contribute to its programming. These include Radio Rozana (www.rozana.fm), which airs from Turkey and is focused on Syria; Sout Raya (Banner voice) radio (www.soutraya.fm), which airs in Idlib, Hama, and the rural areas of Aleppo in Syria; Shadda Radio FM (www.chadafm.net) from Morocco; and Al-Wassat Radio (www.alwasat.ly) from Libya.

As for Radio Monte Carlo (www.mc-doualiya.com), it is a French radio station that broadcasts its programs from Paris in 14 languages and has over 8 million listeners. It is part of France Médias Monde media group, which includes Radio France International (RFI) and France24 TV; together, these two broadcasters have over 90 million listeners and viewers each week and over 25 million followers on social media (MC n.d.). Similar to RNW, France Médias Monde runs a media academy for the training of radio journalists that is mostly active in Africa. Its Arabic service was established on May 1, 1972 and transmits its programs on FM wave to t Middle and Near East, Djibouti, South Sudan, and Mauritania and on medium wave from Cyprus. The station airs updated daily news, features, music, and a variety of cultural programs; however, it is mostly famous for its news programs, which air throughout the week. The radio station's website allows comments on news articles, but only by logging in with a valid Facebook or Twitter account or by creating a user account on the website itself.

In general, these radio stations post news and features on their websites as well as on their SNS outlets. On Facebook, the page administrator posts the news headline, a hyperlink that leads to the article on the organization's website, and a blurb containing a brief description of the article. In many cases, a video link or photo accompanies the news article. Importantly, sometimes changes are made to the headlines by introducing them as questions aimed at engaging the online audience, since SNS outlets are part of Web 2.0 wherein audiences are expected to be active prosumers.

As for the TV channels, the first one investigated here is Al Jazeera Arabic TV, which started broadcasting in 1996. It is supported by the state of Qatar and broadcasts from Doha. It used to have credibility among segments of Arab TV viewers (Auter et al. 2005), especially before the Arab Spring events. In fact, Al Jazeera caused a great deal of diplomatic tension between Qatar and the US government, as well as many other Arab countries like Jordan, Algeria, Iraq, Saudi Arabia, and Libya, because of its reporting of certain political issues and conflicts in the Middle East, while rarely mentioning criticism against Qatar (Bahry 2001; El-Nawawy and Iskander 2003; Lynch 2006; Seib 2008). The channel was also harshly criticized for its allegedly biased reporting. For example, it largely ignored the Shiite protests in Bahrain against the Sunni monarchy (Al-Rawi 2015). After the toppling of Hosni Mubarak, Al-Jazeera sided with the Muslim Brotherhood, prompting 22 journalists to resign in July 2013 due to this one-sided coverage (NPR 2013). The station's editorial line coincided with the views of Qatari authorities, who, for ideological reasons, showed great support for the Muslim Brotherhood (Williams 2014). Al Jazeera has had much trouble in Egypt due to this alleged bias, which "made many Arab viewers question its veracity" (Economist 2013) and prompted Egyptian authorities to close its offices. In one incident, "al-Jazeera's reporters were kicked out of a news briefing held by the Egyptian military in Cairo after the shooting of dozens of supporters of Mohammad Morsi" (Farhi 2013). Later, several Al Jazeera journalists, including Peter Greste, Mohamed Fahmy, and Baher Mohamed, were imprisoned for allegedly supporting the Muslim Brotherhood (Al Jazeera 2015). Despite all of these controversies, Al Jazeera has remained supportive of the movement, which lost over 1000 members and followers during various protests against the military regime (BBC News 2013). This support is evident in the network's decision to allow the famous pro-Muslim Brotherhood preacher, Yousif Qaradawi, to air a religious program in which he attacked several Gulf countries that supported Abdulfatah Al-Sisi, leading to a serious diplomatic crisis (Williams 2014). The political rift was partly bridged when Al Jazeera later canceled Qaradawi's program. In general, the channel maintains a strong following among supporters of the Muslim Brotherhood in Egypt because it frequently invites prominent figures to talk about the movement's activities and concerns.

Al Arabiya, which began broadcasting in 2003, appeals to a different audience. It is a Saudi news channel that is among the most popular in the Arab world, and together with Al Jazeera is considered among the important opinion-makers in the Arab world (Rinnawi 2006; Wessler and Adolphsen 2008, p. 441; Nisbet and

Myers 2011). Saudi Arabia, together with Kuwait and the UAE, strongly opposes the Muslim Brotherhood because it regards it as a threat to its monarchy. It has shown direct support for regime change and the establishment of military rule in Egypt. These three rich countries, in fact, pledged $12 billion as aid to consolidate the new regime after the Muslim Brotherhood government was ousted. The same countries, especially Saudi Arabia, also oppose Bashar Assad's regime in Syria (Butler 2015).

Despite the claim that some pan-Arab channels provide balanced coverage since they follow journalistic principles, the fact is that the majority, including Al Arabiya and Al Jazeera, are directly linked to their state sponsors (Mellor 2011, pp. 17–18). In fact, such channels are used as political tools in the hands of their respective governments to pressure other countries in the region, and the political rivalries and ideological differences between different Arab countries are directly manifested in the media landscape (Fandy 2007, pp. 39–40). For example, the regional director of the Saudi-MBC, which owns Al Arabiya, once mentioned to a US diplomat that there were concerns over the Qatari-owned Al Jazeera's influence in the region, so the decision was made to make Al Arabiya present a new editorial policy that "counters the influence of al-Jazeera and fosters 'moderate' perspectives among the country's youth" (Wikileaks 2009). Indeed, the two channels follow the policies of the states that own them, and the competition between them has been clearly evident for a long time (Seib 2008, p. 22).

This competition manifested in years of tension and mistrust. For example, Al Jazeera journalists always need to be vetted by the Saudi Ministry of Interior before being allowed to enter the kingdom, according to revelations found in the Wikileaks "Saudi Cables" (Wikileaks 2015a). These cables also reveal that Qatar supported radical movements in Sudan and Syria, and backed opposition parties during the 2009 election in Lebanon, in contrast to Saudi Arabia, Jordan, UAE, and Egypt, all of which backed moderate parties (Wikileaks 2015b). Furthermore, Saudi officials repeatedly expressed their concern about Qatar's use of Al Jazeera as a political tool in the region; for example, they pointed out that Qatar, which hosts the International Union of Muslim Scholars (IUMS), actively tries to promote the "Qatari Project," which advocates political Islam as a better alternative to Arab totalitarian rule and dictatorships (Wikileaks 2015c). This seems to be one of the reasons that Qaradawi heads IUMS from Qatar. This context helps shed light on the kinds of online audiences that comment on the news posted on Al Arabiya's and Al Jazeera's Facebook pages.

In the following section, the selective exposure theory is presented as an explanation for the kind of general and often polarized sentiments expressed by the online audiences of these broadcasters.

Selective Exposure on Social Media

The theory of selective exposure is rooted in Leon Festinger's concept of cognitive dissonance, which asserts that human beings seek consistency when confronted with contradictory views (Zillmann and Bryant 2013). In other words, when there is some kind of inconsistency or dissonance, people tend to become intellectually or psychologically distressed or unstable, and, among other potential remedies, they seek information that corresponds with their existing beliefs and values (Cooper 2007). This is because we are "seldom passive absorbers of data; rather, we selectively seek, choose, and screen information we use" (Cotton 2013, p. 11).

There seems to be a close correlation between selective exposure and partisan preferences, which significantly affects the kind of media messages one searches for (Chaffee et al. 2001; Meffert et al. 2006). Over-time analyses indicate that partisan selective exposure leads to polarization and that people's political beliefs motivate their media use (Stroud 2010). In this context, Tsfati et al. (2013) found that opinion climate perceptions have an influence on the selective exposure to some ideological media channels; several other scholars found evidence to support this idea by investigating various media outlets (Donsbach 1991; Mutz and Martin 2001; Sunstein 2001; Galston 2003; Graf and Aday 2008). Furthermore, exposure to similar media messages might lead to a "narrowed domain of political discourse," as the different parties engaged in discussions become more likely to exhibit rigid views (Brundidge and Rice 2009, p. 150). Indeed, this can lead to the creation audience enclaves (Sunstein 2009), in which opposing views are often met with flaming or the venting of negative sentiments.

The Internet contributes to polarization by offering an "amplification in selectivity" (Brundidge 2010, p. 683). Johnson et al. (2009) found that blog users practice selective exposure when seeking political information. This is especially true among active users who are highly educated, partisan, and politically active both online and offline. Further, Johnson et al. (2011) studied how their respondents practiced selective exposure in viewing political websites, but there was no evidence of selective avoidance practiced. In one study of Facebook, news articles shared on the platform were investigated and the authors found evidence that selective exposure did exist, since "users predominantly share like-minded news articles and avoid conflicting ones, and partisans are more likely to do that" (An et al. 2013, p. 51).

On the other hand, there are other media studies that challenge this theory. For example, Webster and Ksiazek (2012) used network analysis metrics with Nielsen data on television and Internet use and found overlapping patterns of public attention rather than enclaves of audiences with distinct media preferences. In relation to social media use, Lee et al. (2014) found that "political discussion moderates the relationship between network heterogeneity and the level of partisan and ideological polarizations." Brundidge and Rice discuss how heterogeneous Internet users practice selective exposure to political disagreements, since it is useful in enhancing democracy, the public sphere, and the whole political process (2009, p. 145). The authors admit that studies examining "heterogeneous political discussion networks" are still under-researched (Brundidge and Rice 2009, p. 149). Results are, at first blush at least, conflicting. Knoblach-Westerwick and Meng (2008), for example, studied how people who are politically active and engaged are more likely to seek views that oppose their beliefs since they are more certain that they can counter them. Johnson et al. (2011) basically agree with this proposition, as they found that politically active respondents were significantly less likely to avoid information that opposes their beliefs. In this context, Kushin and Kitchener (2009) conducted a study on a Facebook group and found that there are two main online camps within its membership: the majority (73%), which expresses support for the stated position, and the minority (17%), which expresses opposition to it. The authors did find evidence of flaming, as 25% of the online discussions they studied were deemed inflammatory. As will be explained later, the theory of selective exposure in its twofold arguments – the homogenous and the heterogeneous views – seems to offer answers to how SNS communities are formed and how they are engaged in online discussions. SNS thus function similarly to traditional media viewership, wherein audience fragmentation and ideological selectivity are well documented (Iyengar and Hahn 2009; Feldman et al. 2012).

Methodologically, a webometric tool called NVivo 10 – N-Capture was used to mine the comments of the Radio Monte Carlo and RNW Facebook pages in February 2014. The Arabic-language RNW Facebook page (http://www.facebook.com/hunasotak) had 425616 likes while France 24 and Radio Monte Carlo's Facebook page (https://www.facebook.com/Monte.Carlo.Doualiya) had 1306100 likes as of December 2014. On RNW's page, there were 2807 stories posted, which generated 31068 comments by the online Arab public.

It is important to indicate the demographic details of the commenters. Based on the self-declared information provided by users, males constituted 79.1% (n = 24598) and females only 20.8% (n = 6470) of RNW's Facebook community. On Radio Monte Carlo's Facebook page, there were 12356 news articles and 153136 comments. Males made up 81.1% (n = 125, 271) of users, while females constituted 18.1% (n = 27865). The reason for the large number of news articles and comments on this page compared with RNW's is that it is shared by the radio station's affiliated TV channel, France24 in Arabic. In total, we analyzed 184204 comments generated from 15163 news stories, and the average gender distribution across both pages was 80.1% males and 19.4% females.

Detailed information on the Facebook page commentators was collected to help understand the demographic variations, especially with relation to gender.

Information units included Arabic, English, and Latinized Arabic posts uploaded by the news organizations and comments made by the public. The collected comments were then analyzed for sentiment analysis using QDA Miner 4 – WordStat. This approach has been used by many scholars to understand the general sentiments toward different issues, including public sentiment (Pang and Lee 2008) toward the 2012 US general elections (Groshek and Al-Rawi 2013), collective ethnic identity (Al-Rawi 2017a, 2018), citizens' political preferences in Italy and France (Ceron et al. 2014), predictions of general elections (Tumasjan et al. 2010), political activism (Al-Rawi 2017b), and how newspapers and blogs cover events while expressing attitudes toward certain places and figures (Godbole et al. 2007). The majority of previous studies, however, were confined to Twitter (Go et al. 2009; Pak and Paroubek 2010; Agarwal et al. 2011; Kouloumpis et al. 2011); sentiment analysis studies involving Arabic or Facebook are rare (Neri et al. 2012). With this method, the researcher is able to examine the most recurrent phrases by adjusting the number of words and identifying the ranking of words and phrases based on their occurrence. This method fit well with our aim of analyzing the general sentiments toward the most recurrent topics discussed, as the dominant sentiments and issues can be identified through their ranking and occurrence in the data set. The Jaccard coefficient was used to accurately calculate the associations among the words and phrases (Tan et al. 2006), similar to the approach described in Chapter 3.

Another level of analysis involved examining the top 20 most liked news stories posted by the two radio stations. This allowed for further understanding of what the social media audience reacts to, and how it reacts. Looking at these top posts gives a better indication of the nature of content that actively engages the radio stations' social media audiences. The Facebook page administrator, who works for the radio station, cannot moderate or change the number of likes. (This is in contrast to the social media audience, who can of course delete comments.) So we can be sure that the top-ranked posts are an accurate indicator of likeability and appeal.

A similar approach was followed for the TV news analysis. NVivo 10 – N-Capture was used to mine the posts and comments of the Al Jazeera Arabic and Al Arabiya Facebook pages in January 2014. Similarly, the collected comments (n = 626 576) were analyzed using QDA Miner 4 – WordStat. The top 100 most commented-on news stories on the Al Arabiya and Al Jazeera Facebook pages were also examined. (Note that any unrelated posts such as questions, greetings, surveys, and general statements that were not news were excised from the top 100 rankings.) In total, 11 685 posts, mostly comprising news stories or links to news reports, which generated over 626 000 comments from the online audience, were retrieved. On average, each Facebook page had 5842 news stories and 313 288 comments. Based on the average number of comments per news story, Al Jazeera

Table 4.1 Number of page likes and news story comments on the two TV channels' Facebook pages.

Channels	Total page likes	Total no. of all news stories (links and posts)	No. of comments for all news stories and posts	Average number of comments for each news story	No. of comments and percentage for top 100 news stories	
1) Al Arabiya	5 508 959	6974	246 504	35.3	90 390	36.6%
2) Al Jazeera	6 149 325	4711	380 072	80.6	75 443	19.8%
Total for all channels	11 658 284	11 685	626 576	116	165 833	
Average for two channels	5 829 142	5842	313 288	58	82 916	28.2%

seems to be a more active Facebook page in terms of audience engagement with an average of 80.6 comments per story, compared to 35.3 for Al Arabiya (see Table 4.1). In total, the top 200 news stories studied generated over 165 000 comments, constituting 26.4% of the total comments on news stories. The reason why it's worth looking at the top Facebook comments is that commenting on news stories indicates an overall interest and engagement from the online audience toward certain stories, which directly corresponds with the selective exposure theory. Online audiences mostly comment on news that they either agree or disagree with, as noted earlier.

After identifying the 100 most commented-on news stories, news topics were categorized following Riffe et al.'s (1986) and Davie and Lee's (1995) studies on news mix. Six broad news topics were identified, as follows: (i) internal politics and conflict, (ii) regional and international politics and conflict, (iii) science, culture, and arts, (iv) economy and business, (v) sports and human interest, and (vi) health and medicine. For internal politics and conflict, the country the news story deals with was identified. Two coders examined over 10% of the sample (n = 30 news stories), and intercoder reliability was acceptable based on Cohen's kappa (Landis and Koch 1977).

Radio News Analysis

In relation to radio news, this chapter attempts to understand the dominant sentiments expressed by Arab Facebook users commenting on Radio Monte Carlo's and RNW's news articles, as well as the kinds of posts Arab Facebook users mostly

Table 4.2 Most recurrent words used by the audience of Radio Monte Carlo's Facebook page.

Rank	Word	Frequency	Rank	Word	Frequency
1	Allah [two formats]	24846	9	Algeria	3122
2	Syria [three formats]	20950	10	France	2628
3	Bashar and Assad	13332	11	Libya	2580
4	people	8828	12	Israel	1957
5	Arabs [two formats]	6432	13	Tunisia	1803
6	army	3925	14	Mohammed	1725
7	Egypt	3645	15	Iraq	1699
8	regime	3925			

Table 4.3 Most recurrent phrases used by the audience of Radio Monte Carlo's Facebook page.

Rank	Phrase	Frequency	Rank	Phrase	Frequency
1	Syrian people	2733	6	Arab countries	569
2	we choose three only: Allah, Syria, Bashar, and that's it [different formats]	1988	7	Syrian regime	562
3	Syrian army	769	8	thanks to Allah	560
4	Allah, Muammar and Libya	627	9	President Bashar	479
5	the people's demand	577	10	Allah is the Greatest	475

like and engage with. The most frequent and prominent words and phrases used by the commentators on the Facebook page of Radio Monte Carlo in Arabic are shown in Tables 4.2 and 4.3, while those for RNW are listed in Tables 4.4 and 4.5. These comments, voiced by the public on social media, are less moderated than what is found on the websites of these news organizations.

We find that some religious terms are highly recurrent. This, however, does not necessarily mean that these social media audiences are characterized by a devout or overtly religious nature, since religious terms are typical of Arabic language and are common expressions in daily use. Our findings point to an obvious difference between the sentiments expressed on RNW's Facebook page and those on

Table 4.4 Most recurrent words used by the audience of RNW's Facebook page.

Rank	Word	Frequency	Rank	Word	Frequency
1	Allah [two formats]	3634	7	world	690
2	Arabs [three formats]	1523	8	Islam	654
3	Egypt	1475	9	human beings	549
4	peoples	1087	10	Holland	524
5	Morocco	823	11	Syria	455
6	Libya	713	12	Muslim brothers	399

Table 4.5 Most recurrent phrases used by the audience of RNW's Facebook page.

Rank	Phrase	Frequency	Rank	Phrase	Frequency
1	the Sahara is Moroccan	226	6	Allah's messenger	85
2	Allah is the best Disposer of affairs	139	7	sufficient for me is Allah	84
3	Arab countries	134	8	Egyptian people	76
4	thanks to Allah	108	9	Arab world	73
5	Syrian people	85			

Radio Monte Carlo's. On the latter, the Syrian crisis is far more prominent, as the words "Syria" and "Bashar Assad" are mentioned more than 34 000 times, making them the second and third most used words (see Table 4.2). Unlike other Arab countries that witnessed swift political changes during the Arab Spring, the conflict in Syria is still unfolding. Sunni rebels formed the Free Syrian Army and other armed factions to fight Assad's regime. The conflict, more recently, has taken on the characteristics of a sectarian civil war rather than a revolution against Assad's totalitarian rule. It has resulted in one of the worst humanitarian crises of modern times, with different armed factions like the Free Syrian Army, Al-Nusra Front, and the Islamic State fighting one another as well as the regime.

As for Radio Monte Carlo's emphasis on Syria, this can be understood in relation to the colonial history of France, which occupied Syria after the First World War. Many Syrians still feel an affinity for French culture and language, and of course there is also the French involvement in the current Syrian conflict. It's apparent that Radio Monte Carlo's coverage of the conflict in Syria is anti-Assad, which is related to France's pro-rebel policy. The page's comments turn up voluminous pro-Assad voices that accuse the station of spreading lies. Selective exposure theory would suggest the station's editorial line is one of the main reasons for finding large numbers of pro-Assad comments on this Facebook page. Politically active people, remember, have been found to be more likely to seek views that oppose their beliefs, since they are more certain that they can counter them (Knobloch-Westerwick and Meng 2008; Johnson et al. 2011).

When it comes to the most recurrent phrases, we find again that Syria was the most discussed country. Interestingly, the popular pro-Assad Arabic chant, "We choose three only: Allah, Syria, Bashar, and that's it" was the second most used phrase, followed by comments containing reference to "Assad's army" (see Table 4.3). Furthermore, the ninth most recurrent term, a more neutral one, was "President Bashar." Strangely enough, this audience also used the pro-Gaddafi chant, "Allah, Muammar and Libya," even though Gaddafi was killed by the Libyan rebels back in October 2011. Finally, the term "Viva Syria" is first and strongly associated with "Bashar Assad" (coefficient = 0.042), followed by "Muammar Gaddafi" (coefficient = 0.024), both of which show strong pro-Assad and pro-Gaddafi sentiments.

Fewer and less strident voices commented with opposing views. For example, the term "garbage of history" is associated with "Muammar Gaddafi" (coefficient = 0.011), "Bashar Assad" (coefficient = 0.005), and "Arab leaders" (coefficient = 0.005). For the latter, it is a negative sentiment that expresses frustration and disappointment due to the apparent inaction of Arab leaders toward the various crises happening in the Arab world. Further, the term "Syrian revolt," referring to the revolt led by various Sunni rebels, is first associated with "Assad terrorism" (coefficient = 0.012) and "Bashar the terrorist" (coefficient = 0.008). In fact, the word "terrorist" is mostly used with "Bashar Assad" (coefficient = 0.073); the phrase "Bashar the terrorist" occurred 248 times, still a very low number in comparison to the more pro-Assad sentiments expressed. In summary, pro-Assad, and to a lesser extent pro-Gaddafi, sentiments are the most dominant, as illustrated by the salience of expressions like, "Allah, Syria, Bashar, and that's it" and "Allah, Muammar and Libya."

The sentiments expressed on RNW's Facebook page, on the other hand, show a clear emphasis on Morocco and Egypt instead of Syria, which came in at the 11th rank (see Table 4.4). This is understandable, as it is well known that the Moroccan immigrant community is one of the largest Arab diasporic groups in the Netherlands (Van Heelsum 2005). As for Egypt, the military takeover of political power that was led by General Sisi against the Muslim Brotherhood and its prominent members, including the former president, Mohamed Morsi, was a significant event that attracted most of RNW's audience's attention.

Regarding the most recurrent phrases (see Table 4.5), the first and most popular term is "the Sahara is Moroccan," a nationalistic slogan uttered by those who oppose the movement by inhabitants of the Western Sahara region for independence from Morocco (Maghraoui 2003). It is not surprising that the "the Sahara is Moroccan" phrase is repeatedly found on this platform, since many Moroccans interact on RNW due to immigrant flows and the cultural proximity between Morocco and the Netherlands. Furthermore, a similar but longer term is ranked number 18 on the platform, "the Sahara is Moroccan and Hala'ib is Egyptian," which is a reference to the highly contested Hala'ib Triangle separating Sudan and Egypt. This is another overtly nationalistic slogan. Unlike Radio Monte Carlo's Facebook page, we find that references to "Bashar Assad" are not prominent and are mostly negative. For example, the term "Allah's curse" is first and strongly associated with "Bashar Assad" (coefficient = 0.010), which clearly indicates anti-Assad sentiment and the backing of the rebels' cause. Further, the term "military rule," which is connected to Egypt, has its third strongest connection with the phrase "sufficient for me is Allah who is the best Disposer of affairs" (coefficient = 0.008). This is a kind of supplication, in which the person asks for God's help to intervene in a difficult situation, especially when faced by an unjust or powerful adversary. In this context, it is understood as an expression of support for the Muslim Brotherhood and a rejection of Sisi's military rule.

One similarity between RNW and Radio Monte Carlo is that we find religious terms using "Allah" and various formulations thereof are the top phrases used on the two Facebook pages. Again, this is not an indication that the online audiences are necessarily religious or supportive of political Islam, since "Allah" is frequently used in daily Arabic language.

The online audiences differ in the attention they show toward certain countries. RNW's audience is more focused on news and events taking place in Egypt, Morocco, Libya, and Syria, while Radio Monte Carlo's is most interested in Syria, Egypt, Algeria, Libya, and Tunisia. There are of course slight variations in this order in relation to the phrases used, but these differences are sufficient to provide an indication of the geographical bias of the radio stations, their news departments, and their audiences.

In relation to the kinds of posts that Arab Facebook users mostly like and engage with, the top 20 most liked Facebook posts on the two radio stations were closely examined. The rankings are discussed here by number, and can be seen in full in Tables 4.6 and 4.7. The total number of RNW likes is 35 222; 14 out of the 20 most liked posts contain questions for the social media audience. In order to engage the online audience, RNW staff ask questions on different issues. This strategy seems to be effective. Further, top RNW posts cover a large array of Arab countries, including Yemen, Libya, Egypt, Algeria, Morocco, and Syria, which surely broadens RNW's audience. In this context, RNW has actively partnered with several

Table 4.6 Top 20 most liked posts on RNW's Facebook page.

Rank	Post (translated to English and abbreviated)	Likes	Date of creation
1	Libya: Do you expect that the Libyan militias will be embedded with the army and that they will be dissolved? How can unemployment be avoided since it's the fate of hundreds of militia fighters if released? Join us in the debate on the live radio show, "Eye on Libya," in cooperation with Benghazi Radio FM ...	5059	11/19/2013
2	Morocco and Algeria: What is the impact of the tension between Algeria and Morocco on their human relationship since there are many mixed marriages between Algerians and Moroccans? Join us in the debate on the radio show, "Here and There" ...	3124	11/4/2013
3	Ramadan: How many hours do Muslims fast around the world?	3028	7/8/2013
4	Eid: Wishing a happy Eid holiday! You can send your greeting wishes via email and we'll air them during Eid holiday	2321	10/12/2013
5	Egypt: In relation to the police mistreatment of Egyptian protesters, are the police part of society or part of power? Participate and maybe one of our cartoonists will be inspired by your idea to draw something relevant ...	1790	2/5/2013
6	Egypt: Commemorating the day Husni Mubarak left power two years ago and discussing the disparity between the high class and the lower (poor) class in Egypt. How can the ruler balance between the interests of the business (high) class and that of the poor?	1657	2/11/2013
7	Libya: in relation to the kidnapping of the president, what has changed in the past two years [since Qaddafi was deposed]? What is the effect of this change on the Libyan citizen? What does the citizen expect from the constitution? What are the criteria followed in inking the constitution? Join us in the debate on the live radio show, "Eye on Libya," in cooperation with Benghazi Radio FM ...	1590	11/5/2013
8	Ramadan: The Lebanese singer Maher Zain, who is known for his Islamic chants, will hold a concert in Rotterdam ... We'll be pleased to ask Zain questions that you post here ...	1586	12/5/2013

(Continued)

Table 4.6 (Continued)

Rank	Post (translated to English and abbreviated)	Likes	Date of creation
9	Contest: RNW is searching for talented individuals willing to film short clips of young people in your society. Send your CV and some of your works to ...	1522	7/1/2013
10	Libya: Announcing an upcoming radio report on the movement of students' unions.	1513	9/16/2013
11	Yemen: How do Yemeni youth live their emotional lives and how do they express themselves in the age of communication revolution? Have contemporary communication means been able to break the boundaries between the two genders in one of the most conservative and traditional countries in the world? This is the new show on "Yemeni Horizons," the mutual radio show made by RNW and Youth Radio from Sanaa ... We'll read a selection of your Facebook comments ...	1436	3/25/2013
12	Egypt: New protest law ... Follow up on Radio Egypt and RNW and participate with your opinion. Do you support or oppose the new protest law in Egypt? Your comments will enrich the debate.	1406	11/29/2013
13	RNW: What do you want to read, see, and listen? You can contribute in shaping our policies and programs as well as the media content of what we produce	1397	9/11/2012
14	Syria: A documentary film on Al-Zaatri refugee camp in Jordan	1212	9/6/2013
15	Visit: Sameh Saif Al-Bazil, an Egyptian intelligence official, is going to visit the Netherlands ... What is the question that you want to ask him?	1164	11/26/2013
16	RNW: Have you seen our channel, Amsterdam, on Nilesat and Arabsat? Please inform us how many times you have seen it. What do you think of it? Please mention the country where you reside ...	1153	9/13/2013
17	RNW is launching a competition, "Best Iftar Table Photo." Post your picture to enter the competition with the possibility of winning $200 ...	1138	7/26/2013

Table 4.6   (Continued)

Rank	Post (translated to English and abbreviated)	Likes	Date of creation
18	Morocco: The 20th of February movement. A joint program between RNW and Shadda Radio FM from Casablanca ... Did you participate in the movement? Do you agree or disagree with it? Is Morocco an exceptional case that is different from other Arab countries? Write your comment here and it could be aired on the program ...	1084	2/18/2013
19	Women: Is the word "single lady" a pejorative term against women? Have you faced an embarrassing situation because you have been single? Send us your personal story ...	1060	7/19/2013
20	Corruption: Report on police corruption in the Arab world from Transparency International	982	7/9/2013

Table 4.7   Top 20 most liked posts on Radio Monte Carlo's Facebook page.

Rank	Post (translated to English and abbreviated)	Likes	Date of creation
1	Nelson Mandela: "Freedom cannot be obtained in stages since man can either be free or oppressed"	4848	12/5/2013
2	Breaking news: Ariel Sharon, the former Israeli prime minister, died	4560	1/11/2014
3	Henry Ford: "Failure is simply the opportunity to begin again, this time more intelligently"	3704	12/9/2013
4	More than 500 thousand followers on our Facebook page. Thank you for your trust and loyalty as we promise you more contributions	3663	9/11/2013
5	Femen activists urinate on Victor Yanukovich's picture to protests against the persecution of Ukrainian protesters	3601	12/2/2013
6	Najib Mahfouz: "The worst defeat in my life is my inability to enjoy reading after my eyesight faded"	3516	12/19/2013
7	Football: The results of the 2014 Football World Cup in Brazil	3397	12/6/2013
8	Our page has just crossed the one million followers. We thank you so much and promise you more contributions.	3204	12/19/2013

(Continued)

Table 4.7 (Continued)

Rank	Post (translated to English and abbreviated)	Likes	Date of creation
9	Breaking news: Cristiano Ronaldo wins the best player in the world for 2013	3088	1/13/2014
10	This is Paris … continuous coverage on France24 channel and website. Greetings to all our followers …	2978	1/25/2014
11	Charles Dickens: "A very little key will open a very heavy door"	2942	12/11/2013
12	Nelson Mandela: "Freedom cannot be obtained in stages since man can either be free or oppressed"	2771	10/5/2013
13	Poetry: A brief biography of the Tunisian poet, Abu Al-Qassim Al-Shabi, without naming him	2757	9/15/2013
14	Breaking news: Saudi Arabia refuses Iran's participation in the Geneva 2 conference because of Tehran's rejection of the establishment of a transitional government and its sending soldiers to fight along the Syrian regime.	2733	1/20/2014
15	Saint Augustine: "The world is a book, and those who do not travel only read one pag"	2721	12/13/2013
16	Emile Zola: "If you shut up truth and bury it under the ground, it will but grow, and gather to itself such explosive power that the day it bursts through it will blow up everything in its way"	2668	10/27/2013
17	Arthur Schopenhauer: "We rarely think of what we own but more of what we lack"	2488	12/8/2013
18	Hafiz Ibrahim: "Mothers are like a school. If you educate them well, you make up a well-mannered nation"	2415	1/26/2014
19	Saudi Arabia: A picture that was circulated in social media outlets showing religious police in Saudi Arabia stopping women from sitting on swings	2413	1/17/2014
20	Najib Mahfouz: "Freedom is the crown man places on his head to be worthy of his humanity"	2392	12/7/2013

local radio stations in these countries to air special programs that cover important issues like political activism, corruption, and marriage and sexual relationships. Some of these topics are regarded as taboo in many Arab societies. Another method that seems effective is RNW's focus on sharing the celebration of the holy month of Ramadan and the Eid holiday, and using the occasions to generate audience engagement; four posts emphasized these events by sending good wishes and encouraging the audience to post its greetings, some of which were subsequently aired (No. 4 – 2321 likes). Other special Ramadan appeals by RNW included asking questions (No. 3 – 3028 likes), encouraging the audience to post inquiries (No. 8 – 1586 likes), and even organizing a photo competition (No. 17 – 1138 likes). Finally, the audiences were repeatedly encouraged to interact with and even shape the policy and content of RNW's programs (No. 16 – 1153 likes) and to get involved through contests with specific rewards (Nos. 9 and 17).

As for Radio Monte Carlo's top 20 most liked posts, they received a total of 62 859 likes, a little less than the number of likes generated by the top posts on RNW's Facebook page. We found that 10 posts, or half of the sample, were made up of wise sayings by famous figures. Of the other half, only six dealt with news, such as the announcement of the death of Ariel Sharon (4560 likes), the former prime minister of Israel, which was the second most liked post. The remaining posts were related to greeting and celebrating with the online audience. Unlike with RNW's approach, Radio Monte Carlo's top posts do not include any questions for the social media audience, except for one indirect question on the Tunisian poet Abu Al-Qassim Al-Shabi, whose short biography was cited without naming him. Radio Monte Carlo's lack of direct questions and emphasis on wise sayings and breaking news indicate that the two radio stations follow different approaches in appealing to their social media audiences.

To elaborate on the differences between RNW and Radio Monte Carlo in relation to their top 20 most liked posts, while the latter has six breaking news stories, we note that RNW's posts address larger, ongoing issues like corruption, the status of women, and the rise of militias in Libya. RNW's page contains no posts of wise sayings by famous authors. Instead, its top posts contain announcements of programs, contests, and Ramadan greetings. As for similarities, both Facebook pages include news stories, though they remain marginal in comparison to other top posts.

Social media platforms, including Facebook, offer what Hermida (2010) calls "ambient journalism" or a non-moderated platform for online readers, which is not normally found in traditional media. Our analysis showed evidence of selective media exposure, with audiences mostly drawn to the nature of coverage of some issues or a focus on certain events. Our examination of the most liked Facebook posts, furthermore, showed that the two radio stations use a variety of methods to appeal to their audiences, including asking them direct or indirect questions and soliciting their opinions to draw them more into relevant debates. The top posts, however, included very few breaking news stories, which suggests that the social media audiences of these two radio channels are more engaged with posts about other issues, be they celebrations or sayings from famous figures. These findings have implications not only for social media research on radio studies but also for research on other outlets like TV and print media.

TV News Analysis

In relation to the analysis of TV news on social media, this section examines the kinds of sentiments expressed by Arab Facebook users commenting on the Al Jazeera Arabic and Al Arabiya news articles as well as the kinds of news stories and countries that attracted most of the online audience comments. Before discussing the results, it is important to indicate the demographic details of the commenters. On Al Jazeera's Arabic page, 4711 stories were posted, which generated 380 072 comments by the online public. Based on the information provided by users, males constituted 83.2% (n = 303 569) of the total number of users (n = 364 430), while females made up only 16.7% (n = 60 861). As for Al Arabiya's Facebook page, there were 6974 news articles and 246 504 comments. Based on the information users provided about themselves, males made up 73.9% (n = 181 231) of the total number of commenters (n = 245 052), while females constituted 26% (n = 63 821): still very low, but higher than for Al Jazeera's page. In total, this chapter analyzed 626 576 comments generated from 11 685 news stories, and the average overall gender distribution was 78.5% males and 21.3% females.

The most recurrent words and phrases used by the commenters on Al Jazeera's Facebook page are listed in Tables 4.8 and 4.9. The most recurrent words and phrases on Al Arabiya's Facebook page are shown in Tables 4.10 and 4.11. As for the most frequently recurring phrases on both pages, a combination of two to six words was used to identify them.

The results show that internal politics and conflict was the top news topic on Al Jazeera and the second-ranked topic on Al Arabiya (n = 73), followed by regional and international politics and conflict (n = 37) and science, culture, and arts (n = 12) (see Table 4.12). As for the most referenced country in the internal politics and conflict topic, Egypt came first on Al Jazeera with a total of 40 stories, followed by Syria with 23 stories; on Al Arabiya, Syria came first (see Table 4.13).

Again, we are looking at unmoderated, or barely moderated, online comments, so they provide a very good representation of the online public. In relation to the kinds of sentiments expressed by Arab Facebook users commenting on the Al Jazeera and Al Arabiya news articles, I have examined each channel separately, but there is again a general trend across the two with frequent use of religious terms.

Table 4.8 Top 20 most frequent words in the comments on Al Jazeera's Facebook page.

Rank	Word	Frequency	Rank	Word	Frequency
1	Allah	90556	11	greatest	7433
2	my Allah	20063	12	sufficient for us	7204
3	Egypt	19172	13	Syria	7102
4	Disposer	12124	14	the Muslims	6761
5	Al-Sisi	11509	15	by Allah	6597
6	best	11379	16	the army	6175
7	people	10148	17	Bashar	5904
8	and Allah	8959	18	oh God	5837
9	Morsi	8813	19	Hell	5718
10	the Arabs	7503	20	the brothers	5520

Table 4.9 Most frequent comment phrases on Al Jazeera's Facebook page.

Rank	Phrase	Frequency
1	Allah is the Greatest [there are many other occurrences of this phrase, coming in multiple repetitions e.g. twice (n = 1896) and thrice (n = 1429)]	6022
2	sufficient for us is Allah, and [He is] the best Disposer of affairs	5708
3	sufficient for me is Allah, and [He is] the best Disposer of affairs	3099
4	Allah bestow victory	2007
5	Hell and the worst fate	1647
6	there is no might nor power except in Allah	1570
7	prayers for Allah and peace be upon the prophet	977
8	let the military rule fall	779

On Al Jazeera TV's page, the most recurrent words included several prominent political figures like "Sisi," "Morsi," and "Bashar," as well as many words used in supplication and prayers, especially to express negative sentiments like cursing or condemning someone (see Table 4.8). This, in fact, is one of the main differences found between Al Jazeera and Al Arabiya, which sheds light on the kinds of online attitudes expressed on the former. When we examine the proximity plot for the word "fall," we find that it is first associated with the words "rule" and

Table 4.10 Top 20 most frequent words in the comments on Al Arabiya's Facebook page.

Rank	Word	Frequency	Rank	Word	Frequency
1	Allah	85451	11	our God	4815
2	glorious	20019	12	power	4152
3	my Allah	13329	13	thankfulness	4099
4	and best	7566	14	Egypt	3965
5	thy God	7331	15	the Glorious	3926
6	sufficient	7206	16	my Disposer	3751
7	by Allah	6097	17	might	3728
8	greatest	5893	18	Hell	3508
9	and Allah	5717	19	Syria	3377
10	for Allah	5544	20	our Disposer	3280

Table 4.11 Most frequent comment phrases on Al Arabiya's Facebook page.

Rank	Phrase	Frequency
1	glory be to Allah	17943
2	Allah is the Greatest (repeated twice n = 732)	5026
3	sufficient for me is Allah, and [He is] the best Disposer of affairs	2891
4	sufficient for us is Allah, and [He is] the best Disposer of affairs	2664
5	thanks to Allah	2497
6	there is no might nor power except in Allah	1761
7	Hell and the worst fate	1196

"military" (coefficient = 0.282 and 0.226), followed by the words "coup" (coefficient = 0.021), "Sisi" (coefficient = 0.015), and "the army" (coefficient = 0.010). Further, if we look at the proximity plot for the phrase "bestow victory," we find that it is first associated with the words "Islam" (coefficient = 0.050), "Muslims" (coefficient = 0.037), and "Morsi" (coefficient = 0.017). These words are clearly being used by the commentators to refer to their dissatisfaction with the current military rule in Egypt and its army chief, Sisi, who removed the former Egyptian president, Morsi, from power. Even the term "Saddam Hussein" is linked to "President Morsi" (coefficient = 0.007) and "Allah have mercy on

Table 4.12 News topic distribution for the top 100 most commented-on news stories.

Topic	Al Jazeera	Al Arabiya	Total
1) Internal politics and conflict	60	13	73
2) Regional and international politics and conflict	23	14	37
3) Science, culture, and arts	4	8	12
4) Economy and business	0	1	1
5) Sports and human interest	8	16	24
6) Health and medicine	0	1	1

Table 4.13 Most commented-on countries in news topics.

Country	Al Jazeera	Al Arabiya	Total
1) Egypt	38	2	40
2) Syria	14	9	23
3) Saudi Arabia	2	0	2
4) UAE	1	1	2
5) Algeria	2	0	2
6) Morocco	1	0	1
7) Sudan	1	0	1
8) Libya	0	1	1
9) Lebanon	1	0	1
10) Iraq	0	0	0

you" (coefficient = 0.007); online commentators make such a connection allegedly because both Arab presidents were imprisoned and put on trial. On the other hand, weaker associations with the word "fall" include "Morsi" (coefficient = 0.007) and "the brothers" (coefficient = 0.007), in reference to Morsi's Muslim Brotherhood. The different and opposing associations with the word "fall" show the kinds of conflicting strong sentiments expressed on the same online platform.

In relation to Syria, another word associated with "fall" is "Bashar" (coefficient = 0.008), in reference to the current Syrian president. The same kind of sentiment is evident when examining the proximity plot for the word "[go to] Hell," a kind of curse, as "Bashar" is closely linked to it (coefficient = 0.010), followed by "Sisi" (coefficient = 0.007). When looking at the word "Bashar" itself, we find that it is closely linked to "take revenge" (coefficient = 0.030) and "kill" (coefficient = 0.016). On the other hand, the phrase "bestow victory [to]" is only weakly associated with "Bashar" (coefficient = 0.011), indicating the disparity among online groups and their sentiments toward Assad.

As for the most frequent phrases on Al Jazeera (see Table 4.9), we find "Allah is the Greatest," used in a variety of ways, at the top of the list. For example, the phrase is closely related to supporting the Syrian rebels, as there are relevant connected phrases like "Free Army'," "Nusra Front," and "Devil's Party." The latter is a distortion of the Lebanese Hezbollah, which literally means "Allah's Party," meant as a rebuke for its backing of Assad's regime for sectarian reasons. The sentiments clearly indicate the dominant pro-rebel and anti-Assad views found on the platform. Another phrase examined is "take revenge from," which is a form of curse. Interestingly, it seems that the Arab public on Al Jazeera's page has mostly directed its curses toward "Arab rulers" (coefficient = 0.008), followed by the "Syrian regime" (coefficient = 0.004), and "Egyptian army"; "Saud family," the rebels' "Free Syrian Army," "Hezbollah," and Sisi's "military rule" all come in with the same weaker coefficient (0.002). Finally, the phrase "let Allah bestow victory" is first linked to the phrase "Islamic state" (coefficient = 0.003), which is related to Al Qaida in Syria; this is an indication of the kind of extreme religious sentiment expressed online.

Regarding Al Arabiya's Facebook page (see Table 4.10), if we examine the proximity plot of the word "Hell," we find it is not used in association with political figures, unlike in the case of Al Jazeera. Also, the term "oh God," which is a normally linked to "preserve" as a supplication, is first linked to "Muslims" (coefficient = 0.026) in a general sense, followed by "Syria" (coefficient = 0.024) and "Egypt" (coefficient = 0.015). There are a few exceptions, however. For example, the phrase "bestow victory to" is first linked to "righteous" (coefficient = 0.063), followed by "Islam" (coefficient = 0.058), "Muslims" (coefficient = 0.029), "Syria" (coefficient = 0.023), "Morsi" (coefficient = 0.011), and "brothers" (coefficient = 0.008), in reference to Egypt's Muslim Brotherhood. On the other hand, the phrase "take revenge from" is first linked to "brothers" (coefficient = 0.009), followed by "Army" (coefficient = 0.005) and "Morsi" (coefficient = 0.004). Finally, the term "Disposer of affairs," which is a reference to God and is used to express powerlessness and reliance on God's action in punishing the unjust, is first linked to "revenge" (coefficient = 0.011) and "Syria" (coefficient = 0.008) in a general sense. This is a common way of expressing sympathy and prayers for the victims of the conflict in Syria. In relation to the phrases used, we find that there is a great deal of supplication and prayer, especially directed toward Syria (see Table 4.11). For instance, the phrase "Allah preserve" is linked to "Syrian people" (coefficient = 0.002) in the fourth rank, while the phrase "Free Army," which is a reference to the Syrian rebels, is first linked to "Allah supports them" (coefficient = 0.003) but has a similar association with "take revenge from [them]" (coefficient = 0.003); this indicates the presence of two opposing sentiments.

The online audiences often express opposing sentiments on both Al Jazeera and Al Arabiya's Facebook pages, but there is a general sympathy and a sense of help-lessness toward events taking place in the Arab and Islamic world. This is especially true of events in Syria and Egypt. On Al Jazeera's page, references to Egypt are more dominant than those to Syria, and there is a much stronger positive sentiment and support for Morsi and the Muslim Brotherhood, with clear antagonism and negative sentiments, articulated in different ways, against General Sisi and Bashar Assad. There is also evidence that some extreme Islamic views and anti-Shiite sentiments are expressed, especially in terms of support for Al Qaida affiliate groups in Syria. As for Al Arabiya's page, references to Egypt and Syria are more dominant than for any other Arab country, and there is much less antagonism and inflammatory commentary toward Assad and Morsi.

The fact that Al Jazeera's page has a higher percentage of pro-Morsi sentiments can be explained by what is known as audience selective exposure (Sunstein 2001; Stroud 2010) and ideological selectivity (Iyengar and Hahn 2009; Feldman et al. 2012). Users who frequently express pro-Morsi sentiments choose Al Jazeera's Facebook page and its news stories as a platform for expressing their beliefs. In fact, the current political situation in Egypt is discussed far more than Syria in Al Jazeera's commentary despite the ongoing conflict and dire humanitarian situation in the latter. This indicates that Al Jazeera's page attracts more Egyptians and more supporters of the Muslim Brotherhood, especially those who sympathize with Morsi and oppose Sisi's military rule. As mentioned earlier, Al Jazeera was in fact banned in Egypt due to its alleged bias toward the Muslim Brotherhood movement (Watkins 2014).

Al Arabiya's Facebook page, in contrast, is almost equally divided among those who express positive sentiments toward Morsi and the Muslim Brotherhood in Egypt and those who express negative sentiments toward them. There is also less antagonism against Assad than is the case with Al Jazeera. In general, there is evidence of opposing sentiments. This reflects the fact that Facebook can be a highly divided online platform due to the ideological differences among its users. Van Dijk (1998, p. 65) emphasized the way ideology determines how members of a group perceive and express themselves, and these conditioning factors are one explanation for the trends and difference in online comments across the two channels' Facebook pages.

Our results indicate that the news topic of internal politics and conflict – in other words, stories that deal with one country – attracted most of the public online comments (n = 73), followed by regional and international politics and conflict (n = 37) and sports and human interest (n = 24). When it comes to the individual channels, Al Arabiya's audience mostly commented on sports and human interest news stories (n = 16), followed by regional and international politics and conflict (n = 14) and internal politics and conflict (n = 13). On the other hand, Al Jazeera's online public mostly commented on internal politics and conflict (n = 60), regional and international politics and conflict (n = 23), and sports and human interest (n = 8) (see Table 4.12). These variations give an insight into the difference in news preferences and consumption patterns between the online audiences of Al Arabiya's and Al Jazeera's Facebook channels. Indeed, this is due to the audiences' selective exposure practices, as they choose to read and comment on certain stories, while the majority of other news reports do not receive the same kind of attention. As discussed earlier, audiences usually engage with posts that either conform with their views or that contradict them, if they have strong ideological beliefs. It is assumed here that the top 100 comments fall within such a theoretical categorization attributed to differences in ideology. Further, the sentiment analysis of the online comments also showed existing differences and sometimes opposing sentiments that correspond with the selective exposure theory.

In relation to the most referenced countries mentioned in internal politics and conflict news stories across the two channels, the results show that Egypt came first, mostly because of Al Jazeera's news stories (n = 38), with almost double the total amount (n = 40) of stories as Syria (n = 23). On Al Arabiya, Syria came first (n = 9), followed by Egypt (n = 2). On Al Jazeera, Syria came second (n = 14). It is important to mention here that the top news stories that deal with Egypt refer either to Sisi or the Muslim Brotherhood, or both, while those dealing with Syria cover Assad's regime and the ongoing conflict there. Many other news stories dealing with regional and international politics and conflict cover a variety of Arab countries, especially Egypt and Syria, while many human interest stories deal with the plight of Syrian children and refugees. Again, these selective exposure practices of the online audiences indicate differences in the attention given to news stories and varied news preferences. Finally, these findings are supported by statistics on Al Jazeera's Arabic Facebook page by Socialbakers (www. socialbakers.com), which show that fans from Egypt constitute the largest segment at 28.4%, followed by Tunisia 8.2%, Morocco 7.8%, and Saudi Arabia 5.9%.

To sum up, this TV news analysis reveals that there are some opposing sentiments expressed on these two Facebook pages, but some trends are more dominant than others. Many clusters of sentiments expressed by the online audience show evidence of selective media exposure, mostly related to the kinds of news stories posted and the ideological nature of the TV channels. The empirical findings of this chapter show that the voices of Muslim Brotherhood supporters are more dominant on Al Jazeera because they find in it an outlet that conveys their political views and general sentiments. As for the top 100 most commented-on news stories, internal politics and conflict news that deals with one country attracted most of the online public's comments, especially on Al Jazeera, while

Egypt and then Syria was the general focus of news stories. These findings closely correspond with the sentiment analysis of the online public comments. Indeed, the SNS outlets of news organizations can offer researchers new venues and chances to conduct further research, whether by examining news posted on SNS or interviewing audiences and news organization staff members who are actively engaged with these outlets.

A note on this chapter's limitations: it has not been possible, for example, to provide full details on each word and phrase listed in the tables due to space limitations. A more focused analysis and contextualization needs to be presented. Also, the software used to retrieve social media data is limited because of Facebook API restrictions, so it is not clear whether all comments are collected. Another limitation is that the chapter did not investigate the photos posted by the Facebook pages' administrators, as the focus is on the commentary of the online news readers and their news preference. Finally, and most importantly, more insights on radio and TV channels' use of social media and audience motivations for engagement on social media can be further explained by conducting interviews with online audience members and journalists working for these news stations.

References

Agarwal, A., Xie, B., Vovsha, I. et al. (2011). Sentiment analysis of Twitter data. In: *Proceedings of the Workshop on Languages in Social Media* (eds. M. Nagarajan and M. Gamon), 30–38. Stroudsburg, PA: Association for Computational Linguistics.

Al Jazeera (2015). Egypt postpones retrial of Al Jazeera journalists. Available from: http://www.aljazeera.com/news/2015/05/150509055832040.html (accessed November 28, 2019).

Al-Rawi, A.K. (2015). Sectarianism and the Arab Spring: framing the popular protests in Bahrain. *Global Media and Communication* 11 (1): 25–42.

Al-Rawi, A. (2017a). Facebook and virtual nationhood: social media and the Arab Canadians community. *AI and Society* 34 (3): 559–571.

Al-Rawi, A. (2017b). Online political activism in Syria: sentiment analysis of social media. *Sage Research Studies Cases* https://doi.org/10.4135/9781473994829.

Al-Rawi, A. (2018). Regional TV & collective ethnic identity: investigating the SNS outlets of Arab TV shows. *Social Media+Society* 4: 1–40.

An, J., Quercia, D., and Crowcroft, J. (2013). Fragmented social media: a look into selective exposure to political news. *Proceedings of the 22nd International Conference on World Wide Web Companion*, pp. 51–52.

Auter, P., Arafa, M., and Al-Jaber, K. (2005). Identifying with Arabic journalists: how Al-Jazeera tapped parasocial interaction gratifications in the Arab world. *International Communication Gazette* 67 (2): 189–204.

Bahry, L.Y. (2001). The new Arab media phenomenon: Qatar's Al-Jazeera. *Middle East Policy* 8 (2): 88–99.

BBC News (2013). Egypt crisis: Al-Jazeera journalists arrested in Cairo. Available from: http://www.bbc.com/news/world-middle-east-25546389 (accessed November 28, 2019).

Brundidge, J. (2010). Encountering "difference" in the contemporary public sphere: the contribution of the Internet to the heterogeneity of political discussion networks. *Journal of Communication* 60 (4): 680–700.

Brundidge, J. and Rice, R.E. (2009). Political engagement online: do the information rich get richer and the like-minded more similar. In: *Routledge Handbook of Internet Politics* (eds. A. Chadwick and P.N. Howard), 144–156. London: Taylor & Francis.

Butler, D. (2015). APNNewsBreak: Turkey, Saudi in pact to help anti-Assad rebels. Associated Press. Available from: https://apnews.com/97e2ec0b591c4a43a319ff2fd895dc4e (accessed November 28, 2019).

Ceron, A., Curini, L., Iacus, S.M., and Porro, G. (2014). Every tweet counts? How sentiment analysis of social media can improve our knowledge of citizens' political preferences with an application to Italy and France. *New Media & Society* 16 (2): 340–358.

Chaffee, S.H., Saphir, M.N., Grap, J. et al. (2001). Attention to counter-attitudinal messages in a state election campaign. *Political Communication* 18 (3): 247–272.

Cooper, J. (2007). *Cognitive Dissonance: 50 Years of a Classic Theory*. London: Sage.

Cotton, J. (2013). Cognitive dissonance in selective exposure. In: *Selective Exposure to Communication* (eds. D. Zillmann and J. Bryant), 11–34. London: Routledge.

Davie, W.R. and Lee, J.S. (1995). Sex, violence, and consonance/differentiation: an analysis of local TV news values. *Journalism and Mass Communication Quarterly* 72 (1): 128–138.

Donsbach, W. (1991). Exposure to political content in newspapers: the impact of cognitive dissonance on readers' selectivity. *European Journal of Communication* 6 (2): 155–186.

Economist (2013). Al Jazeera: must do better. Available from: http://www.economist.com/news/middle-east-and-africa/21569429-arabs-premier-television-network-bids-american-viewers-must-do-better (accessed November 28, 2019).

El-Nawawy, M. and Iskander, A. (2003). *Al-Jazeera: The Story of the Network that is Rattling Governments and Redefining Modern Journalism*. Boulder, CO: Westview Press.

Fandy, M. (2007). *(Un) Civil War of Words: Media and Politics in the Arab World*. New York: Greenwood.

Farhi, P. (2013). Mideast journalists allege bias in al-Jazeera's reports on Morsi, Muslim Brotherhood *Washington Post*. Available from: http://www.washingtonpost.com/lifestyle/style/mideast-journalists-allege-bias-in-al-jazeeras-reporting-on-morsi-and-muslim-brotherhood/2013/07/08/9166c364-e80e-11e2-aa9f-c03a72e2d342_story.html (accessed November 28, 2019).

Feldman, L., Maibach, E.W., Roser-Renouf, C., and Leiserowitz, A. (2012). Climate on cable the nature and impact of global warming coverage on fox news, CNN, and MSNBC. *International Journal of Press/Politics* 17 (1): 3–31.

Galston, W.A. (2003). If political fragmentation is the problem, is the Internet the solution? In: *The Civic Web: Online Politics and Democratic Values* (eds. D.M. Anderson and M. Cornfield), 35–44. Oxford: Rowman & Littlefield.

Go, A., Huang, L., and Bhayani, R. (2009). Twitter sentiment analysis. *Entropy* 17: 252.

Godbole, N., Srinivasaiah, M., and Skiena, S. (2007). Large-scale sentiment analysis for news and blogs. In: *International Conference on Weblogs and Social Media (ICWSM '07).*

Graf, J. and Aday, S. (2008). Selective attention to online political information. *Journal of Broadcasting & Electronic Media* 52 (1): 86–100.

Groshek, J. and Al-Rawi, A. (2013). Public sentiment and critical framing in social media content during the 2012 US presidential campaign. *Social Science Computer Review* 31 (5): 563–576.

Hermida, A. (2010). Twittering the news: the emergence of ambient journalism. *Journalism Practice* 4 (3): 297–308.

Iyengar, S. and Hahn, K.S. (2009). Red media, blue media: evidence of ideological selectivity in media use. *Journal of Communication* 59 (1): 19–39.

Johnson, T.J., Bichard, S.L., and Zhang, W. (2009). Communication communities or "cyberghettos?": a path analysis model examining factors that explain selective exposure to blogs. *Journal of Computer-Mediated Communication* 15 (1): 60–82.

Johnson, T.J., Zhang, W., and Bichard, S.L. (2011). Voices of convergence or conflict? A path analysis investigation of selective exposure to political websites. *Social Science Computer Review* 29 (4): 449–469.

Knobloch-Westerwick, S. and Meng, J. (2008). Looking the other way: selective exposure to attitude-consistent and counter-attitudinal political information. In: *International Communication Association Conference*. Montreal, QC, Canada.

Kouloumpis, E., Wilson, T., and Moore, J. (2011). Twitter sentiment analysis: the good the bad and the omg! In: *Proceedings of the Fifth International Conference on Weblogs and Social Media*. Barcelona, Catalonia, Spain, July 17–21.

Kushin, M.J. and Kitchener, K. (2009). Getting political on social network sites: exploring online political discourse on Facebook. *First Monday* 14 (11).

Landis, J.R. and Koch, G.G. (1977). The measurement of observer agreement for categorical data. *Biometrics* 33 (1): 159–174.

Lee, J.K., Choi, J., Kim, C., and Kim, Y. (2014). Social media, network heterogeneity, and opinion polarization. *Journal of Communication* 64 (4): 702–722.

Lynch, M. (2006). *Voices of the New Arab Public: Iraq, Al-Jazeera, and Middle East Politics Today*. New York: Columbia University Press.

Maghraoui, A. (2003). Ambiguities of sovereignty: Morocco, the Hague and the Western Sahara dispute. *Mediterranean Politics* 8 (1): 113–126.

MC (n.d.). About us. Available from: http://www.mc-doualiya.com/about-us (accessed November 28, 2019).

Meffert, M.F., Chung, S., Joiner, A.J. et al. (2006). The effects of negativity and motivated information processing during a political campaign. *Journal of Communication* 56 (1): 27–51.

Mellor, N. (2011). *Arab Media: Globalization and Emerging Media Industries*. Cambridge: Polity.

Mutz, D.C. and Martin, P.S. (2001). Facilitating communication across lines of political difference: the role of mass media. *American Political Science Review* 95 (1): 97–114.

Neri, F., Aliprandi, C., Capeci, F., Cuadros, M., and By, T. (2012). Sentiment analysis on social media. In: *Proceedings of the 2012 International Conference on Advances in Social Networks Analysis and Mining (ASONAM 2012)*. IEEE Computer Society, pp. 919–926.

Nisbet, E.C. and Myers, T.A. (2011). Anti-American sentiment as a media effect? Arab media, political identity, and public opinion in the Middle East. *Communication Research* 38 (5): 684–709.

NPR (2013). Al-Jazeera staffers quit over alleged bias in Egypt coverage. Available from: http://www.npr.org/2013/07/10/200823466/al-jazeera-staffers-quit-over-alleged-bias-in-egypt-coverage (accessed November 28, 2019).

Pak, A. and Paroubek, P. (2010). Twitter as a corpus for sentiment analysis and opinion mining. In: *Proceedings of the International Conference on Language Resources and Evaluation, LREC 2010*, pp. 1320–1326.

Pang, B. and Lee, L. (2008). Opinion mining and sentiment analysis. *Foundations and Trends in Information Retrieval* 2 (1–2): 1–135.

Riffe, D., Ellis, B., Rogers, M.K. et al. (1986). Gatekeeping and the network news mix. *Journalism and Mass Communication Quarterly* 63 (2): 315–321.

Rinnawi, K. (2006). *Instant Nationalism: McArabism, Al-Jazeera, and Transnational Media in the Arab World*. Lanham, MD: University Press of America.

RNW (n.d.a). About us. Available from: https://www.rnw.org/about-us/ (accessed November 28, 2019).

RNW (n.d.b). History of RNW media. Available from: https://www.rnw.org/history/ (accessed November 28, 2019).

Seib, P. (2008). *The Al Jazeera Effect: How the New Global Media Are Reshaping World Politics*. New York: Potomac.

Stroud, N.J. (2010). Polarization and partisan selective exposure. *Journal of Communication* 60 (3): 556–576.

Sunstein, C. (2001). *Republic.com*. Princeton, NJ: Princeton University Press.

Sunstein, C.R. (2009). *Going to Extremes: How like Minds Unite and Divide*. Oxford: Oxford University Press.

Tan, P., Steinbach, M., and Kumar, V. (2006). *Introduction to Data Mining*. New York: Pearson.

Tsfati, Y., Stroud, N.J., and Chotiner, A. (2013). Exposure to ideological news and perceived opinion climate: testing the media effects component of spiral-of-silence in a fragmented media landscape. *International Journal of Press/Politics* 19 (1): 3–23.

Tumasjan, A., Sprenger, T.O., Sandner, P.G., and Welpe, I.M. (2010). Predicting elections with Twitter: what 140 characters reveal about political sentiment. In: *International Conference on Weblogs and Social Media (ICWSM '07)*, pp. 178–185.

Van Dijk, T.A. (1998). Opinion and ideologies in the press. In: *Approaches to Media Discourse* (eds. A. Bell and P. Garrett), 22–63. Oxford: Blackwell.

Van Heelsum, A. (2005). Political participation and civic community of ethnic minorities in four cities in the Netherlands. *Politics* 25 (1): 19–30.

Watkins, T. (2014). Al Jazeera demands release of journalists still held by Egypt. CNN. Available from: http://edition.cnn.com/2013/12/31/world/meast/egypt-journalists-detained (accessed November 28, 2019).

Webster, J.G. and Ksiazek, T.B. (2012). The dynamics of audience fragmentation: public attention in an age of digital media. *Journal of Communication* 62 (1): 39–56.

Wessler, H. and Adolphsen, M. (2008). Contra-flow from the Arab world? How Arab television coverage of the 2003 Iraq war was used and framed on Western international news channels. *Media, Culture and Society* 30 (4): 439.

Wikileaks (2009). Ideological and ownership trends in the Saudi media. 09RIYADH651 May 11. E.O. 12958. Embassy Riyadh. Available from: http://wikileaks.org/cable/2009/05/09RIYADH651.html (accessed November 28, 2019).

Wikileaks (2015a). Saud Al Faysal cable to the Ministry of Interior. Available from: https://wikileaks.org/saudi-cables/doc118353.html (accessed November 28, 2019).

Wikileaks (2015b). Royal Embassy of Saudi Arabia – Doha. Available from: https://wikileaks.org/saudi-cables/doc67345.html (accessed November 28, 2019).

Wikileaks (2015c). Directorate of General Intelligence – Kingdom of Saudi Arabia. Available from: https://wikileaks.org/saudi-cables/doc85590.html (accessed November 28, 2019).

Williams, L. (2014). Inside Doha, at the heart of a GCC dispute. *The National*. Available from: http://www.thenational.ae/world/qatar/inside-doha-at-the-heart-of-a-gcc-dispute (accessed November 28, 2019).

Zillmann, D. and Bryant, J. (eds.) (2013). *Selective Exposure to Communication*. London: Routledge.

5

Viral News on Social Media

Introduction

There are few studies that have examined viral and popular news on social media; the majority deal instead with comparisons between editors' news selections and readers' news preferences. This chapter attempts to fill this gap by investigating the elements that constitute news virality on YouTube, Twitter, and Facebook. In particular, it discusses the way social networking sites (SNS) allow news readers to choose which news stories to read and subsequently to disseminate them to their friends or followers by sharing, liking, or commenting on them; this ultimately enhances online news engagement and interaction.

The first part of the chapter compares the social media channels (YouTube and Twitter) of four elite newspapers based in the United Kingdom and United States: the *Guardian*, the *New York Times*, the *Washington Post*, and the *Wall Street Journal*. These four papers were selected due to their wide outreach and fame. According to SimilarWeb (www.similarweb.com), which ranks the most popular websites in the world, theguardian.com was ranked second in 2016, followed by nytimes.com at third, while washingtonpost.com was tenth. As for wsj.com, it was ranked as the third most visited website for business news. As of 2016, the total number of the four newspapers' YouTube subscribers was over 1.2 million, while their total number of Twitter followers was over 51 million. The *New York Times* was the most followed outlet, with more than 27.8 million Twitter followers.

This chapter is adapted from two previously published papers: Al-Rawi, A. (2017). Viral news on social media. *Digital Journalism*, 7 (1), pp. 1–17, available at: https://doi.org/10.1080/21670811. 2017.1387062; and Al-Rawi, A. (2017). Audience preferences of news stories on social media. *Journal of Social Media in Society*, 6 (2), pp. 343–367, available at: https://thejsms.org/tsmri/index.php/TSMRI/article/view/284.

The rest of the chapter investigates a large Facebook data set taken from 10 news organizations, examining the most liked and commented-on Facebook stories from various Arabic-language news organizations: Deutsche Welle (DW) Arabic (German), Russia Today (RT) Arabic (Russian), CNN Arabic (American), BBC Arabic (British), Al Arabiya (Saudi), Al Jazeera Arabic (Qatari), France 24 and Radio Monte Carlo (French), Radio Netherlands Worldwide (RNW) (Dutch), SkyNews Arabia (UAE and British), and Al-Alam (Iranian). The US Department of State's Radio Sawa and Al Hurra TV are not included because the majority of their Facebook posts are questions addressed to their online audience. Arabic-language outlets that belong to ideologically and geographically diverse news organizations are incorporated into the chapter in order to provide a better picture of international news preferences. The scope of coverage is usually broad, encompassing the whole Arab world and targeting Arabic-speaking audiences.

The following section presents a literature review on the meaning of viral content and its elements.

What Is Viral Content?

Virality has many definitions, one of which refers to "what stands out as *remarkable* in a sea of content" (Nahon and Hemsley 2013, p. 2). According to the Oxford English Dictionary, "to go viral" means to "spread widely and rapidly." Indeed, virality is regarded as one of the mysteries of the Internet era because it is difficult to know why certain songs, movies, video clips, or news articles gain sudden and wide popularity while others that are equal (or better) in quality, content, and presentation do not. For example, "Alex from Target" became famous overnight after someone posted his photo on Twitter and it was shared by thousands of teenagers. Andrew Lih, commenting on Alex's sudden fame, stated: "There is a whole attempt at making sense of this now. But I can't find any" (Kaufman 2014). Jonah Berger (2013) refers to another example related to a *New York Times* article on coughing that went viral, for reasons that were at first mysterious. According to Berger, it boiled down to "emotion," since "When we care, we share." However, there are two other important elements that can explain the popularity of the coughing news article: relevance to all people and practical use. In this context, Jenkins et al. rightly state that when it comes to virality, "not all content is created equal" (2013, p. 198), due to the availability of certain elements that will be discussed in detail later.

Some of the first studies that investigated viral content were conducted by advertising and marketing researchers, mostly relying on emotion studies. The term "viral marketing" is believed to have first been used by the "firm Draper

Fisher Jurvetson in 1997 to describe Hotmail's use of advertisements ... to promote its free email service" (Jenkins et al. 2013). It was later used in a *PC User* magazine article in 1989 comparing Macintosh SE and Compaq computers (Kirby 2006, p. 89). Some scholars think that viral content is an extension of word of mouth (Phelps et al. 2004). The analogy is to the way rumors and gossip spread virally in certain times and contexts. Other scholars call this phenomenon "word-of-Mouse" (Mills 2012, p. 162).

It seems that one of the elements of virality is its practical information utility. For example, Berger refers to the six elements that drive virality, which can be abbreviated as STEPPS: social currency, triggers, emotion, public, practical value, stories (2013, p. 209). Furthermore, when André et al. (2012) asked respondents about tweets that are worth reading, they identified the following elements: information, humor, and conciseness. Tweets that are informative come first (48%), followed by humorous ones (24%) (André et al. 2012). Rudat and Buder (2015) found that tweets that carry "high informational value" as well as agent awareness information lead to retweeting. This is confirmed by other studies (e.g. Bobkowski 2015), since "consumers may share ... practically useful content for altruistic reasons," like when they want "to help others, generate reciprocity, or boost their reputation (e.g. show they know entertaining or useful things)" (Berger and Milkman 2012, pp. 193 and 201). This is related to the ego-oriented appeals cited later.

In their study on spreadable media, Jenkins et al. claim that some kinds of content can become viral if there is a "perceived social value" (2013, p. 199). By relying on John Fiske's notion of "producerly" – the sense that audiences internalize cultural meanings – Jenkins et al. believe that viral content can include the "use of shared fantasies, humor, parody and references, unfinished content, mystery, timely controversy, and rumors" (2013, p. 202). Also, Mills (2012) refers to the need to have some kind of likeability or appeal in the message itself. Content goes viral only "to the degree to which the message is stimulating or engaging in some emotional or intellectual way" (Mills 2012, pp. 166–167). Mills identifies four motivators for viral marketing, known as the SPIN framework: "the spreadability of content based on personal factors, the propagativity of content based on media type, the integration of multiple media platforms and the successive reinforcement of messaging" (2012, p. 166).

Though it is not addressed in this chapter, content relevance is indeed another important factor highlighted in previous studies that can be explored by conducting ethnographic research. In general, audiences tend to share content online that is most related to their personal beliefs and values (Hermida 2014). In this regard, Cohen et al. (1990) mention the concept of "psychological proximity," which is similar to the notion that people have "zones of relevance" that they use to decide whether to read and share news.

Viral content, therefore, is determined by a number of factors. In this chapter, I have drawn on a number of relevant news elements identified in previous studies, such as information utility and practical value (Berger and Milkman 2012; Berger 2013; Rudat and Buder 2015), humor, and social value (Jenkins et al. 2013), which is similar to the social significance identified in studies on news values.

Emotions and Virality

As noted, marketing scholars were among the first researchers to examine viral content with a clear focus on the role of emotions. Phelps et al. (2004), for example, found that emails were forwarded when Internet users experienced the following positive emotions: good, happy, excited, connected, rewarded, anticipation, inspired, and unique. In relation to negative emotions, they found that Internet users forwarded emails if they experienced one of the following feelings: irritated, angry, disappointed, skeptical, burdened, overwhelmed, and uninterested. Phelps et al. (2004) emphasized that connecting messages to specific audiences is an effective viral strategy. Porter and Golan (2006) conducted a study on viral advertising by examining 501 advertisements and six advertising appeals. They found that sex, nudity, and violence are more linked to virality. Dobele et al. (2007) also investigated viral campaigns by examining six primary emotions: surprise, joy, sadness, anger, fear, and disgust. They concluded that these strong emotions are all linked to virality. The authors highlighted the importance of the surprise element in capturing attention, yet they also pointed out gender differences in what constitutes virality, noting that "disgust-based and fear-based campaigns [are] more likely to be forwarded by male recipient[s]" (Dobele et al. 2007). Golan and Zaidner (2008, p. 966) content-analyzed 360 viral advertisements and found that ego-oriented appeals are highly important in making videos viral, including sexuality (28.1%), humor (91%), violence (14.4%), animals (17.8%), and children (12.8%). Nahon and Hemsley (2013) also referred to the virality of pet animals on YouTube and other SNS outlets, while Guadagno et al. (2013) found that strong emotional reactions, such as anger, can drive the virality of videos.

In relation to Twitter, Bakshy et al. (2011) studied the most popular influencers by examining 1.6 million Twitter users and 74 million diffusion events in 2009. They found that the largest influencers are those who have some previous fame or popularity that can be translated into news dealing with celebrities. The authors pointed out that "content that is rated more interesting tends to generate larger cascades on average, as does content that elicits more positive feelings" (Bakshy et al. 2011, p. 7). Yet, the attribute "interesting" remains relative and vague. In this regard, Khan and Vong (2014) also found that celebrity status or offline fame plays a crucial role in making YouTube videos viral. It is important to note here that previous research shows that having a high number of online followers does not necessarily secure a large number of retweets or mentions (Cha et al. 2010). As for YouTube views, Southgate et al. (2010) studied 102 viral videos by investigating the elements of distinctiveness, celebrity endorsement, enjoyment, and branding. They found that involvement and enjoyment are the main elements that determine the virality of a video. In terms of viral video games, Cohen studied players' decisions to share the pro-social "Darfur is Dying" game and found that "positive emotions predicted sharing while students played the game, but negative emotions predicted whether the game was shared after initial game play" (2014, p. 321).

Other scholars discuss the importance of high physiological arousal in virality. This refers to the activation of the nervous system as part of determining whether certain kinds of content should be shared (Berger 2011, p. 891). Additionally, Nelson-Field, Riebe, and Newstead examined two emotional responses that can make videos viral: arousal and valence (positive vs. negative content). The authors found that high arousal emotions play a far more important role than valence in the decision to share a video (Nelson-Field et al. 2013). Finally, one of the most relevant studies on viral news was conducted by Berger and Milkman (2012), who investigated a list of the most emailed *New York Times* articles from a total sample of about 7000 news stories. They found that content that evokes high arousal emotions such as awe (positive emotion), anger, and anxiety (both negative emotions) tends to be more viral than other types of content. Berger and Milkman emphasize that the opposing "emotions characterized by activation or arousal (i.e., awe, anxiety, and anger) are positively linked to virality, while emotions characterized by deactivation (i.e., sadness) are negatively linked" (2012, p. 199). The results of their study reveal that awe content is more viral, while sadness-inducing content is less viral. However, they found that "some negative emotions are positively associated with vitality. More anxiety – and anger-inducing stories are both more likely to make the most e-mailed list" (Berger and Milkman 2012, p. 197).

In this chapter, valence (positive vs. negative content) and arousal (awe, anger, anxiety, and sadness) are examined subsequent to previous research on virality (Phelps et al. 2004; Dobele et al. 2007; Berger and Milkman 2012; Guadagno et al. 2013; Nelson-Field et al. 2013; Cohen 2014). Valence is coded as bad news versus good news, based on previous research on news values. In this regard, Shoemaker and Cohen assert in their study of international news that people generally prefer to "be presented with 'good' news" but are biologically programed to "pay more attention to bad or deviant news items because it is in their best interest to do so" in terms of survival (2012, p. 12). In other words, bad news is more important or newsworthy than good news. Other news elements that have been incorporated into this chapter include news stories on or involving celebrities (Bakshy et al. 2011; Khan and Vong 2014), animals and pets (Nahon and Hemsley 2013), children, violence/conflict, humor, and sexuality (Porter and Golan 2006; Golan and Zaidner 2008).

Viral News and Newsworthiness

For the purposes of this chapter, viral news can be defined as networked news stories that spread online mostly through social media in a much faster and wider manner than other news stories. Since there is a gap in the literature on viral news, the concept of newsworthiness is a relevant field of research because it sheds light on the elements that make some events very newsworthy among readers. The reason to include research on newsworthiness in this chapter was that it provides a "set of rules" that journalists and editors use to "plan and execute the content of a publication or a broadcast" (Brighton and Foy 2007, p. 3). Previous studies on news values highlighted several conventions that are popular among journalists and editors in their news selection decisions. Unlike emotions, newsworthiness is regarded as a "cognitive concept" or a "mental judgment made by individual people" (Shoemaker and Cohen 2012, p. 337) in order to filter events and produce news. Newsworthiness provides a "matrix which sets out the variables and allows them to be applied to news stories as a means of prioritising items" or events (Brighton and Foy 2007, p. 3).

As discussed in Chapter 2, there are different criteria that can be followed to explore news values (Galtung and Ruge 1965; Harcup and O'Neill 2001; Shoemaker and Cohen 2012). Recently, Harcup and O'Neill recommended examining new elements in news values, including what they called "shareability," which refers to "stories that are thought likely to generate sharing and comments via Facebook, Twitter and other forms of social media" (2016, p. 13). But they do not elaborate on or clarify what constitutes "shareability" and its features. In this regard, Jenkins, Ford, and Green elaborate on content shareability and emphasize that it can be achieved if one or all of these five conditions are met: "It's available when and where audiences want it, portable (quotable and grabbable) to make it easier to be shared, easily reusable in a variety of ways, relevant to multiple audiences e.g. shared nostalgia, and part of a steady stream of material e.g. brands invest all their energy in a particular media text that is expected to generate exponential hits" (2013, pp. 197–198). These conditions, however, are mostly focused on the format and presentation rather than the content that makes it sharable, while the "quotable or grabbable" element remains vague. In this regard, Mills defines "shareability" as a reference to "the degree to which the consumer feels that the content will have a similar effect (of stimulation or engagement) on others in their social network" (2012, pp. 166–167). Kalsnes and Larsson (2017) conducted an empirical study on the frequency of sharing news articles on news organizations' websites rather than directly via social media. They used the RSS feed tool to collect the necessary data and found that soft news topics, rather than hard news, were more likely to be shared by readers of the outlets they studied, with the exception of the Norwegian TV2 channel. Furthermore, Larsson (2016) studied news posted on four Facebook pages belonging to Norwegian news organizations. He classified 800 news items into nine categories based on previous studies: "Accidents, Crime/Conflict/War, Economy, Entertainment, Health, Human Interest, Other, Politics, Sports, and Technology" (Larsson 2016). The news examined in this chapter, however, was randomly selected from a larger sample (n = 21 717), so it is not focused on virality. Larsson found that news organizations often post news on politics followed by human interest, entertainment, and accidents/crimes/conflict. On the other hand, Facebook users were more likely to share and like news on human interest stories and to comment on political news (Larsson 2016).

For this chapter, a relevant selection of news elements has been chosen in order to investigate virality or newsworthiness among audiences; these include good news, bad news, unexpectedness/odd/surprising, elite people (celebrity), entertainment, social significance/magnitude, human interest, and conflict/violence (Galtung and Ruge 1965; Harcup and O'Neill 2001; Shoemaker and Cohen 2012; Larsson 2016).

As for the issue of online news popularity among readers, Boczkowski and Mitchelstein mention that online news readers exhibit a kind of "human interactivity" (2013, p. 113) by either clicking on the news article, emailing it, or commenting on it. To provide some kind of justification, the authors state that clicking is usually associated with what is interesting, emailing is associated with what is bizarre, and commenting is associated with controversial topics, so the three activities are often quite different. A much earlier study conducted by Tewksbury (2003, p. 704) examined the online behavior of news readers and found that online audiences mostly prefer to read certain news topics such as sports, business and money, arts and entertainment, features, and US national news consecutively. It is important to note that readers' choice of news seems to follow a different process than editors' and journalists', especially during times of "normal political activity," as "journalists choose stories about political, international, and economic subjects substantively more than consumers" (Boczkowski and Mitchelstein 2010, p. 420). Boczkowski et al. (2012) examined the thematic gap between news dissemination by journalists and news consumption by readers during the 2008 US presidential campaign. They found that there is a difference between what journalists promote on their news organizations' websites and what readers like to read. In general, journalists prefer "public affairs news (stories about politics, economics, and international topics)" (Boczkowski et al. 2012, p. 347) more than do readers, though this gap changes during campaign times and across different outlets. In a similar study, the same authors examined the gap in online news choices in Western Europe and Latin America, and reached similar conclusions (Boczkowski et al. 2011). In their study of international news in 10 countries, Shoemaker and Cohen also reached similar conclusions, stating that "there seems to be a universal dissatisfaction [by the participants in ten countries] with the prominence given to the various news items in newspapers" (2012, p. 89). They concluded that there "is no systematic pattern of agreement between newspaper and public relations practitioners, low SES [socioeconomic status] audience members, or high SES audience members" on what constitutes newsworthiness (Shoemaker and Cohen 2012, p. 88). Yet, one of the major limitations of Boczkowski's studies with his colleagues is that the classification of news is generic: public affairs versus non-public affairs news, which makes it difficult to clearly understand the most and least popular news subtopics, while other important factors like emotions are not incorporated in previous news values research. In this regard, a few studies used ethnographic approaches to investigate the emotional aspects of news consumption (Perloff 1989; Perse 1990; Bucy 2003) in what Knobloch et al. (2004) call "affective news," but they examine neither virality nor the different elements of news content. In this chapter, viral news is examined on social media platforms instead of on news organizations' websites, and the investigation is focused on the various cognitive and emotional elements that make news viral. The chapter also combines quantitative and qualitative analyses of viral news, since the majority of previous studies relied on ethnographic research (Bright and Nicholls 2014).

In terms of method, the first part of the chapter examines the top 50 most popular or viral news stories, which constitute 40.2% of total YouTube views (257 709 980 views out of a total of 640 847 335) and 3% of the audience's retweets (337 813 retweets out of a total of 11 207 902). A detailed list of the news organizations examined can be found in Table 5.1, including information on the total number of subscribers, views, and videos posted for each, as well as the dates on which they joined each platform. The metadata at the top of each video is also documented, such as the number of total comments, views, likes, and dislikes. It is important to mention here that two measurements of virality have been used in this chapter because they are widely regarded by scholars, media, and the social media companies themselves as the most common ones. YouTube, for example, uses number of views to calculate advertising revenues; other measurements like the number of comments, likes, and dislikes remain relevant, but do not seem to be equal in importance (Greenburg 2017). For Twitter, retweets are considered the most popular method of evaluating virality – more important than replies, mentions, and likes (Luckerson 2016).

As there is so much "noisy data" on SNS (Agarwal et al. 2011) that can be difficult to make sense of, many scholars have found solutions to understand what matters most to their online readers and audiences. For example, some studies investigating big data limited their attention to the most popular posts or tweets. Naaman et al. (2011) examined a large data set collected from New York City Twitter users by examining the top 50 Twitter trends. Afterwards, the trends were classified into four categories. Similarly, Wilkinson and Thelwall (2012) studied

Table 5.1 News stories on YouTube and Twitter.

YouTube stats[a]	*Guardian*	NYT	WP	WSJ	Total
Videos	6073	7648	4553	19753	38027
Subscribers	211427	661374	58729	349636	1281166
Views	109395343	269363519	38080837	224007636	640847335
Date joined	Feb. 14, 2006	Oct. 13, 2006	Jun. 30, 2006	Jun. 18, 2007	—

Twitter stats[b]	*Guardian*	NYT	WP	WSJ	Total
Stories	75887	47198	30923	41424	195432
Retweets	2573789	3640773	2222741	2770599	11207902
Replies	448356	630314	369060	330442	1778172
Total engagement	3022145	4271087	2591801	3101041	12986074
Date joined	Nov. 5, 2009	Mar. 2, 2007	Mar. 27, 2007	Mar. 31, 2007	—

[a] Data as of April 1, 2016.
[b] Data from December 12, 2013 to February 17, 2015.

about half a billion tweets from six countries by investigating the top 50 trending keywords.

In relation to the data sample for this chapter, the YouTube channel for each newspaper was examined. The platform allows users to select the "Most Popular" option from among the list of videos posted, based on the number of views counted from the day the channel was created until the current date (our data was collected on April 1, 2016). In relation to Twitter news, the data was collected via Crimson Hexagon through its social media impact program. As the company has access to Twitter's firehose, tweets dating from December 19, 2013 until February 17, 2015 (the date of retrieval) could be collected. Retweeting a news story, unlike YouTube views, involves potentially viewing it and sharing it with one's Twitter followers. However, the two online activities both entail active engagement with the news story and can be clear indicators of virality when compared to other stories. In total, 38027 YouTube videos and 195432 Twitter stories posted by the four elite newspapers were included in the sample for this chapter. Since only the top 50 news stories were selected on each platform, the 400 most viral news stories on YouTube and Twitter are studied here. The unit of analysis for Twitter is the news story as a whole, as hyperlinked via the platform. In relation to YouTube, the unit of analysis is also the news story, which in this case is the whole video.

The codebook was designed based on relevant previous research on viral content as well as a selected number of studies on newsworthiness, which is why this chapter is based on a mixed model. The decision to combine these two types of studies is related to the limitation each one has, since studies on virality are mostly focused on emotions in advertising and marketing, while studies on news values largely ignore the emotional aspect in virality. Hence, this chapter, which investigates 17 elements that are identified in previous research on viral news, combines relevant emotional and cognitive elements that drive virality: positive (good news), negative (bad news), unexpectedness/odd/surprising, elite people (celebrity), entertainment, social significance/magnitude, humor, human interest, sexuality, animals, children, practical value or utility, conflict/violence, sadness, anger, anxiety, and awe. A news story can contain more than one of these categorical variables, so they are not mutually exclusive. Finally, two coders examined over 10% of the sample (n = 50 news stories), and intercoder reliability was acceptable using Cohen's kappa (Landis and Koch 1977).

As for Facebook news, the chapter attempts to understand the types of news stories online audiences mostly comment on and like to read, and whether there are significant differences between liking and commenting on popular social media news. In addition, the chapter examines the countries that garnered most of the online audience attention based on the top news stories they were exposed to and investigates whether there is any attention given to non-Arab countries. To this end, I used NVivo-N-Capture in January and February 2014 to mine Facebook posts, comments, and other details from 10 Arabic-language news organizations. The webometric tool provided over 85 000 Facebook posts, mostly comprising news stories or links to news reports, which garnered over 26.4 million likes from the online audience. In relation to the most commented-on news stories, they garnered over 1.9 million comments from the online audience. On average, each Facebook page had 8515 news stories and 193 122 comments. Based on the average number of comments per news story, BBC Arabic seems to be the most active Facebook page in terms of audience engagement with 85.3 comments per story, followed by Al Jazeera (80.6), RT (47), Al Arabiya (35.3), and SkyNews Arabia (22) (see Table 5.2).

Next, I investigated the top 100 most liked and commented-on news stories from each news organization, especially in relation to the kinds of news audiences most like to consume them. For accuracy, I removed any non-news posts like general greetings or statements. In total, 2000 news stories were studied, which generated over 4.1 million likes, constituting 17.6% of the total news stories likes. As for the most commented-on posts, they generated over 487 000 comments or 25.2% of the total news stories comments. The reason I chose Facebook likes is that, according to a Pew Research Center survey, Facebook users more often like a page, photo, or post than comment, send private messages, or update their profiles (Smith 2014). Back in 2012, Facebook announced that over 2.7 billion likes are given every single day, making this online behavior the most active one among Facebook users (Tam 2012). As for Facebook comments, they are also regarded as

Table 5.2 Number of page and news story likes and comments along the 10 news organizations.

Channel	Total page likes	Total no. of all news stories (links and posts)	No. of likes for all news stories and posts	No. of likes and percentage for top 100 news stories	No. of comments for all news stories and posts	Average no. of comments for each news story	No. of comments and percentage for top 100 news stories	
1) Al-Alam	531 538	7986	6 572 900	972 315 (14.7%)	313 872	1.7	98 594	31.40%
2) CNN	581 145	7961	167 366	20 333 (12.1%)	111 264	13.9	19 787	17.70%
3) Al Arabiya	5 508 959	6974	8 196 770	1 402 241 (17.1%)	246 504	35.3	90 390	36.60%
4) Al Jazeera	6 149 325	4711	3 785 830	607 110 (16%)	380 072	80.6	75 443	19.80%
5) RT	2 155 248	5741	3 218 913	440 763 (13.6%)	270 250	47	69 810	25.80%
6) DW	377 855	26 782	505 951	68 504 (13.5%)	96 533	3.6	11 709	12.10%
7) SkyNews	2 503 101	4985	1 494 880	177 919 (11.9%)	110 007	22	21 979	19.90%
8) France24	1 402 378	12 356	1 042 832	153 294 (14.6%)	155 000	12.5	25 390	16.30%
9) RNW	279 249	5114	129 233	61 934 (47.9%)	30 975	6	11 131	35.90%
10) BBC	2 104 697	2540	1 379 365	209 671 (15.2%)	216 752	85.3	63 301	29.20%
Total for all channels	21 593 495	85 150	26 494 040	4 114 084	1 931 229	307.9	487 534	
Average for all channels	2 159 349	8515	2 649 404	411 408 (17.6%)	193 122	30.7	48 753	24.40%

an important online activity, since commenting on news stories indicates a certain degree of engagement. In fact, commenting requires some kind of reflection and the writing of a relevant response. When a Facebook user comments on news stories posted on another Facebook page, his or her friends can see the comment on their News Feed, so this is one way of disseminating or diffusing news, allowing others to like, share, or comment on it in turn. Since in this chapter over 85 000 news stories are examined, producing over 26.4 million likes and 1.9 million comments, it becomes extremely hard to make sense of how the online audience collectively interacts on the Facebook pages of the news organizations under investigation. To narrow down the focus, only the top 100 most commented-on and liked news stories are examined. In this way, I aim to cut through the noise on social media and reveal key trends related to virality.

In order to understand the types of news stories online audiences liked and commented on most, they are categorized into 22 topics following previous studies on news values, including those by Atwater (1984), Riffe et al. (1986), and Shoemaker and Cohen (2012). The latter, for example, examined news values in 10 countries and identified 26 main topics. In this chapter, order, politics, and sports are all classified based on three levels: internal, referring to one specific Arab country, regional, involving two or more Arab countries, and international, involving non-Arab countries. One added news topic, which is similar to Riffe et al.'s (1986) religion topic, is religious commemoration, which includes describing pilgrimage season, Ramadan, or the Eid holiday (see Table 5.3). Finally, two coders who are fluent in Arabic coded over 10% of the sample (n = 220 news stories), and intercoder reliability was acceptable using Cohen's kappa (Landis and Koch 1977).

YouTube and Twitter News Analysis

This chapter, as discussed, seeks to understand the prominence of the various elements that make news viral, as well as the differences between viral news on Twitter and on YouTube (and on Facebook). The results of the Twitter news analysis show that, in total, there were 337 813 retweets of the top 50 news stories among the four newspapers. The highest number of retweets came from the *Wall Street Journal* (100 308), followed by the *Washington Post* (91 193), the *New York Times* (88 221), and the *Guardian* (58 091). The total engagement on these 200 news stories, including replies and retweets, was 369 527 (see Table 5.4).

The findings indicate that the element of unexpectedness/odd/surprising, at 15.3% (n = 168), is the most appealing in terms of making news viral on Twitter. News stories that deal with unusual or odd events have attracted people from the

Table 5.3 News topic distribution along the 10 news organizations.

No.	News topic
1)	Local politics (confined to one Arab country)
2)	Regional politics (limited to the Arab world or to one Arab country and one non-Arab one)
3)	International politics (involving non-Arab countries)
4)	Local order (civil war, demonstrations, crimes, terrorism, violent incidents, etc.)
5)	Regional order
6)	International order
7)	Local sports
8)	Regional sports
9)	International sports
10)	Human interest
11)	Economy, business, commerce, and industry (combined)
12)	Military and defense
13)	Entertainment, fashion, and beauty
14)	Health/welfare/social services
15)	Weather and environment
16)	Cultural events and ceremonies (political and ethnic commemorations)
17)	Disasters and epidemics
18)	Housing and transportation
19)	Science, technology, and energy
20)	Education
21)	Religious commemoration
22)	Odd and/or funny stories

beginning of time, and previous research on news values has identified this element as an important one in news production. The second most appealing element is social significance, or the magnitude of economic, cultural, public, or political events, coming in at 14.1% (n = 155). As noted earlier, practical information is a very appealing news element because of its usefulness in people's lives, especially as it is linked to ego-oriented appeals, and the results show that this element is in the top five at 8.2% (n = 91), followed by human interest at 8.1% (n = 90).

When it comes to valence, online readers prefer positive news (58.2%, n = 113) to negative news (41.7%, n = 81) when these two elements are considered separately. This finding is interesting because journalists and editors often believe bad

Table 5.4 Viral news on the four newspapers' Twitter accounts.

Element	NYT	WSJ	*Guardian*	WP	Total
Retweets	88 221	100 308	58 091	91 193	337 813
Replies	10 771	8983	4402	7558	31 714
Total engagement	98 992	109 291	62 493	98 751	369 527
1) Positive	27	34	26	26	113
2) Negative	22	15	21	23	81
3) Unexpectedness/odd/ surprising	39	44	42	43	168
4) Elite people	15	13	3	17	48
5) Entertainment	14	10	5	0	29
6) Social significance/magnitude	44	38	36	37	155
7) Humor	0	2	4	6	12
8) Human interest	24	24	23	19	90
9) Sexuality	0	1	1	0	2
10) Animals	0	1	4	1	6
11) Children	0	0	0	3	3
12) Practical value or utility	14	32	21	24	91
13) Conflict/violence	19	13	20	14	66
14) Sadness	12	10	10	10	42
15) Anger	14	7	22	12	55
16) Anxiety	5	6	6	9	26
17) Awe	25	35	24	27	111

news is more appealing or more important to readers, but there is a clear preference by news readers on Twitter to view and share positive news. This corresponds with previous studies that found a gap between journalists' selection of news and readers' consumption patterns (Boczkowski et al. 2011; Shoemaker and Cohen 2012). In relation to the three arousal elements when calculated separately, awe, which is associated with positive emotions, comes far ahead at 57.8% (n = 111), while arousal, which is linked to negative feelings like anger, comes in at 28.6% (n = 55), followed by anxiety at 13.5% (n = 26). Similar to these findings on valence, we find news stories that contain arousal elements associated with positive emotions drive virality more than those that contain negative emotions. And yet, news stories that contain sadness (3.8%, n = 42) exceed those that have entertainment (2.6%, n = 29) or humor (1%, n = 12) elements.

   As for the analysis of YouTube news, the top 200 videos garnered 257 709 980 views, 710 830 comments, and 113 658 081 likes, in comparison to only 106 193 dislikes (see Table 5.5). The *New York Times* has the highest number of YouTube views (112 877 429), comments (351 258), likes (113 228 687), and dislikes (52 504). In terms of the number of views, the next highest are the *Wall Street Journal* (71 272 778), the *Guardian* (49 397 913), and the *Washington Post* (24 161 860), respectively. As for the number of comments on the top 200 YouTube videos, the *Washington Post* comes second (191 274), followed by the *Guardian* (102 996) and the *Wall Street Journal* (65 302).

Table 5.5   Viral news on the four newspapers' YouTube channels.

Element	NYT	WSJ	*Guardian*	WP	Total
Views	112 877 429	71 272 778	49 397 913	24 161 860	257 709 980
Comments	351 258	65 302	102 996	191 274	710 830
Likes	113 228 687	216 065	127 767	85 562	113 658 081
Dislikes	52 504	21 837	22 677	9175	106 193
1) Positive	29	41	39	31	140
2) Negative	14	8	11	9	42
3) Unexpectedness/ odd/surprising	16	25	24	23	88
4) Elite people	22	25	11	27	85
5) Entertainment	21	30	27	14	92
6) Social significance/ magnitude	27	20	24	36	107
7) Humor	6	3	2	4	15
8) Human interest	32	24	20	19	95
9) Sexuality	4	2	5	0	11
10) Animals	3	4	5	2	14
11) Children	1	0	0	1	2
12) Practical value or utility	15	10	14	20	59
13) Conflict/violence	8	7	10	7	32
14) Sadness	8	1	4	4	17
15) Anger	7	7	5	6	25
16) Anxiety	6	3	7	6	22
17) Awe	23	26	34	24	107

Similar to Twitter news, positive YouTube stories (77.1%, n = 140) score higher on valence than those that are negative (22.8%, n = 42). The gap between positive and negative news stories is larger on YouTube than on Twitter, which provides an indication of the differences in the two social media platforms' audience demographics and their news preferences. As for the arousal elements, when calculated separately, awe comes first (69.4%, n = 107), followed by anger (16.2%, n = 25) and anxiety (14.2%, n = 22). These findings are generally similar to those for Twitter news; news stories that generate positive emotions tend to be more viral than those that induce negative ones. Unlike news on Twitter, YouTube news stories that contain sadness are even less likely to be viral (1.7%, n = 17), while entertainment news (9.6%, n = 92) is among the top five most appealing elements. However, news stories that contain humor are not that significant (1.5%, n = 15) in the selected sample.

Other viral news elements that are prominent in the top YouTube videos include social significance/magnitude (11.2%, n = 107), human interest 9.9%, n = 95), unexpectedness/odd/surprising (9.2%, n = 88), and stories that deal with elite people or celebrities (8.9%, n = 85). It is interesting to note that other elements found to be viral in advertising and marketing research such as the use of children, animals, and sexuality are not highly prominent in the study of viral news.

As for the differences between Twitter and YouTube, there seem to be different types of audience that consume news and other types of content online. In order to examine the similarities between YouTube and Twitter news, the Spearman correlation coefficient ranking test was used (rs 0.8529). The results showed statistically significant differences between the two platforms (see Table 5.6). Despite some general similarities, especially in relation to valence and arousal elements, this ranking test provides another indication of the differences in the news consumption patterns of online audiences between different social media platforms. This is not surprising, since a Pew Research Center report on SNS use found several differences among people and their preferred platforms and ways of accessing them according to various factors like age, gender, socio-economic status, racial and ethnic background, and community (Perrin 2015).

Though there are slight differences in valence between the two social media platforms, online news viewers and readers on YouTube and Twitter prefer to consume and share positive news stories with an average of 67.2%, in contrast to 32.7% for negative news. As for arousal, awe-inspiring elements that are associated with positive emotions exceed other arousal factors with an average of 63%, while arousal elements that are linked to negative emotions come much later, with an average of 23.1% for anger and 13.8% for anxiety. These findings partially correspond with previous research on viral news (Berger and Milkman 2012), and

Table 5.6 Ranking of news stories on YouTube and Twitter.

No.	Element	YouTube	Twitter
1)	Positive	1	3
2)	Negative	9	7
3)	Unexpectedness/odd/surprising	6	1
4)	Elite people	7	10
5)	Entertainment	5	12
6)	Social significance/magnitude	2	2
7)	Humor	14	14
8)	Human interest	4	6
9)	Sexuality	16	17
10)	Animals	15	15
11)	Children	17	16
12)	Practical value or utility	8	5
13)	Conflict/violence	10	8
14)	Sadness	13	11
15)	Anger	11	9
16)	Anxiety	12	13
17)	Awe	3	4

Spearman correlation coefficient rs 0.8529, Significance (2-tailed) $P = 0.000014$ (correlation is significant at the 0.05 level [2-tailed]).

they show that the viral news that online readers most want to read, view, and share is significantly positive rather than negative.

In relation to the most appealing element, social significance and magnitude – including its four dimensions, economic, cultural, public, and political – is found to be the most important one (6.3%) to making news viral (see Table 5.7). The second most popular is unexpectedness/odd/surprising (6.2%), followed by positive (6.1%), awe-inspiring (5.3%), human interest (4.4%), entertainment (2.9%), and practical utility (3.6%). On the other hand, the least viral elements are anxiety (1.1%), humor (0.6%), animals (0.4%), sexuality (0.2%), and children (0.09%).

To sum up, by studying 17 viral elements that have been identified in previous research, this chapter found that online news readers overwhelmingly prefer to read and share positive and awe-inspiring news in contrast to negative and angry or anxiety-inducing news. Social significance and unexpectedness/odd/surprising are the most appealing elements in making news viral.

Table 5.7 Average results on YouTube and Twitter in sequence.

No.	Element	Average (percentage)
1)	Social significance/magnitude	131 (6.3%)
2)	Unexpectedness/odd/surprising	128 (6.2%)
3)	Positive	126.5 (6.1%)
4)	Awe	109 (5.3%)
5)	Human interest	92.5 (4.4%)
6)	Entertainment	60.5 (2.9%)
7)	Practical value or utility	75 (3.6%)
8)	Elite people	66.5 (3.2%)
9)	Negative	61.5 (2.9%)
10)	Conflict/violence	49 (2.3%)
11)	Anger	40 (1.9%)
12)	Sadness	29.5 (1.4%)
13)	Anxiety	24 (1.1%)
14)	Humor	13.5 (0.6%)
15)	Animals	10 (0.4%)
16)	Sexuality	6.5 (0.2%)
17)	Children	2.5 (0.09%)

Facebook News Analysis

As noted, online audiences who read and engage with news on social media outlets distribute stories to their followers and friends by either liking or commenting on them on Facebook. The examination of the top 100 most liked news stories from among the 10 news organizations showed some important patterns in the online audience news consumption of popular social media content (see Tables 5.8 and 5.9).

In relation to the kinds of news stories that the online audiences are collectively exposed to by likes count, the results show that news topics dealing with local order, including security issues, in specific Arab countries garnered the most attention, making up 16.3% (n = 180) of the most liked stories. This was expected, due to the ongoing turmoil in the Middle East, especially after the Arab Spring events. The second most liked news topic was local politics, which made up 15.2% (n = 168) of the most liked stories. This topic deals with election news, political rivalry, and government formation and issues related to a specific country. The third most liked topic was human interest 13.3% (n = 147), which mostly deals with emotional, heartbreaking, or moving stories. Interestingly, the scope of the majority of these stories was the Arab or Muslim world. The fourth most liked topic was international

Channel	Topic 1	Topic 2	Topic 3	Topic 4	Topic 5	Topic 6	Topic 7	Topic 8	Topic 9	Topic 10	Topic 11
Al-Alam	13	4	15	22	1	0	0	0	1	10	0
CNN	35	13	5	15	1	1	2	2	0	4	1
Al Arabiya	1	0	2	8	0	0	0	0	0	19	0
Al Jazeera	35	12	11	29	0	0	2	1	0	7	0
RT	15	5	8	18	1	3	0	1	1	8	0
DW	19	1	3	8	0	0	0	0	0	31	0
SkyNews	24	9	11	17	3	4	0	3	4	6	1
France24	5	11	10	20	2	4	3	3	7	7	0
BBC	11	8	15	24	3	0	2	1	0	11	0
RNW	10	4	0	11	3	0	0	0	0	31	4
Total	168	71	98	180	15	18	9	12	18	147	18
Percentage	15.2%	6.4%	3.9%	16.3%	1.3%	1.6%	0.8%	1.09%	1.6%	13.3%	1.6%

Channel	Topic 12	Topic 13	Topic 14	Topic 15	Topic 16	Topic 17	Topic 18	Topic 19	Topic 20	Topic 21	Topic 22
Al-Alam	17	2	0	1	1	0	0	1	0	12	0
CNN	5	0	0	4	3	0	0	2	0	1	6
Al Arabiya	0	1	0	9	7	1	0	4	0	12	36
Al Jazeera	0	0	0	1	0	0	0	2	0	0	0
RT	12	3	2	1	1	0	0	10	2	1	8
DW	0	2	0	2	3	2	0	4	6	12	7
SkyNews	0	1	1	2	5	0	0	3	0	0	6
France24	2	2	0	1	10	2	0	3	0	0	8
BBC	0	3	0	2	3	1	0	5	1	1	9
RNW	1	1	2	8	3	0	0	1	2	8	11
Total	37	15	6	33	41	14	0	42	11	50	97
Percentage	3.3%	1.3%	0.5%	3%	3.7%	1.2%	0%	3.8%	1%	4.5%	8.8%

Table 5.9 Most commented-on news topic distribution along the 10 news organizations.

Channel	Topic 1	Topic 2	Topic 3	Topic 4	Topic 5	Topic 6	Topic 7	Topic 8	Topic 9	Topic 10	Topic 11
Al-Alam	22	21	2	28	4	0	0	1	0	4	0
CNN	58	16	1	20	1	0	0	0	0	1	0
Al Arabiya	4	6	5	9	3	0	0	0	0	16	1
Al Jazeera	39	11	6	21	5	1	0	0	0	8	0
RT	18	11	7	16	12	1	0	1	1	8	0
DW	32	8	6	14	3	0	0	0	2	18	0
SkyNews	30	8	16	10	2	0	1	3	7	6	1
France24	11	8	7	12	4	4	1	4	7	8	1
BBC	33	8	4	29	7	1	1	2	0	8	0
RNW	15	11	1	13	5	0	1	0	2	23	0
Total	262	108	55	172	46	7	4	11	19	100	3
Percentage	26.2%	10.8%	5.5%	17.2%	4.6%	0.7%	0.4%	1.1%	1.9%	10%	0.3%

Channel	Topic 12	Topic 13	Topic 14	Topic 15	Topic 16	Topic 17	Topic 18	Topic 19	Topic 20	Topic 21	Topic 22
Al-Alam	5	1	0	0	0	1	0	0	0	6	5
CNN	0	0	0	0	3	0	0	0	0	0	0
Al Arabiya	0	4	1	5	1	2	1	3	0	5	34
Al Jazeera	2	0	0	2	3	0	0	1	1	0	0
RT	5	9	0	0	2	0	0	2	0	1	6
DW	1	0	1	2	3	0	0	1	1	7	1
SkyNews	0	5	1	1	4	2	0	2	0	0	1
France24	1	4	0	0	25	1	0	1	0	0	1
BBC	0	1	0	0	2	0	0	1	0	0	3
RNW	0	2	1	9	5	0	0	0	2	5	5
Total	14	26	4	19	48	6	1	11	4	24	56
Percentage	1.4%	2.6%	0.4%	1.9%	4.8%	6%	0.1%	1.1%	0.4%	2.4%	5.6%

politics (8.9%, n = 98), dealing with world powers and non-Arab countries. The fifth most liked topic, however, was odd and/or funny stories (8.8%, n = 97). This was not expected, as the other top topics involved some level of online civic engagement with the news, especially with important events taking place in the Arab region. These results, with some differences, roughly correspond with Shoemaker and Cohen's (2012) study on the kinds of news stories TV news organizations themselves focus on. For example, internal politics came second (13.3%), international politics fifth (7.4%), local order sixth (6.8%), and human interest seventh (6.1%).

As for the least liked topics, housing and transportation news came last (n = 0), while health/welfare/social services (0.5%, n = 6), local sports (0.8%, n = 9), education (1%, n = 11), and regional sports (1.09%, n = 12) all did slightly better. For local and regional sports, it had been expected that the online audience would like such story topics more than others based on Shoemaker and Cohen's (2012) study, in which sports came in first place (14.1%).

In relation to the kinds of news stories that the online audience is collectively exposed to by the comments counts, the results show that stories dealing with local politics including political rivalry, government formation, and election issues in specific Arab countries garnered the highest attention, making up 26.2% (n = 262) of the most commented-on stories. This was also expected due to the ongoing political changes in the Middle East, especially after the Arab Spring events. Local order came second, making up 17.2% (n = 172) of the most commented-on stories. This topic deals with security issues, protests, arrests, and terrorism. This was also expected, because of the ongoing military operations in the Middle East, especially in countries like Syria, Iraq, and Yemen. The third most commented-on topic was regional politics (10.8%, n = 108), which mostly deals with official meetings, negotiations, and treaties with more than one Arab country. The fourth most commented-on topic was human interest (10%, n = 100), content that involves emotional or tragic stories. Interestingly, the scope of the majority of these stories was the Arab or Muslim world. The fifth most commented-on topic was odd and/or funny news (5.6%, n = 56), while the sixth was international politics, dealing with non-Arab countries (5.5%, n = 55). This is an interesting finding, showing that there is some kind of online civic engagement with more local news, especially important events taking place in the Arab region. These results, again with some differences, correspond to some extent with Shoemaker and Cohen's (2012) study on the kinds of news stories TV news organizations themselves focus on. For example, internal politics came second in their study (13.3%), followed by international politics in fifth (7.4%), internal order in sixth (6.8%), and human interest in seventh (6.1%).

As for the least commented-on topics, housing and transportation news again came last 0.1% (n = 1), followed by economy, business, commerce, and industry (0.3%, n = 3), local sports (0.4%, n = 4), health/welfare/social services (0.4%, n = 4), education (0.4%m n = 4), disasters and epidemics (0.6%, n = 6), and international order (0.7%, n = 7). It's not surprising that local sports would rank higher than many other topics. Shoemaker and Cohen's (2012) study found sports came in first place (14.1%) in terms of news organizations' emphasis, though the online audience preference differed somewhat. As for the statistical differences between liking and commenting on Facebook news, Spearman correlation coefficient test of ranking R 0.177, P = 0.431, indicated no significant differences between the two online activities (see Table 5.10).

Table 5.10   Ranking of news stories.

Likes ranking	Comments ranking
1	1
4	4
10	2
3	10
22	3
2	5
21	9
19	8
16	15
12	6
15	16
6	21
9	22
11	7
5	11
13	13
17	20
8	14
20	12
7	17
14	18
18	19

Spearman correlation coefficient R 0.177,
Significance (2-tailed) P = 0.431 (Correlation
is significant at the 0.05 level [2-tailed]).

Regarding the top countries to which the online audience was exposed, Egypt topped the list (54.3%, n = 194) as the country that is mostly referenced in the top 100 news stories, followed by Syria (20.7%, n = 74), Iraq (5.8%, n = 21), and Saudi Arabia (4.7%, n = 17) (see Table 5.11). Regarding the most commented-on news topics, the results indicate that Egypt again came first with 27.5%, followed by Syria (6.7%), Iraq (2.4%), and Saudi Arabia (2.1%) (see Table 5.12). As for the differences between liking and commenting on news, the Spearman correlation coefficient test of the rankings (R 0.601, P = 0.039) showed no significant differences between the two online activities. The results also show that online audiences were mostly interested in news on Arab countries; no Western or other non-Arab countries show up in the top countries list. According to two previous studies on social media news, Arabic-language news organizations make ample references to Western countries as part of their core media coverage (Al-Rawi 2016a,b), yet Arab online audiences seem to prefer consuming news that is more related to their own local, national, or regional surroundings. This finding should be interesting for news organizations, which seem to follow certain news-making rules in determining

Table 5.11 References to specific countries in local order, politics, and sports in most liked news topics.

Country	Frequency	Percentage
Egypt	194	54.3%
Syria	74	20.7%
Iraq	21	5.8%
Saudi Arabia	17	4.7%
Lebanon	12	3.3%
Libya	7	1.9%
Yemen	7	1.9%
Tunisia	7	1.9%
Palestine	7	1.9%
Morocco	5	1.4%
UAE	4	1.1%
Jordan	1	—
Algeria	1	—
Total	357	

Spearman correlation coefficient for the ranking test between commenting and liking news is R 0.601, Significance (2-tailed) P = 0.039 (Correlation is significant at the 0.05 level [2-tailed]).

Table 5.12   References to specific countries in local order, politics, and sports in most commented-on news topics.

Country	Frequency	Percentage
Egypt	275	27.5%
Syria	67	6.7%
Iraq	24	2.4%
Saudi Arabia	21	2.1%
Algeria	9	0.9%
Libya	7	0.7%
Yemen	5	0.5%
Morocco	5	0.5%
UAE	4	0.4%
Tunisia	3	0.3%
Palestine	3	0.3%
Lebanon	2	0.2%
Total	425	

Spearman correlation coefficient for the ranking test between commenting and liking news is R 0.601, Significance (2-tailed) P = 0.039 (Correlation is significant at the 0.05 level [2-tailed]).

what is worthy of being reported, while online audiences have their own criteria in determining what is worthy of being read and shared with others.

As for Egypt's first-place ranking in news topics, this is unexpected since the current conflicts in Syria and Iraq are obviously more newsworthy topics due to the high number of people being killed there. The demographics of the online audience are relevant in explaining this. Facebook data provided by Socialbakers (www.socialbakers.com) on the top 10 users by country for the news organizations investigated in this chapter reveal that Egypt comes first with over 11.2 million users for all 10 Facebook pages, followed by Iraq (5.3 million), Morocco (over 3 million), and Syria (2.8 million) (see Table 5.13). These figures clearly explain why Egypt scores first as the country most mentioned in local order, politics, and sports news topics.

In summary, the findings indicate that social media audiences mostly prefer to read stories about local order, internal politics, human interest, international politics, and odd and/or funny subjects. The findings of other studies conducted on news organizations' news selection practices show that these same topics score high. The results of this chapter indicate that there is a genuine interest in local order and politics, which partly explains the kind of civic and political engagement users have. Meanwhile, social media audiences mostly prefer to comment on stories

Table 5.13 Total number of Facebook users by country for the 10 news organizations.

Rank	Country	Users	Rank	Country	Users
1	Egypt	11 206 127	6	Libya	2 555 362
2	Iraq	5 362 604	7	Tunisia	2 282 594
3	Morocco	3 072 001	8	Algeria	2 186 975
4	Syria	2 810 879	9	Jordan	1 854 127
5	Saudi Arabia	2 637 699	10	Yemen	1 101 372

about local politics, local order, regional politics, human interest, odd and/or funny, and international politics subjects. The two statistical tests conducted show no significance differences between liking and commenting on Facebook news. Further, the results indicate that the most referenced countries, in terms of likes and comments on news stories about local order, politics, and sports, are Egypt, Syria, and Iraq. This, we can conclude, is mainly due to the large number of Egyptian Facebook users who follow news from these pages. News organizations find SNS outlets to be extremely useful because they can help them understand their audiences and target them with advertising. This research confirms the view that there are differences between what news organizations focus on in their news coverage and production and what their audiences actually want from their news stories.

This chapter has limitations, in particular given the importance of studying the demographics of social media use by conducting ethnographic research on Twitter, YouTube, and Facebook news users. Future research could focus on other social media platforms, like Instagram and Reddit, that are used by news organizations to disseminate news. Other important features that have not been included in this chapter include the timeliness or recency of news stories, the relevance of viral content to certain audiences, and the esthetic quality of news, including the quality of writing or of video and audio editing. Other research areas to explore further in relation to viral news include the length and depth of news stories, and whether images and illustrations accompany viral textual news. In addition, future studies should investigate international differences among speakers of other languages and their online news consumption habits when it comes to popular and viral content.

References

Agarwal, A., Xie, B., Vovsha, I., Rambow, O., and Passonneau, R. (2011). Sentiment analysis of Twitter data. In: *Proceedings of the Workshop on Languages in Social Media*. Association for Computational Linguistics, pp 30–38.

Al-Rawi, A. (2016a). News values on social media: news organizations' Facebook use. *Journalism* 18 (7): 871–889.

Al-Rawi, A. (2016b). News organizations 2.0: a comparative study of Twitter news. *Journalism Practice* 11 (6): 705–720.

André, P., Bernstein, M., and Luther, K. (2012). Who gives a tweet? Evaluating microblog content value. In: *Proceedings of the ACM 2012 Conference on Computer Supported Cooperative Work*. ACM.

Atwater, T. (1984). Product differentiation in local TV news. *Journalism Quarterly* 61 (4): 757–762.

Bakshy, E., Hofman, J., Mason, W., and Watts, D. (2011). Everyone's an influencer: quantifying influence on Twitter. In: *Proceedings of the Fourth ACM International Conference on Web Search and Data Mining*. ACM, pp. 65–74.

Berger, J. (2011). Arousal increases social transmission of information. *Psychological Science* 22 (7): 891–893.

Berger, J. (2013). *Contagious: Why Things Catch On*. New York: Simon & Schuster.

Berger, J. and Milkman, K.L. (2012). What makes online content viral? *Journal of Marketing Research* 49 (2): 192–205.

Bobkowski, P. (2015). Sharing the news: effects of informational utility and opinion leadership on online news sharing. *Journalism & Mass Communication Quarterly* 92 (2): 320–345.

Boczkowski, P. and Mitchelstein, E. (2010). Is there a gap between the news choices of journalists and consumers? A relational and dynamic approach. *International Journal of Press/Politics* 15 (4): 420–440.

Boczkowski, P. and Mitchelstein, E. (2013). *The News Gap: When the Information Preferences of the Media and the Public Diverge*. Cambridge, MA: MIT Press.

Boczkowski, P., Mitchelstein, E., and Walter, M. (2011). Convergence across divergence: understanding the gap in the online news choices of journalists and consumers in Western Europe and Latin America. *Communication Research* 38 (3): 376–396.

Boczkowski, P., Mitchelstein, E., and Walter, M. (2012). When burglar alarms sound, do monitorial citizens pay attention to them? The online news choices of journalists and consumers during and after the 2008 US election cycle. *Political Communication* 29 (4): 347–366.

Bright, J. and Nicholls, T. (2014). The life and death of political news: measuring the impact of the audience agenda using online data. *Social Science Computer Review* 32 (2): 170–181.

Brighton, P. and Foy, D. (2007). *News Values*. Thousand Oaks, CA: Sage.

Bucy, E. (2003). Emotion, presidential communication, and traumatic news: processing the World Trade Center attacks. *Harvard International Journal of Press/Politics* 8 (4): 76–96.

Cha, M., Haddadi, H., Benevenuto, F., and Gummadi, K. (2010). Measuring user influence in Twitter: the million follower fallacy. In: *AAAI Conference on Weblogs and Social Media*, p. 14.

Cohen, E. (2014). What makes good games go viral? The role of technology use, efficacy, emotion and enjoyment in players' decision to share a prosocial digital game. *Computers in Human Behavior* 33: 321–329.

Cohen, A., Bantz, C., and Adoni, H. (1990). *Social Conflict and Television News.* Thousand Oaks, CA: Sage.

Dobele, A., Lindgreen, A., Beverland, M. et al. (2007). Why pass on viral messages? Because they connect emotionally. *Business Horizons* 50 (4): 291–304.

Galtung, J. and Ruge, M.H. (1965). The structure of foreign news: the presentation of the Congo, Cuba and Cyprus crises in four Norwegian newspapers. *Journal of Peace Research* 2 (1): 64–90.

Golan, G.J. and Zaidner, L. (2008). Creative strategies in viral advertising: an application of Taylor's six-segment message strategy wheel. *Journal of Computer-Mediated Communication* 13 (4): 959–972.

Greenburg, Z. (2017). How 'Despacito' became the most popular YouTube video of all time. *Forbes*. Available from: https://www.forbes.com/sites/zackomalleygreenburg/2017/08/07/how-despacito-became-the-most-popular-youtube-video-of-all-time/#71eb24657185 (accessed November 28, 2019).

Guadagno, R.E., Rempala, D.M., Murphy, S., and Okdie, B.M. (2013). What makes a video go viral? An analysis of emotional contagion and Internet memes. *Computers in Human Behavior* 29 (6): 2312–2319.

Harcup, T. and O'Neill, D. (2001). What is news? Galtung and Ruge revisited. *Journalism Studies* 2 (2): 261–280.

Harcup, T. and O'Neill, D. (2016). What is news? News values revisited (again). *Journalism Studies* 18 (12): 1470–1488.

Hermida, A. (2014). *Tell Everyone: Why We Share and Why It Matters.* Toronto, ON: Doubleday.

Jenkins, H., Ford, S., and Green, J. (2013). *Spreadable Media: Creating Value and Meaning in a Networked Culture.* New York: NYU Press.

Kalsnes, B. and Larsson, A.O. (2017). Understanding news sharing across social media: detailing distribution on Facebook and Twitter. *Journalism Studies* 19 (11): 1669–1688.

Kaufman, L. (2014). Known as "Alex From Target," teenage clerk rises to star on Twitter and talk shows. *New York Times*. Available from: http://nyti.ms/1AlZalP (accessed November 28, 2019).

Khan, F. and Vong, S. (2014). Virality over YouTube: an empirical analysis. *Internet Research* 24 (5): 629–647.

Kirby, J. (2006). Viral marketing. In: *Connected Marketing: The Viral, Buzz and Word of Mouth Revolution* (eds. J. Kirby and P. Marsden), 87–106. Burlington, MA: Butterworth-Heinemann.

Knobloch, S., Patzig, G., Mende, A.M., and Hastall, M. (2004). Affective news: effects of discourse structure in narratives on suspense, curiosity, and enjoyment while reading news and novels. *Communication Research* 31 (3): 259–287.

Landis, R. and Koch, G. (1977). The measurement of observer agreement for categorical data. *Biometrics* 33 (1): 159–174.

Larsson, A. (2016). "I shared the news today, oh boy": news provision and interaction on Facebook. *Journalism Studies* 19 (1): 43–61.

Luckerson, V. (2016). These are the 10 most popular tweets of all time. *Time*. Available from: http://time.com/4263227/most-popular-tweets (accessed November 28, 2019).

Mills, A. (2012). Virality in social media: the SPIN framework. *Journal of Public Affairs* 12 (2): 162–169.

Naaman, M., Becker, H., and Gravano, L. (2011). Hip and trendy: characterizing emerging trends on Twitter. *Journal of the Association for Information Science and Technology* 62 (5): 902–918.

Nahon, K. and Hemsley, J. (2013). *Going Viral*. Oxford: Polity.

Nelson-Field, K., Riebe, E., and Newstead, K. (2013). The emotions that drive viral video. *Australasian Marketing Journal (AMJ)* 21 (4): 205–211.

Perloff, R. (1989). Ego-involvement and the third person effect of televised news coverage. *Communication Research* 16 (2): 236–262.

Perrin, A. (2015). Social media usage: 2005–2015. Pew Research Center. Available from: http://www.pewinternet.org/2015/10/08/social-networking-usage-2005-2015 (accessed November 28, 2019).

Perse, E. (1990). Involvement with local television news cognitive and emotional dimensions. *Human Communication Research* 16 (4): 556–581.

Phelps, J., Lewis, R., Mobilio, L. et al. (2004). Viral marketing or electronic word-of-mouth advertising: examining consumer responses and motivations to pass along email. *Journal of Advertising Research* 44 (4): 333–348.

Porter, L. and Golan, G. (2006). From subservient chickens to brawny men: a comparison of viral advertising to television advertising. *Journal of Interactive Advertising* 6 (2): 30–38.

Riffe, D., Ellis, B., Rogers, M.K. et al. (1986). Gatekeeping and the network news mix. *Journalism & Mass Communication Quarterly* 63 (2): 315–321.

Rudat, A. and Buder, J. (2015). Making retweeting social: the influence of content and context information on sharing news in Twitter. *Computers in Human Behavior* 46: 75–84.

Shoemaker, P. and Cohen, A. (2012). *News Around the World: Content, Practitioners, and the Public*. London: Routledge.

Smith, A. (2014). What people like and dislike about Facebook. Pew Research Center. Available from: https://www.pewresearch.org/fact-tank/2014/02/03/what-people-like-dislike-about-facebook/ (accessed November 28, 2019).

Southgate, D., Westoby, N., and Page, G. (2010). Creative determinants of viral video viewing. *International Journal of Advertising* 29 (3): 349–368.

Tam, D. (2012). Facebook processes more than 500 TB of data daily. CNET. Available from: http://www.cnet.com/news/facebook-processes-more-than-500-tb-of-data-daily (accessed November 28, 2019).

Tewksbury, D. (2003). What do Americans really want to know? Tracking the behavior of news readers on the Internet. *Journal of Communication* 53 (4): 694–710.

Wilkinson, D. and Thelwall, M. (2012). Trending Twitter topics in English: an international comparison. *Journal of the American Society for Information Science and Technology* 63 (8): 1631–1646.

Part III

Producers

6

Celebrity Journalists 2.0 and Branding

Introduction

This chapter investigates the social media posts of eight well-known Arab journalists who draw significant audience attention on Twitter and Facebook. It introduces the concept of celebrity journalists 2.0 and examines audiences' top engagement with journalists, which remains under-researched despite its importance to contemporary and future investigation. According to Lasorsa et al., little "is known about whether and to what extent" social media is used for "public discourse (i.e., tweeting news and information about current events) and interactions with the public" (2012, p. 2). A number of research studies have empirically examined online audiences' responses toward journalists' social media posts by specifically investigating what drives audience attention. Many empirical studies have content analyzed journalists' social media outlets by looking at specific samples (Nuernbergk 2016).

The journalists and media figures investigated in this chapter have been chosen for their high number of followers, exceeding 17 million users on Twitter and 29 million on Facebook between them. Only a few empirical studies have examined the use of social media by journalists in the Arab world (e.g., Mansour 2018). Most other studies on journalists' social media use have focused on Twitter or relied on ethnographic research (Gulyas 2013; Sacco and Bossio 2015; Saldaña et al. 2016; Weaver and Willnat 2016), investigating either their news sources (Hladík and Štětka 2015) or guidelines regarding social media use (Opgenhaffen and Scheerlinck 2014; Sacco and Bossio 2016). Most have focused on journalists from Western countries (Djerf-Pierre et al. 2016; Nuernbergk 2016; Olausson 2016), leaving those from other regions severely under-researched.

———

This chapter is first published as follows: Al-Rawi, A. (2020). Social media & celebrity journalists' audience outreach in the MENA region. *African Journalism Studies*. 1–30. DOI: 10.1080/23743670.2020.1754266.

Celebrity Journalists

The majority of news organizations have found that using social networking sites (SNS) in disseminating news and reaching out to different audiences is indispensable in today's news market (Beckett 2011; Knight and Cook 2013). This commitment to using new technologies has required investments of time, effort, and money to harness the power of SNS in order to better disseminate news, self-promote, advertise, and engage with audiences in what is known as news 2.0. Among the other benefits of these new technologies, news organizations often use SNS to encourage audiences to personalize the news experience by communicating directly with journalists online (Pew Research Center 2011, p. 28). Journalists' use of social media thus now plays an integral role in the news production process (Wilson 2008), further connecting audiences to news organizations, incorporating audience feedback, and providing access to new information: what is known as "networked journalism" (Beckett and Mansell 2008; Knight 2012; Van der Haak et al. 2012; Jordaan 2013). Lawrence et al. believe journalists act as gatekeepers because people follow them on social media; journalists are "curators or guides in the sea of digital information" (2014, p. 922).

In this sense, social media functions as a virtual bridge that connects audiences with their favorite journalists and news organizations. Journalists 2.0 are the new reality of making and sharing the news. Phillips (2012, p. 676) suggests that journalists' SNS use can increase audience reach and enhance the popularity of news organizations, while Holton and Molyneux (2015, pp. 4–5) look at how journalists use social media to brand themselves and their news organizations. According to survey data collected from the United Kingdom, United States, Italy, and Australia, journalists and news organizations are very popular on social media, with about 32% of people surveyed stating they follow them (Newman et al. 2015, p. 82). On Twitter, this means clicking "follow" on the journalist or news organization's account, while on Facebook it means liking or following a page. Weeks and Holbert (2013, p. 227) state that connecting with a journalist's social media account in this way indicates more active engagement with news.

Social media, however, is not without peril for the people who report the news. A number of journalists have been penalized, or even lost their jobs, for tweeting something controversial, as in the case of CNN's Octavia Nasr (Walker 2010). Some journalists, furthermore, find it difficult to share the kinds of personal views are opinions that are expected on social media. Rogstad observes that unlike political commentators, "very few [political] reporters are comfortable sharing political opinions or blurring the boundaries between the personal and the professional" (2014, p. 688). In this regard, Holton and Molyneux (2015, p. 14) refer to the challenges journalists face on social media and the paradox of using social media, stressing the need for journalists to set a balance between disclosing personal information and reporting news.

Famous journalists usually attract audiences, since many people prefer to have a "personal" connection with news; they are more likely to pay attention if it comes from someone they like or who is a well-known "media personality" (Nordlund 1978; Grant et al. 1991). A great number of studies have been done on what is known as "personality journalism" or "celebrity journalism" (Forde 2001; Day 2004; Petersen 2011; Conboy 2014), highlighting the impact of media personalities in drawing an audience's attention. The phenomenon is similar to fandom. More than ever, in this age of social media, popular journalists and media figures hold an influence over their followers and audiences. This relatively new phenomenon can be called celebrity journalism 2.0. The two-step flow theory of communication pioneered by Katz and Lazarsfeld (1955), though somewhat outdated, seems relevant here. The theory focuses on how ideas flow from traditional media like radio, TV, and print outlets to policy makers and opinion leaders, who in turn influence the public (Katz 1957, p. 61). In the age of social media, some studies have asserted that this theory is still valid in the sense that opinion leaders can generate interest and communication flows among ordinary people (Hilbert et al. 2016). Choi (2015), for example, relies on Katz and Lazarsfeld's theory to explain how opinion makers in South Korea are more effective and influential than online content creators. Southgate et al. (2010) find that celebrity status or offline fame plays a crucial role in making content such as YouTube videos viral. Several other studies confirm that celebrities have a clear impact on making some online media content popular (Wu and Wang 2011; Nahon and Hemsley 2013, p. 78; Feroz Khan and Vong 2014). When journalists and media figures are famous offline, their influence on their followers is more likely to increase.

Journalists and Social Media Use

As indicated, the majority of journalists use social media in their daily work because it has become indispensable. Weaver and Willnat (2016, p. 1) find that many journalists regard social media as having a positive impact on their profession, especially in terms of news gathering, identifying suitable stories, and staying in touch with audiences. In a study of Dutch journalists, 78% of those interviewed said they use SNS every day and 56% said they could not perform their job well without it. Among journalists, Twitter is the most popular SNS (90%), followed by Facebook (81%) and LinkedIn (64%), which is used mostly for business (ING 2015). In Ireland, about 99% of journalists use social media (especially Twitter) for work (Heravi 2015). Through conducting interviews with various Australian journalists, Bossio and Sacco (2016) identified three types of SNS user. The first uses social media for purely professional purposes by creating public accounts, but also has a separate personal account. The second only has a professional account, while the third merges his or her professional and personal accounts together. Hanusch and Bruns (2016) looked at the Twitter profiles and accounts of 4189 Australian journalists to investigate their strategies of self-presentation and branding. The results indicate that journalists mostly identify through professional characteristics, though a large number mix in personal information. The study found that about one-third of them include a disclaimer that their opinions are their own and do not represent their news organization. In another study of journalists' use of social media in Finland, Germany, Sweden, and the United Kingdom, Gulyas (2013) emphasizes that journalists exhibit varied uses of social media, suggesting there is a kind of fragmentation similar to that found in online audiences. In a study of sports journalism, Reed (2011) found that 46% of the journalists used Facebook for professional use, while 80% used Twitter professionally. Different social media platforms are used for different purposes, and it is clear many journalists prefer Twitter for professional work, whereas Facebook tends to be more connected to conducting general research or exclusively devoted to family, friends, and other personal networks (Santana and Hopp 2016).

Further, Cozma and Chen (2013) identified a few SNS functions by studying Twitter use by foreign correspondents working at major US networks and print publications. They found that journalists mainly use Twitter to "break news, promote their work and their news organization, and communicate with their audiences" (Cozma and Chen 2013). Though no gender differences were noted, the authors observed a few differences between broadcast and print journalists, as the former tended to break news while the latter preferred to share their views, as well as links from other news outlets. Hedman and Djerf-Pierre (2013) conducted a survey of Swedish journalists in 2011/2012 and categorized their different motivations for using social media. They identified 14 different functions, the most important of which was following ongoing discussions, followed by finding ideas or angles for stories, using social media for research, and trend spotting. Finally, Brems et al. (2016, p. 1) interviewed Dutch and Flemish journalists in order to better understand personal branding on Twitter. They concluded that creating a personal brand on social media gives journalists many benefits and amplifies their role as a source of news and opinions. The results show that journalists "struggle with being factual or opinionated, being personal or professional, how to balance broadcasting their message with engagement and how to promote themselves strategically" (Brems et al. 2016). Some of the journalists examined, it is worth nothing, had Twitter accounts but no Facebook pages or vice versa. This could be due to the time demands of using multiple social media outlets.

There are some recent empirical studies that have examined journalists' social media posts, albeit exclusively focused on Twitter. For example, Mourão (2015) content analyzed 5700 tweets by 430 US political journalists during the 2012 general election debates, finding that about one-fifth used humor on Twitter and that many provided opinions on the news. Nuernbergk (2016) conducted a content analysis of 2210 tweets posted by German political journalists during one week in March 2014. The study revealed that journalists mostly interacted with other journalists, with audiences given little room to become active participants in the process of making the news. Hedman (2016) conducted a content analysis of 1500 tweets posted by Swedish journalists during one week in Spring 2014, categorizing tweets into three main types: disclosure transparency, which is related to work and how news is created; participatory transparency, which involves explicit references to the audience, encouraging it to get involved in the news-making process; and personal transparency, which is focused on disclosing personal information such as family news. The results showed that 24% of journalists' tweets were transparent in relation to the way news is produced, though there was a distinct lack of personal information or personal transparency. Swedish journalists, it seems, are reticent about allowing audiences to interact with them or to be involved in the news-making process.

In addition, Lasorsa et al. (2012) content analyzed over 22 000 tweets and categorized the posts into seven types: major opining, minor opining, retweeting, job talking, discussing, personalizing, and linking (for transparency and credibility). They found three main categories: conveying information, seeking information, and expressing opinion. The study revealed that journalists' tweets mostly express minor opinions, followed by major ones; the third largest category was retweeting. Finally, Lee et al. (2015) studied Korean journalists' tweets and found that 62% were focused on public affairs and 56% involved engagement with the audience. The authors also found some partisan differences among journalists: those working for liberal media outlets were more likely to interact with their audience and talk about public affairs (Lee et al. 2015, p. 15).

This chapter examines eight celebrity journalists from the Arab world, looking at their top tweets and Facebook posts. The journalists have been selected based on number of social media followers and social media page rankings, as identified by Socialbakers (www.socialbakers.com). One limitation of SocialBakers is that many journalists' Facebook and Twitter pages are not categorized as belonging to "media personalities" or "broadcast stars." Therefore, a general search on Google was conducted to find more top journalists on social media from different locations in the Arab world. Certain celebrity journalists, such as Amr Khaled, who has a whopping 21.6 million Facebook followers, were excluded because in addition to practicing journalism they are also preachers, politicians, or artists.

The celebrity journalists selected for this study include: Faisal Al Qassem from Al Jazeera Arabic (Syrian, 3.46 million Twitter followers), well known for his show, *The Opposite Direction*; Khadija Ben Guena, the Al Jazeera Arabic anchorwoman (Algerian, 8.04 million Facebook followers); Turki Al Dakhil, general manager of the Saudi-owned Al Arabiya network (Saudi, 3.34 million Twitter followers); the satirist Bassem Youssef, known for his TV show, *Al-Barnameg* (Egyptian, 7.41 Twitter followers); Yosri Fouda, the editor and presenter of *The Last Word* on ONTV (Egyptian, 2.84 million Twitter followers); Ahmad Al-Shugairi, host of *Khawatter* on MBC (Saudi, 13.83 million followers); Mohammed Al Wakeel, a radio and TV presenter (Jordanian, 6.56 million Facebook followers); and Nasser Al Laham, the editor-in-chief of the Maan news agency (Palestinian, 1.22 million Facebook followers). In total, these eight media figures have about 47 million followers on social media (see Tables 6.1 and 6.2).

Data retrieved from social media outlets can be useful in understanding the nature of news coverage, as well as audiences' reactions toward news. It is not clear why particular Arab journalists have great popularity on social media, but cultural values certainly play a role (Amin 2002). Mellor argues that authority figures like leaders and "those in the public eye" (2005, p. 91) receive far more public attention, and some journalists certainly fall into this category.

This study analyzed the top 100 tweets and Facebook posts for each celebrity journalist, for a total of 800 social media posts. Previous studies analyzing large datasets extracted from social media followed a similar procedure by choosing the top posts (Naaman et al. 2011; Wilkinson and Thelwall 2012) because there is so much noise on SNS. These top posts were measured based on the intensity of the online audience's engagement in terms of the top 100 most replied-to tweets and most commented-on Facebook posts. Retweeting or liking social media posts is less laborious and time consuming than replying to and commenting on the same posts; hence, the decision was made to choose the second type of online activity because it signifies more engagement. It is important to note here that data extracted from Twitter has been used in other relevant studies. For example, Chorley and Mottershead (2016) used 11 million tweets to examine who spread information about news and the nature of interaction. They found that news organizations as well as journalists and their audiences are active on Twitter, allowing researchers "to build a rich picture of interaction around news media" (Chorley and Mottershead 2016, p. 1).

For this selected sample, tweets were collected via Crimson Hexagon. Tweets dating between December 19, 2013 and March 17, 2015 were extracted from four accounts. In total, over 15 700 posted tweets were extracted, constituting an average of 11.5% of the total posted tweets from the time the four Twitter accounts were created until June 18, 2016. The collected tweets received over 1.2 million retweets and 400 000 replies, with Bassem Youssef receiving 69 699 replies for his 100 top tweets, Faisal Al Qassem 23 442, Turki Al Dakhil 18 619, and Yosri Fouda 2756. As for Facebook posts, NVivo's webometric tool N-Capture was used to extract data from four pages on April 28, 2015. In total, 2466 posts generated 13 892 149 likes and 852 802 comments between them. Al Shugairi comes out on top, receiving 224 951 comments for his top 100 Facebook posts, followed by Al Wakeel at 157 303, Ben Guena at 156 200, and Al Laham at 32 831.

Table 6.1 Statistics on the journalists' Twitter accounts.

Name[a]	Date of joining Twitter[a]	Total no. of tweets (thousands)[a]	Extracted tweets[b]	Retweets[b]	Replies[b]	Followers (millions)[b]	Hyperlink[b]
Yosri Fouda	Sep. 2010	3.1	318 (10%)	8060	4393	2.84	twitter.com/YosriFouda
Turki Al Dakhil	Jun. 2009	23.2	2874 (12.3%)	141061	48339	3.34	twitter.com/turkialdakhil
Faisal Al Qassem	Dec. 2009	68.2	11936 (17.5%)	897745	263209	3.46	twitter.com/kasimf
Bassem Youssef	Mar. 2011	9.7	611 (6.2%)	230906	96191	7.41	twitter.com/DrBassemYoussef
Total	—	104.2	15739	1277772	412132	17.05	—

[a] Figures collected on June 18, 2016.
[b] Data collected for the period between December 19, 2013 and March 17, 2015.

Table 6.2 Statistics on the journalists' Facebook pages.

Name[a]	Date of joining Facebook[a]	Total posts[a]	Dates of posting[b]	Likes[b]	Comments[b]	Followers (millions)[b]	Hyperlink[b]
Khadija Ben Guena	Mar. 2011	581	Feb. 12, 2015– Apr. 27, 2015	2 843 793	245 524	8.04	www.facebook.com/BenguenaKhadija
Ahmad Al-Shugairi	—	239	Jul. 10, 2013– Apr. 28, 2015	273 757	289 262	13.83	www.facebook.com/AhmadAlShugairi
Mohammed Al Wakeel	Jun. 2011	1346	Apr. 12, 2015– Apr. 25, 2015	9 477 316	274 049	6.56	www.facebook.com/ MohammadAlwakeelshow
Nasser Al Laham	—	300	Feb. 20, 2015– Apr. 26, 2015	1 297 283	43 967	1.22	www.facebook.com/Nasser.Allaham
Total	—	2466	—	13 892 149	852 802	29.65	—

[a] Figures collected on June 18, 2016.
[b] Data collected April 28, 2015.

In terms of the classification of social media posts, the decision was made to rely on previous relevant studies. In this regard, Brems et al. (2016) classified the tweeting behavior of journalists into 14 categories, covering the kinds of posted tweets, their functions, and types of interaction. The authors found that sharing news came first, followed by providing opinion, and then by arguing or debating. Tweets were categorized as follows: sharing news; live reporting; self-promotion; promoting other individual journalists; opinion, critique, and interpretation; arguing and debating; requesting non-journalistic input; requesting journalistic input; giving advice or helping someone; acknowledgment; sharing personal information; correcting an error; reflecting on journalism practice; and other. Further, Lawrence et al. (2014) studied Twitter use by political reporters and commentators during the 2012 US Republican and Democratic conventions. They classified tweets into nine types and found that expressing opinions came first, followed by discussing job talk (which revolves around personal experiences at the workplace), policy, and candidates' characteristics. Tweets were classified as follows: opinion; job talk; policy; candidate characteristics; voter strategy; horse race; information-seeking; fact-checking; and personal. Finally, Cozma and Chen (2013) categorized broadcast and print correspondents' tweets into nine types: discuss current events where stationed; discuss current events elsewhere; break news; share opinion; make random observations; post personal information; promote own media outlet; promote other media outlets; and ask questions. For the purpose of this study, the classification of the journalists' social media posts is mostly borrowed with a few minor modifications from Brems et al.'s (2016) study because it is the most relevant to this research and most exhaustive in its classification. Just one category has been added: the use of humor, which is often referenced in other studies on journalists' social media use (Molyneux 2015; Mourão et al. 2015). Two coders examined over 10% (n = 90) of the selected sample, and the agreement was acceptable using Cohen's kappa (Landis and Koch 1977).

As indicated, this chapter attempts to understand the nature of celebrity journalists' popular posts and branding on Twitter and Facebook. We found that self-promoting comes first at 26.6% (n = 247), followed by sharing news (26.5%, n = 246), providing opinion, critique, and interpretation (20.7%, n = 193), giving advice, helping others (7%, n = 65), requesting non-journalistic input (3.9%, n = 37), and humor (3.6%, n = 34). On the other hand, the lowest degree of engagement on the two platforms is as follows: correcting an error (n = 4), acknowledging an issue (n = 4), requesting journalistic input (n = 5), reflecting on journalism practice (n = 5), promoting other individual journalists (n = 11), arguing, debating with others (n = 13), breaking news or live reporting (n = 14), and sharing personal information (n = 18).

In relation to Twitter, we find that self-promotion is at the top, making up 36.4% of the top tweets, with Fouda using it the most (n = 85), followed by Al Dakhil (n = 50), Youssef (n = 40), and Al Qassem (n = 6) (see Table 6.3). This self-promotion includes providing information on the time a TV show will air and providing a hyperlink where readers can view details of the journalist's work. It seems that audiences want these media figures to highlight their activities in order that they can discuss and provide personal opinions on them. As in the case of Dutch and Flemish journalists (Brems et al. 2016), Arab journalists are interested in self-promotion and audiences seem to be most actively engaged with such posts.

The second highest category on Twitter is providing opinion, critique, and interpretation, which constitutes 25.6% of the top tweets, with Al Dakhil coming first (n = 46), followed by Al Qassem (n = 38), Youssef (n = 25), and Fouda (n = 19). It is important to note here that these media figures, with the exception of Al Qassem, are very much confined to providing opinions on issues related to their respective countries. Al Qassem is the only one who really tries to expand his

Table 6.3   Categories of journalists' posts on Twitter.

Category	Yosri Fouda	Turki Al Dakhil	Faisal Al Qassem	Bassem Youssef	Total
Opinion, critique, interpretation	19	46	38	25	128 (25.6%)
Sharing news	9	22	25	1	57 (11.4%)
Break news or live reporting	0	1	2	0	3 (0.3%)
Self-promotion	86	50	6	40	182 (36.4%)
Promoting other individual journalists	2	2	1	1	6 (0.6%)
Arguing, debating with others	0	0	4	1	5 (0.5%)
Request for non-journalistic input	0	2	22	3	27 (5.4%)
Request for journalistic input	0	0	5	0	5 (0.5%)
Giving advice, helping someone	4	22	0	5	31 (6.2%)
Acknowledgement	0	0	0	3	3 (0.3%)
Share personal information	2	8	1	5	16 (3.2%)
Correcting an error	0	0	0	4	4 (0.4%)
Reflecting on journalism practice	0	0	0	3	3 (0.3%)
Humor	0	1	10	16	27 (5.4%)
Other	1	0	0	1	2 (0.2%)

arguments internationally, though the Syrian conflict is most emphasized due to his national attachment and interest. He also articulates a clear condemnation of the Islamic State of Iraq and the Levant (ISIS) and its ideology; for example, the following tweet got 236 replies: "When you see what the enemies of civilization did to Mosul's Museum, you thank God that many Arab treasures and archeological artifacts are stored in Western museums and away from the hands of savages." As for Al Dakhil, he also repeatedly provides his judgment of ISIS. In some instances, he tries to broaden his topics, including a tweet describing how to reasonably react to the publication of the Muhammed cartoons by *Charlie Hebdo* magazine, which received 1135 replies from his followers.

The third highest category is related to sharing news, which makes up 11.4% of the top tweets. In this regard, Al Qassem comes first (n = 25), followed by Al Dakhil (n = 22), and Fouda (n = 9); Youssef showed no interest in this kind of tweet. However, there is a clear bias, or one-sided way of sharing news, according to the journalist's political or ideological background. For example, Al Qassem's anti-Assad stance is very clear in the kind of news he shares, often focusing on the atrocities committed by Assad's government against Syrians. In this regard, celebrity journalists are, in fact, gatekeepers, because they filter news and present certain perspectives for their audience (Lawrence et al. 2014).

Other top tweets that received audience attention include giving advice, helping someone, which constitutes 6.2% of the tweets. Al Dakhil comes first on this metric (n = 22), with many pieces of advice on how to stop radicalization and how to avoid wasting water, all directed to his Saudi audience. Indeed, one recurrent theme is that many journalists consistently attack ISIS: an indication that they feel they have a responsibility to inform and possibly educate their audiences. For example, Al Dakhil frequently tweets about articles he publishes in his column "The Heart's Ink," published in the Saudi newspaper *Okaz*, many of which focus on the danger of ISIS and how to counter it (e.g., Al Dakhil 2014). He also often uses the Arabic hashtag (#nototerrorism #notoradicalism), urging extremists to abandon their ideology; one such tweet got 95 replies. This is reminiscent of the social responsibility concept of the press that is known among some Arab journalists (Amin 2002, pp. 127–128) and within some parts of the Arab media system (Rugh 2004, p. 24). In the examples given mentioned here, many of the journalists seem to function as reformers, because of their self-perceived role in enlightening citizens.

Requesting non-journalistic input makes up 5.4% of tweets, with Al Qassem coming first here (n = 22). Al Qassem actively engages his social media audience with questions in order to solicit their feedback, which can help him get more ideas for his *Opposite Direction* show, centered on debates. In some instances, he even tries to expose and discredit ISIS sympathizers in this manner. For example, the following tweet received 197 replies: "A question to the heads' choppers: Do you think that by acting in this way you will build civilized societies that people fought for or will you make those people regret revolting against their dictators?"

Humor, finally, is most used by Youssef (n = 16), especially in relation to his satirical attacks against Egyptian politicians and his opponents. For instance, the following tweet got 2481 replies: "The decision to revoke my citizenship, expel me from the country and at the same time prohibit me from travelling! Ok but how? Like what someone [sic] says: 'Please God, I neither want to win nor lose; let the ball remain offside.'" In another tweet that received 894 replies, he comments on the funny Arabic hashtag #Bassemforpresident, saying: "the hashtag has been trending worldwide in less than 15 minutes. I'll give a villa and yacht for each citizen:)." Al Qassem, meanwhile, often expresses a kind of dark humor in his political criticism.

As for Facebook, sharing news is the most popular practice in terms of attracting the online audience (44%). It is found most among Al Laham's posts (n = 75), followed by Ben Guena's (n = 65), Al Wakeel's (n = 45), and Al Shugairi's (n = 7) (see Table 6.4). It is important to note here that Al Laham and Al Wakeel are very confined in disseminating national and local news within their geographical locations, unlike Ben Guena and Al Qassem, who both tweet about regional news throughout the Arab world. Various Arab audiences seem to gather around these celebrity journalists, who in return respond to some of their information demands. Statistics from Crimson Hexagon with regard to Twitter and Socialbakers in relation to Facebook show the clustering of audiences based on their geographical locations (see Table 6.5).

Similar to Al Qassem on Twitter, there is clear gatekeeping activity with Al Laham and Ben Guena, who have strongly partisan views that they share with their social media audiences. For example, Ben Guena mostly shares news that praises Turkish President Erdogan, sides with Egypt's Muslim Brotherhood, and criticizes Egyptian President Sisi.

The second most popular activity on Facebook is self-promotion (15.1%), tied with providing opinions, critique, and interpretation (15.1%). When it comes to self-promotion, we find that Al Shugaili comes far ahead of the other celebrity journalists (n = 41), especially because he routinely announces the times his TV show is aired. With regard to the second providing opinions, critique, and interpretation, this relates to offering an explanation of events, and Al Shugaili again comes first (n = 23).

The fourth most popular activity on Facebook is providing advice or helping others. Once more, Al Shugaili comes ahead of the other journalists (n = 21), mostly due to his philanthropical work on social causes such as cross-cultural understanding and religious tolerance, which is the main focus of his TV show. For example, a message Al Shugairi posted about the need to donate money to help Syrian refugees from Saudi Arabia got 3762 comments. Al Shugairi is similar

Table 6.4 Categories of journalists' posts on Facebook.

Category	Al Shugaili	Al Laham	Ben Guena	Al Wakeel	Total
Opinion, critique, interpretation	23	15	13	14	65 (15.1%)
Sharing news	7	75	62	45	189 (44%)
Break news or live reporting	0	5	1	5	11 (2.5%)
Self-promotion	41	11	13	0	65 (15.1%)
Promoting other individual journalists	0	2	3	0	5 (1.1%)
Arguing, debating with others	3	0	2	3	8 (1.8%)
Request for non-journalistic input	4	0	5	1	10 (2.3%)
Request for journalistic input	0	0	0	0	0 (0%)
Giving advice, helping someone	21	0	2	11	34 (7.9%)
Acknowledgement	1	0	0	0	1 (0.2%)
Share personal information	1	0	1	0	2 (0.4%)
Correcting an error	0	0	0	0	0 (0%)
Reflecting on journalism practice	2	0	0	0	2 (0.4%)
Humor	0	1	3	3	7 (1.6%)
Other	8	0	2	20	30 (6.9%)

to Al Dakhil on Twitter. Both seem to act like activists who feel that they must influence their Arab audience in general, and their Saudi followers in particular. Arab journalists, similar to their Dutch and Flemish counterparts (Brems et al. 2016), appear to place major importance on their social role. This phenomenon, and its various contexts, can be difficult to explain or understand without interviewing journalists from these places.

In summary, audiences on Facebook mostly comment on posts that deal with sharing news, self-promotion, and providing advice. Interestingly, the results show that celebrity journalists' top posts do not include requests for journalistic input, with the except of Faisal Al Qassem, who frequently engages his online audience by asking them questions on journalism as well as politics. As noted

Table 6.5 Geographical locations of journalists' social media followers.

Ben Guena		Al Wakeel		Al Shugaili		Al Laham	
Country	FB local fans[a]	Country	FB local fans	Country	FB local fans	Country	FB local fans
Egypt	1 943 623 (24.1%)	Jordan	2 616 015 (39.8%)	Egypt	3 161 841 (22.8%)	Palestinian Territory	556 034 (45.5%)
Algeria	1 133 846 (14.1%)	Egypt	1 057 919 (16.1%)	Algeria	526 897 (11%)	Israel	218 744 (17.9%)
Morocco	596 061 (7.4%)	Iraq	367 606 (5.6%)	Jordan	1 219 314 (8.8%)	Egypt	103 292 (8.5%)
Jordan	483 955 (6.0%)	Algeria	297 105 (4.5%)	Morocco	1 141 047 (8.2%)	Jordan	67 581 (5.5%)
Saudi Arabia	465 676 (5.8%)	Morocco	290 403 (4.4%)	Iraq	1 052 290 (7.6%)	Algeria	36 237 (3.0%)

Faisal Al Qassem		Bassem Youssef		Turki Al Dakhil		Yosri Fouda	
Country	No. of Twitter posts[b]	Country	No. of Twitter posts	Country	No. of Twitter posts	Country	No. of Twitter posts
Saudi Arabia	312 599 (40.3%)	Egypt	188 057 (68.9%)	Saudi Arabia	51 100 (59.4%)	Egypt	11 610 (77.1%)
Turkey	100 830 (13%)	Saudi Arabia	16 843 (6.1%)	Turkey	6571 (7.6%)	Saudi Arabia	947 (6.2%)
Kuwait	38 806 (5%)	United States	16 278 (5.9%)	United Arab Emirates	5562 (6.4%)	United States	575 (3.8%)
Egypt	37 047 (4.7%)	United Arab Emirates	6353 (2.3%)	Kuwait	3491 (4%)	Turkey	271 (1.7%)
United States	32 298 (4.1%)	Turkey	5617 (2%)	United States	3286 (3.8%)	United Arab Emirates	227 (1.5%)

[a] Data provided by Socialbakers (www.socialbakers.com).
[b] Data collected for the period between December 19, 2013 and March 17, 2015.

earlier, this is due to his need to get new ideas for his TV show. Another interesting finding is the lack of interest in debating with the online audience or sharing personal information. Molyneux rightly claims that the goal behind posting personal information is "to build a personal brand and relationships with their audience" (2015, p. 1). However, the 800 social media posts contain only 18 references to personal information such as family photos or other details that could create some kind of rapport with online audiences.

Further, it is important to note the way some celebrity journalists manage their social media accounts, especially in relation to dealing with personal attacks, flaming, and trolls. It seems that many of these media figures, especially Al Qassem, directly inform their audiences about specific attacks they receive, which might be an indirect way of mobilizing followers. For instance, in a tweet that received 182 replies, Al Qassem mentions the name and refers to the Twitter handle of one female user, saying: "[this lady] demands killing Faisal Al Qassem as soon as possible least his likes multiply. Does Twitter allow such language?" Bassem Youssef also refers once to the Twitter handle of a user in order to remind him that his "mother is dead," implying that there is no need to curse her. The user's tweet received 753 replies from Youssef's followers. As for Ben Guena, she once posted, "I'm forced to block some users for uttering unethical and obscene comments that are not up to the standards of debate..." Her post received 3743 comments from her followers. The interesting aspect here is that some of these journalists try to protect themselves online by soliciting the assistance of their loyal followers in silencing or rebutting hostile voices. Previous studies on journalists' use of social media have not focused on this phenomenon, and it warrants further study.

In conclusion, this chapter focused on an important aspect of media practice that is popular today and is expected to remain important in the future. The research has examined the top social media posts of eight celebrity journalists in the Arab world and has showed a variety of responses by the online audience. Arab celebrity journalists are largely confined in their social media posts to their geographical locations, with the exceptions of Al Qassem and Ben Guena, the two Al Jazeera journalists, while gatekeeping is actively practiced in terms of the kinds of news shared and views disseminated. The findings show that audiences mostly engage with social media posts on self-promotion (26.6%), sharing news (26.5%), providing opinion (20.7%), giving advice (7%), requesting non-journalistic input (3.9%), and humor (3.6%) on both Twitter and Facebook. The selected journalists mostly refrain from asking their followers for feedback on journalism-related reporting, and some of them, especially Al Dakhil and Al Shugairi, seem to regard themselves as reformers whose role is to inform and correct social ills.

Most Arab celebrity journalists are preoccupied with self-promotion, since social media outlets seem to function as marketing platforms for them (Holton and Molyneux 2015). It is not clear, though, whether this kind of self-promotion is done to gain more credibility, attain popularity, maintain influence over followers, or all of the above. Certainly, social media complements traditional media outlets, in which these journalists do not have the same time or opportunities to promote their work; thus, the affordances of SNS have become instrumental to their profession and career, similar to the case of journalists from the Netherlands and elsewhere (Weaver and Willnat 2016). One must emphasize here that traditional media and social media outlets enjoy a kind of symbiotic co-existence, since celebrity journalists rely on both to exert their influence. Further, social media gives ample opportunities for sharing news as well as expressing personal opinions, which are the second and third most popular categories of posts identified in this chapter. In some cases, sharing news becomes a very important feature, as news is often personalized or elaborated upon by the journalists themselves, and many audience members rely on these journalists to elaborate on the different dimensions and nuances of certain recent events that are featured in the news. As for expressing personal opinions, this is not always possible in mainstream media (MSM), and it seems helpful in garnering a great deal of attention from audiences; this is especially true in the cases of Ben Guena and Al Qassem. Despite the subjective and partisan nature of this feature, Al Jazeera does not seem to impose any restrictions on its journalists in expressing partisan views, provided that they are not critical of Qatar and the internal politics of some Arab Gulf countries. This is similar to a number of Western news organizations, such as CNN, which have penalized journalists for expressing controversial views on social media, as noted earlier in the chapter. Finally, some journalists regard themselves as social reformers, in a manner reminiscent of the social responsibility model in media systems (Hallin and Mancini 2004).

It is important to mention here that the findings of this chapter may be unique to the Arab world, so conducting research on other regions and examining other case studies will be very useful in providing insight into celebrity journalism. Future studies on journalists' social media use should also further examine the symbiotic nature of traditional and social media, since they complement each other, especially for celebrity journalists. More research that investigates different platforms managed by the same journalists is needed in order to better understand the differences in audience engagements. It is important to compare and contrast non-Western journalists' media practices in order to gain more insight into the challenges and opportunities that social media provides for journalists. Finally, it is relevant for future research to examine and categorize audiences' responses to journalists' posts rather than solely focusing on categorization; however, such studies will require big data analysis due to the high degree of audiences' social media engagement with celebrity journalists.

References

Al Dakhil, T. (2014). Search for Daesh amongst you. *Okaz*. Available from: https://www.okaz.com.sa/article/941530 (accessed November 28, 2019).

Amin, H. (2002). Freedom as a value in Arab media: perceptions and attitudes among journalists. *Political Communication* 19 (2): 125–135.

Beckett, C. (2011). *SuperMedia: Saving Journalism So It Can Save the World*. London: Wiley.

Beckett, C. and Mansell, R. (2008). Crossing boundaries: new media and networked journalism. *Communication, Culture and Critique* 1 (1): 92–104.

Bossio, D. and Sacco, V. (2016). From "selfies" to breaking tweets: how journalists negotiate personal and professional identity on social media. *Journalism Practice* 11 (5): 1–17.

Brems, C., Temmerman, M., Graham, T., and Broersma, M. (2016). Personal branding on Twitter: how employed and freelance journalists stage themselves on social media. *Digital Journalism* 5 (4): 443–459.

Choi, S. (2015). The two-step flow of communication in Twitter-based public forums. *Social Science Computer Review* 33 (6): 696–711.

Chorley, M.J. and Mottershead, G. (2016). Are you talking to me? An analysis of journalism conversation on social media. *Journalism Practice* 10 (7): 1–12.

Conboy, M. (2014). Celebrity journalism – an oxymoron? Forms and functions of a genre. *Journalism* 15 (2): 171–185.

Cozma, R. and Chen, K.-J. (2013). What's in a tweet? Foreign correspondents' use of social media. *Journalism Practice* 7 (1): 33–46.

Day, E. (2004). Why women love journalism. *British Journalism Review* 15 (2): 21–25.

Djerf-Pierre, M., Ghersetti, M., and Hedman, U. (2016). Appropriating social media: the changing uses of social media among journalists across time. *Digital Journalism* 4 (7): 1–12.

Feroz Khan, G. and Vong, S. (2014). Virality over YouTube: an empirical analysis. *Internet Research* 24 (5): 629–647.

Forde, E. (2001). From polyglottism to branding: on the decline of personality journalism in the British music press. *Journalism* 2 (1): 23–43.

Grant, A.E., Guthrie, K.K., and Ball-Rokeach, S.J. (1991). Television shopping a media system dependency perspective. *Communication Research* 18 (6): 773–798.

Gulyas, A. (2013). The influence of professional variables on journalists' uses and views of social media: a comparative study of Finland, Germany, Sweden and the United Kingdom. *Digital Journalism* 1 (2): 270–285.

Hallin, D.C. and Mancini, P. (2004). *Comparing Media Systems: Three Models of Media and Politics*. Cambridge: Cambridge University Press.

Hanusch, F. and Bruns, A. (2016). Journalistic branding on Twitter: a representative study of Australian journalists' profile descriptions. *Digital Journalism* 5 (1): 26–43.

Hedman, U. (2016). When journalists tweet: disclosure, participatory, and personal transparency. *Social Media+ Society* https://doi.org/10.1177/2056305115624528.

Hedman, U. and Djerf-Pierre, M. (2013). The social journalist: embracing the social media life or creating a new digital divide? *Digital Journalism* 1 (3): 368–385.

Heravi, B. (2015). Irish journalists among world's heaviest social media users, study finds. *Irish Times.* Available from: http://www.irishtimes.com/business/media-and-marketing/irish-journalists-among-world-s-heaviest-social-media-users-study-finds-1.2101471 (accessed November 28, 2019).

Hilbert, M., Vásquez, J., Halpern, D. et al. (2016). One step, two step, network step? Complementary perspectives on communication flows in Twittered citizen protests. *Social Science Computer Review* 35 (4): 444–461.

Hladík, R. and Štětka, V. (2015). The powers that tweet: social media as news sources in the Czech Republic. *Journalism Studies* 18 (2): 154–174.

Holton, A.E. and Molyneux, L. (2015). Identity lost? The personal impact of brand journalism. *Journalism* 18 (2): 195–210.

ING (2015). 2014 study impact of social media on news: more crowd-checking, less fact-checking. Available from: https://www.ing.com/newsroom/all-news/nw/2014-study-impact-of-social-media-on-news-more-crowdchecking-less-factchecking.htm (accessed November 28, 2019).

Jordaan, M. (2013). Poke me, I'm a journalist: the impact of Facebook and Twitter on newsroom routines and cultures at two South African weeklies. *Ecquid Novi: African Journalism Studies* 34 (1): 21–35.

Katz, E. (1957). The two-step flow of communication: an up-to-date report on an hypothesis. *Public Opinion Quarterly* 21 (1): 61–78.

Katz, E. and Lazarsfeld, P. (1955). *Personal Influence: The Part Played by People in the Flow of Mass Communications.* Glencoe, IL: The Free Press.

Knight, M. (2012). Journalism as usual: the use of social media as a newsgathering tool in the coverage of the Iranian elections in 2009. *Journal of Media Practice* 13 (1): 61–74.

Knight, M. and Cook, C. (2013). *Social Media for Journalists: Principles and Practice.* Thousand Oaks, CA: Sage.

Landis, J.R. and Koch, G.G. (1977). The measurement of observer agreement for categorical data. *Biometrics* 33 (1): 159–174.

Lasorsa, D.L., Lewis, S.C., and Holton, A.E. (2012). Normalizing Twitter: journalism practice in an emerging communication space. *Journalism Studies* 13 (1): 19–36.

Lawrence, R.G., Molyneux, L., Coddington, M., and Holton, A. (2014). Tweeting conventions: political journalists' use of Twitter to cover the 2012 presidential campaign. *Journalism Studies* 15 (6): 789–806.

Lee, N.Y., Kim, Y., and Kim, J. (2015). Tweeting public affairs or personal affairs? Journalists' tweets, interactivity, and ideology. *Journalism* 17 (7): 845–864.

Mansour, E. (2018). The adoption and use of social media as a source of information by Egyptian government journalists. *Journal of Librarianship and Information Science* 50 (1): 48–67.

Mellor, N. (2005). *The Making of Arab News*. Lanham, MD: Rowman & Littlefield.

Molyneux, L. (2015). What journalists retweet: opinion, humor, and brand development on Twitter. *Journalism* 16 (7): 920–935.

Mourão, R.R. (2015). The boys on the timeline: political journalists' use of Twitter for building interpretive communities. *Journalism* 16 (8): 1107–1123.

Mourão, R., Diehl, T., and Vasudevan, K. (2015). I love Big Bird: how journalists tweeted humor during the 2012 presidential debates. *Digital Journalism* 4 (2): 1–18.

Naaman, M., Becker, H., and Gravano, L. (2011). Hip and trendy: characterizing emerging trends on Twitter. *Journal of the American Society for Information Science and Technology* 62 (5): 902–918.

Nahon, K. and Hemsley, J. (2013). *Going Viral*. Oxford: Polity.

Newman, N., Levy, D., and Nielsen, R.K. (2015). Reuters Institute Digital News Report 2015. SSRN 2619576. Available from: https://reutersinstitute.politics.ox.ac.uk/our-research/digital-news-report-2015-0 (accessed November 28, 2019).

Nordlund, J.-E. (1978). Media interaction. *Communication Research* 5 (2): 150–175.

Nuernbergk, C. (2016). Political journalists' interaction networks: the German federal press conference on Twitter. *Journalism Practice* 10 (7): 1–12.

Olausson, U. (2016). The reinvented journalist: the discursive construction of professional identity on Twitter. *Digital Journalism* 5 (1): 1–21.

Opgenhaffen, M. and Scheerlinck, H. (2014). Social media guidelines for journalists: an investigation into the sense and nonsense among Flemish journalists. *Journalism Practice* 8 (6): 726–741.

Petersen, A.H. (2011). Towards an industrial history of celebrity gossip: *The National Enquirer*, *People Magazine* and "personality journalism" in the 1970s. *Celebrity Studies* 2 (2): 131–149.

Pew Research Center (2011). How mainstream media use Twitter: content analysis shows an evolving relationship. Available from: http://www.journalism.org/analysis_report/how_mainstream_media_outlets_use_twitter (accessed November 28, 2019).

Phillips, A. (2012). Sociability, speed and quality in the changing news environment. *Journalism Practice* 6 (5–6): 669–679.

Reed, S. (2011). Sports journalists' use of social media and its effects on professionalism. *Journal of Sports Media* 6 (2): 43–64.

Rogstad, I.D. (2014). Political news journalists in social media: transforming political reporters into political pundits? *Journalism Practice* 8 (6): 688–703.

Rugh, W.A. (2004). *Arab Mass Media: Newspapers, Radio, and Television in Arab Politics*. New York: Greenwood Publishing Group.

Sacco, V. and Bossio, D. (2015). Using social media in the news reportage of war & conflict: opportunities and challenges. *Journal of Media Innovations* 2 (1): 59–76.

Sacco, V. and Bossio, D. (2016). Don't tweet this! How journalists and media organizations negotiate tensions emerging from the implementation of social media policy in newsrooms. *Digital Journalism* 5 (2): 177–193.

Saldaña, M., Higgins Joyce, V., Schmitz Weiss, A., and Calmon Alves, R. (2016). Sharing the stage: analysis of social media adoption by Latin American journalists. *Journalism Practice* 11 (4): 1–21.

Santana, A.D. and Hopp, T. (2016). Tapping into a new stream of (personal) data assessing journalists' different use of social media. *Journalism and Mass Communication Quarterly* 93 (2).

Southgate, D., Westoby, N., and Page, G. (2010). Creative determinants of viral video viewing. *International Journal of Advertising* 29 (3): 349–368.

Van der Haak, B., Parks, M., and Castells, M. (2012). The future of journalism: networked journalism. *International Journal of Communication* 6: 2923–2938.

Walker, P. (2010). Octavia Nasr fired by CNN over tweet praising late ayatollah. *Guardian*. Available from: http://www.theguardian.com/media/2010/jul/08/octavia nasr-cnn-tweet-fired (accessed November 28, 2019).

Weaver, D.H. and Willnat, L. (2016). Changes in US journalism: how do journalists think about social media? *Journalism Practice* 10 (7): 1–12.

Weeks, B.E. and Holbert, R.L. (2013). Predicting dissemination of news content in social media a focus on reception, friending, and partisanship. *Journalism and Mass Communication Quarterly* 90 (2): 212–232.

Wilkinson, D. and Thelwall, M. (2012). Trending Twitter topics in English: an international comparison. *Journal of the American Society for Information Science and Technology* 63 (8): 1631–1646.

Wilson, K. (2008). In your Facebook: why more and more journalists are signing up for the popular social networking site. *American Journalism Review* 30 (1): 12–14.

Wu, P.C.S. and Wang, Y.-C. (2011). The influences of electronic word-of-mouth message appeal and message source credibility on brand attitude. *Asia Pacific Journal of Marketing and Logistics* 23 (4): 448–472.

7

Who Is Breaking News on Social Media?

Introduction

This chapter examines the issue of breaking news on social media in order to understand who is using it and what is being disseminated, in addition to other aspects. Previous journalism research has not sufficiently focused on the quantitative and qualitative assessment of users and their most retweeted posts. The data set used here contains more than 7 million tweets. The analysis follows a mixed approach including bot detection in order to examine as many aspects as possible of Twitter users' utilization of the term "breaking news" and of the hashtag #breakingnews. Theoretically, this analysis expands on a metajournalistic discourse framework to include the information productions of non-journalistic actors, an aspect that has been overlooked in previous research. Finally, the chapter argues that the breaking news phenomenon needs to be situated within the discussion of clickbait journalism, whose long-term impact can undermine trust in news and democracy.

Based on a Google Ngram search, we find that term "breaking news" has a long history of use in English-language publications. It can be traced back to 1720, when it was used in a literary play by Charles Shadwell. According to the Oxford English Dictionary, it is regarded as a colloquial expression used by journalists that means "To publish or reveal (an item of news); to make available for publication" (OED 2019). The general definition of the term "breaking news," sometimes called "spot news," is as follows:

> news events and issues that are unpredictable and warrant expedited dissemination to inform news organization's audience as they unfold. Currently, this is accomplished through interrupting regular programming on television and radio platforms, or distributing information on websites through text alerts, or on social media platforms. Breaking news can range

News 2.0: Journalists, Audiences, and News on Social Media, First Edition. Ahmed Al-Rawi.
© 2020 John Wiley & Sons, Inc. Published 2020 by John Wiley & Sons, Inc.

from terrorist attacks to earthquakes and is intended to be presented by journalists as a serious issue or event that warrants viewers' attention. Breaking news was initially designed to inform the public about nonroutine events, but has become more common because of the proliferation of legacy and Internet-based sites competing for viewership. (Luchsinger and Barnett 2019, p. 1)

Hence, the term "breaking news" is basically a label attached to news items to suggest that one news organization is ahead in identifying an important story and informing audiences about it.

What Is Breaking News?

At its core, breaking news refers to the speed by which information is transmitted, a vital element of journalism, since "the work of journalists ... [often] involves notions of speed, fast decision-making, hastiness, and working in accelerated real-time" (Deuze 2005, p. 449). It often denotes immediacy (Usher 2018), importance, and up-to-date dissemination. Breaking news can also refer to a "story that emerges or unfolds unexpectedly, as opposed to a diary story" (Harcup 2014). In this regard, Stuart Allan (2006) believes the Oklahoma City bombing of April 19, 1995 was an important landmark in the way news organizations provide up-to-date information on important events that are often hard news in nature. If one takes into account the availability of information today due to social media affordances, the breaking news label becomes a challenge and an added responsibility for news organizations, since every piece of information needs to be verified in a speedy manner (Bruns et al. 2012).

Another aspect of the breaking news "tag" is that it implies "drama" injected into the news business, and carries the potential of hyperbole (Lewis and Cushion 2009, p. 309). In other words, it is often viewed as a hollow term since any news story can be labeled as a breaking news item. David Weigel (2012) calls the breaking news phenomenon today a "joke," while some scholars and journalists even believe that news itself is broken because of several factors, including the trivialization of the journalism profession. This, they argue, threatens to undermine democracy and distract news consumers from what is worthy of their attention (Fallows 1997; Rusbridger 2018). In this chapter, I argue that due to the overuse of the label "breaking news" in journalism, it has become associated with sensational clickbait stories taking the form of emotionality or affective news (Wahl-Jorgensen 2016). Clickbait journalism is often linked to the types of news features that define tabloid stories (Bastos 2016), and is generally understood to be a form of "content designed to increase off-site referral traffic from social media platforms through attention-grabbing (and sometimes tabloid-worthy) headlines and photos" (Caplan and Boyd 2016). On Twitter, the clickbait phenomenon is practiced not only by journalists and news organizations, but also by ordinary people who have appropriated the term and used it to attract attention to their posts, often in an effort to make them go viral. In a study of breaking news, Miller and Leshner (2007) found that its main function is to garner attention, rather than helping in news recall. There is, after all, clear competition on social media between ordinary people (or non-journalistic actors) and journalists, since they are vying for attention through virality; non-journalistic actors have a much harder time in this, since they do not enjoy the same privileges and hierarchy of access as mainstream media (MSM) journalists.

Though it is easy to label these ordinary people as citizen journalists, who are traditionally considered to "report news to the wider public ... 'bear[ing] witness to crisis event unfolding around them'" (Allan and Thorsen 2009, p. x), this conceptualization is limited and remains broad because some Twitter users do not identify as journalists at all, and are aware that their posts are not genuinely regarded as news. It is also inaccurate to label them as fake journalists, as these are understood as people who benefit commercially from the practice (e.g., in Indonesia; Sen and Hill 2010) or, like Jon Stewart, who label themselves as such for satirical entertainment reasons (Tenenboim-Weinblatt 2009). Tony Harcup (2014) emphasizes that critics of citizen journalism research "argue that the phenomenon often has little to do with either citizenship or journalism." Tamara Small (2011) studied the hashtag #cdnpoli (used on tweets related to Canadian politics) and found a very limited number of tweets were related to breaking news or even reporting, though Twitter itself is known for news dissemination. Small argues that "people are clearly using Twitter in a different way than the breaking news frame suggests" (2011, p. 884). In other words, the common understanding of tweets suggests news dissemination and sharing, yet people often use Twitter in ways that fall outside such traditional frameworks.

Previous research on the hashtag #breakingnews has been conducted from a methodological perspective in the field of computer science, mostly in terms of detecting important events (Phuvipadawat and Murata 2010; Gupta and Kumaraguru 2012; Imran et al. 2017; Ramisa et al. 2017). For example, Phuvipadawat and Murata (2010) studied 154 000 tweets that referenced #breakingnews and identified the retweets as well as the popular terms in order to track important events. Using different methods, Lewis and Cushion (2009) found crime stories, followed by accidents and disasters, and then war and celebrity/sport/human interest stories, to be the most common breaking news items (2009). The research highlighted in this chapter, however, employs a mixed method that has not been used in previous journalism studies of breaking news.

Metajournalistic Discourses and Breaking News

In this chapter, I argue that ordinary people using the term "breaking news" and the hashtag #breakingnews on Twitter are employing metajournalistic discourses, or "the discourses produced by journalists about journalism or themselves" (De Maeyer and Le Cam 2015). Since there is "fluidity of journalistic work" (Carlson 2015, p. 356), such discourses are not entirely "owned" by journalists, who "themselves have significantly less control over the discourse that helps shape the understanding of the journalism industry" (Ferrucci 2018, p. 4822). Here, there is a kind of re-territorialization of the journalism profession as its boundaries are becoming "more inclusive of non-traditional journalism and news media, expanding the notion of 'expert'" (Johnston and Wallace 2017, p. 862). In this regard, Matt Carlson argues that metajournalistic discourses are based on three components, including non-journalistic sites and actors that permit "agency" (2015, p. 353) and provide legitimacy and authority. The third component is related to the topics discussed, or reactive and generative metajournalistic discourses. The former refers to responses to "a particular story, journalist, or news outlet," while the latter is defined as "the ability of evaluative texts to spark wider conversations about journalism" (Carlson 2015, p. 358). In this sense, "metajournalistic discourse connects the creation and circulation of journalism's sociocultural meanings to the social practices surrounding news production and consumption" (Carlson 2015, p. 350). Carlson's focus on reactions to journalists is quite limiting; I argue here that such practices must also include reactions to non-journalistic actors, such as in the case study investigated in this chapter.

As mentioned, many users examined here are non-journalistic actors who do not claim to be journalists or practitioners of citizen journalism and yet use the term "breaking news" or the hashtag #breakingnews as a form of clickbait to attract attention to their posts. This is a sign of the new age of liquid journalism (Deuze 2008) we are living in, for "journalists themselves have had an uneasy relationship with their own professionalism. Many journalists have made a point of overtly resisting any formal qualifications for the profession; instead, they view their work as a highly skilled craft best learned through apprenticeship" (Kantola 2016, p. 425).

In relation to non-journalistic sites, which are the second component of the metajournalistic discourses theory, Twitter functions as a non-traditional site for news dissemination, especially popular in breaking news stories (Kwak et al. 2010; Petrovic et al. 2013; Vis 2013; Zubiaga et al. 2015). In this regard, Osborne and Dredze (2014) found that Twitter is faster in disseminating breaking news than Facebook and other social media sites. In fact, Twitter is categorized as a news app in the Apple App Store, where it is described as follows: "From breaking news and entertainment to sports, politics, and everyday interests, when it happens in the world, it happens on Twitter first. See all sides of the story. Join the conversation. Watch live streaming events. Twitter is what's happening in the world and what people are talking about right now" (Twitter n.d.). Other social media platforms like Facebook are actively exploring ways to attract more audiences through fast news dissemination and breaking news notificationFacebook recently announced, for example, that it is making changes to its newsfeed in order to find "new ways to help people stay informed about timely, breaking news that matters to them," adding the "Breaking News" label to the pages of 80 news publishers (Facebook 2018). However, one of the main advantages of news dissemination on Twitter, which keeps it ahead of other social media sites, is its use of hashtags. News items that are "hashtagged" become more "visible to relevant existing user groups" (Bruns et al. 2012). This chapter attempts to examine the following aspects: the main topics of the most retweeted posts and what are their sources; the meaning derived from the most recurrent words, phrases, hashtags, and mentions based on a computational analysis of the tweets; and the nature of the top Twitter users who tweet about breaking news and what is their likelihood of being bots.

As discussed, this chapter uses a mixed-method approach. The computational analyses are conducted using three different Python codes to identify the following: top users, most retweeted posts, and the likelihood of accounts being bots (via Botometer) (Ferrara 2017; Al-Rawi et al. 2019). The Twitter data set of 7 094 488 tweets posted by 2 721 494 unique users was collected from January 23, 2018 to June 4, 2018 using Netlytic's academic subscription. The search terms used were #breakingnews and "breaking news." Data visualization was conducted using Tableau and Microsoft Excel, while identification of the most recurrent words, phrases, hashtags, and mentions was done with QDA Miner WordStat8, a commercial program used for qualitative and quantitative data analysis. After identifying the top 100 Twitter users and the most retweeted posts, a qualitative assessment by two coders, including the author of this chapter, was conducted to understand the nature of those users and the major topics of the retweets. Only the top users and retweets were examined because they provide an indication of the major actors involved in the dissemination of breaking news stories, and the retweets offer an understanding of what the audiences are mostly engaged with. Besides, which such a large data set, it is not possible to investigate the nature of all users and retweets. Based on Grounded theory, the codebooks were inductively designed and individually coded. Wimmer and Dominick (2013) use the term "emergent coding" to describe this method since topics are identified by finding patterns or commonalities in the communicated messages (Strauss and Corbin 1998; Guest et al. 2011).

Regarding the nature of users and building on the theory of metajournalistic discourses, we categorized users as follows: (i) journalistic actors, (ii) non-journalistic actors, and (iii) suspended. To do this, we relied on the available cues on Twitter, including each user's profile description, the nature of their previous tweets, and tweets referencing breaking news found in the data set. If a user claimed to be a journalist or a news organization, whether mainstream, alternative, citizen, or self-proclaimed, we coded them as a journalistic actor because we were unable to make judgements about who should or should not be labeled a journalist or news organization. We combined MSM with alternative media outlets because the boundaries sometimes blur and overlap and it is difficult to categorize non-Western outlets as alternative. Overall, this is linked to the previous theoretical discussion on metajournalistic discourses and the fluidity of the conceptualization and practice of journalism in today's world. As for the most retweeted posts, we identified six major topics by relying on news values theory (Galtung and Ruge 1965; Harcup and O'Neill 2001; Shoemaker and Cohen 2012): human interest, politics, celebrity, sports, environment/climate, and tragic event/death/murder; other topics were categorized as "other." In this regard, human interest stories have a high number of humorous or ironic items, while celebrity news contains a large number of stories that deal with celebrities from the music entertainment industry.

In addition, we examined the sources of the most retweeted posts using the same categorization followed in identifying the top users, sorting as non-journalistic and journalistic sources. Regarding non-journalistic sources, there were seven tweets referencing breaking news that were not available online, either because they were deleted by the users themselves or because the users' accounts were suspended or deleted. We relied on Google searches to lead us to these deleted tweets and their non-journalistic users on other online platforms.

Building on the theory of metajournalistic discourses (Carlson 2015), I argue here that, because of the fluidity of journalism practices and the difficulty of providing an inclusive definition of news and of who journalists are, reactions to non-journalistic actors need to be incorporated into the theory, since its third component is limited to reactions to journalists only.

For an overview of the large data set, comprising over 7 million tweets, see Figure 7.1. We can note, for example, that 120 636 tweets were posted on February 14, 2018 alone: the highest number in the data set. A clear fluctuation is seen in the remaining periods. For example, the second top day is May 23, 2018, with 81 751 tweets. Regarding the nature of the top retweets, and to better understand the reason behind the high number of tweets in the month of February, Table 7.1 identifies the top 10 most retweeted posts. A qualitative assessment indicates that the majority are human interest stories, especially those that are humorous or ironic in nature (6/10), followed by a minority about politics (4/10). The four top retweets were originally made by news organizations, such as MSNBC, CBS News, and eNCA, a South African news organization. On the second top day, the most retweeted post reads as follows: "BREAKING NEWS: All these cows are kissing

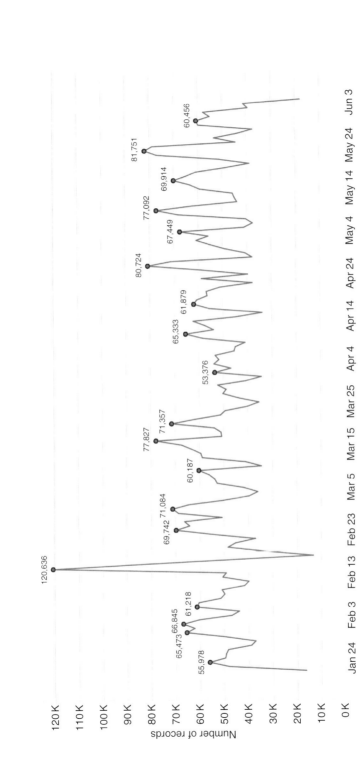

Figure 7.1 Frequency of tweets referencing #breakingnews and "breaking news."

Table 7.1   Top 10 retweets in the data set on February 14, 2018.

No.	Retweet	Frequency
1)	RT @YOONGIFIED: BREAKING NEWS: It\'s been reported Jung Hoseok has been reported missing from his partner in crime, Park Jimin. The pair we ...	4560
2)	RT @keepnhspublic: BREAKING NEWS – we hear @ Jeremy_Hunt is speaking at Kettering General Hospital at 12.30 tomorrow. He's asked that the event not be publicised. So please don't tell anyone who lives nearby.	3382
3)	RT @eNCA: [BREAKING NEWS] Jacob Zuma has resigned as the President of South Africa – "I have come to the decision to resign with immediate ...	3006
4)	RT @stanGotBangtan: Breaking News: iGot7 gave the first 1 Billion+ hearts for a vlive. This is the first vlive reaching Billion of Hearts e ...	2416
5)	RT @CBSNews: There is breaking news of a shooting outside the NSA headquarters in Fort Meade, Maryland. There appears to be an SUV with bul ...	2310
6)	RT @eNCA: [BREAKING NEWS] #ZumaRecall – Mashatile: Jacob Zuma has been recalled. The deadline is today. We will now go ahead with the Motion ...	2106
7)	RT @MSNBC: JUST IN: More students run out of Marjory Stoneman Douglas High School in South Florida. Tune in to @MSNBC for live breaking n ...	2058
8)	RT @_NinoGuapo: BREAKING NEWS: Derrick Rose has been traded back to Simeon for a 6 piece from Harold's with lemon pepper, mild sauce and a ...	2007
9)	RT @stanGotBangtan: Breaking News: iGOT7 has reached 777 777 777 hearts on vlive breaking the record for most number of hearts ever. #IGOT7 ...	1532
10)	RT @naryaselh: [BREAKING NEWS] The prince Park Jimin was spotted in the airport alone and the Sunshine has been reported missing on the #Ha ...	1093

this dog https://t.co/sVyy3kxvRR." This post got retweeted 29 924 times. Here, the top five retweets are human interest stories with an emphasis on humor. Table 7.2 lists the 10 most retweeted posts in the whole data set; most of the remaining retweets deal with politics or hard news.

As mentioned, the qualitative assessment of the top 100 retweeted posts was done by two coders in order to categorize news stories into topics based on news values theory. After excluding five posts that were not in English, the analysis

Table 7.2 Most retweeted posts in the data set.

No.	Retweet	Frequency
1)	BREAKING NEWS: All these cows are kissing this dog https://t.co/sVyy3kxvRR	76 754
2)	BREAKING NEWS: North High teacher fired after being caught selling juul pods to students. She claimed "I was making more money than this shithole was paying me, and a bitch gotta do what she gotta do." https://t.co/iGUEEeubEl	36 816
3)	I\'ve gotten three times as many breaking news emails today about "Roseanne" getting cancelled than I have about the death toll in Puerto Rico being 70 times higher than we thought	34 380
4)	RT @kalenminaj: BREAKING NEWS: Mariah Carey has officially become a gas, making her the skinniest person alive. She says she achieved this …	28 288
5)	Breaking News: Trump to back out of Louisiana Purchase.	27 435
6)	BREAKING NEWS: North and South Korea will sign a peace treaty to formally end the Korean War later this year, 65 years after hostilities ceased https://t.co/cKEMmhZdvj https://t.co/VSJ7sAs9VU	20 290
7)	BREAKING NEWS: The Trump administration today announced that Russia has successfully launched a cyberattack on our nuclear power grid, has compromised the grid, and can shut it down at will. This is on top of what Russia did to our election. We are under attack by a hostile power	18 592
8)	Breaking News on … CNN: Cohen raided by FBI NBC: Cohen raided by FBI CBS: Cohen raided by FBI ABC: Cohen raided by FBI FOX: … https://t.co/DRV9e1Q3ig	14 024
9)	RT @GovMikeHuckabee: Breaking News! Medical personnel being rushed to US Capitol to administer Metamucil to Democrats who appear deeply mi …	13 269
10)	BREAKING NEWS: The crowd in Washington DC has officially reached 1 000 000 protesters. #MarchForOurLives https://t.co/RKgsKXpE8I	12 528

Table 7.3 Most dominant topics in the top retweets in the data set.

No.	Topic	Frequency
1)	Human interest	14
2)	Politics	49
3)	Celebrity	25
4)	Sports	3
5)	Environment/climate	2
6)	Tragic event/death/murder	3
7)	Other	4

shows that politics comes first (49%), followed by celebrity (with a clear emphasis on music entertainment news, especially South Korean K-pop bands like BTS and Got7) (25%), and then human interest stories with a focus on humor or irony (14%) (Table 7.3). Minor topics include sports (3%), tragic event/death/murder (3%), and environment/climate (2%). These findings provide unique insight into the major topics that are most likely to garner audience attention in relation to breaking news on social media. While Lewis and Cushion's (2009) research on breaking news on Sky News and the BBC shows that crime stories, followed by accidents and disasters, are the most common breaking news items as indicated by journalists and news organizations, this chapter demonstrates that politics followed by celebrity and human interest stories are the most important topics for audiences. The latter are regarded as soft news topics due to their entertainment quality and positive tone, as compared to politics or hard news, which is serious in nature (Bell 2009, p. 687). In other words, once you include non-journalistic actors in the analysis, soft news stories play a more prominent role.

Next, I examined the sources of the top retweets and found that the majority are sent by non-journalistic actors (59%), followed by journalistic actors like mainstream and alternative news organizations and journalists (41%). As noted, the line between alternative media and MSM is sometimes too blurry to properly identify, so both are coded as journalistic actors here. One unique example is a tweet by Fox News presenter, Sean Hannity, who used the term "breaking news" and provided a link to a sensational story taken from a right-wing anti-liberal website, saracarter.com, stating: "RT@seanhannity: BREAKING NEWS: FBI informant on Uranium One Breaks Silence Today via @SaraCarterDC https://t.co/CGg5cg36lZ" (n = 6192). In general, the results found here are interesting because they show that the majority of the top retweets actually originate from non-journalistic actors, who appropriate the term "breaking news" in order to draw attention to their own tweets. This is similar to clickbait journalistic practices, and perhaps can be thought of as citizen clickbait. Those users act like journalists, or at least employ their terminology, making full use of the affordances provided by Twitter in terms of information dissemination and outreach. As Hannah Spyksma (2019) describes it, these are an example of "unintentional journalists," defined as "people ... who do the work of journalism without intending to do so."

As for the tweets that reference breaking news using computational methods, I examined the data set as a whole by first focusing on the top words other than terms like "breaking," "news," and "breakingnews". We can see in Table 7.4 that the South Korean pop band "BTS" comes first (n = 59 157), followed by "Trump" (n = 47 967), and then words like "school," in reference to a mass-shooting incident in the United States (n = 42 863). As with the topics of the top retweets, we find that most of the top words carry political meanings, including "South" (Korea) and (Jacob) "Zuma," the former South African president. This is also

Table 7.4 Top 20 most recurrent words in the Twitter data set.

No.	Word	Frequency
1)	News	710 799
2)	Breaking	707 060
3)	Breakingnews	127 151
4)	BTS	59 157
5)	Trump	47 967
6)	School	42 863
7)	Today	39 110
8)	Btsarmyna	38 408
9)	President	32 627
10)	AMP	31 912
11)	Florida	30 172
12)	Shooting	28 083
13)	Nytimes	24 164
14)	Live	23 223
15)	March	22 094
16)	CNN	21 714
17)	South	21 614
18)	Zuma	21 605
19)	Police	19 291
20)	High	18 982

confirmed in Table 7.5, which lists the most recurrent phrases after removing any redundant or repeated ones (e.g., "breaking news"). As far as the major topics found in the most retweeted posts, we again find politics to be the most dominant in the data set, followed by celebrity news. Regarding the most recurrent hashtags, and aside from the top three ones related to breaking news, we find that the few top ones are also political in nature. For example, the top hashtag is #Resignsheriffisrael (n = 7796), in reference to news on Scott Israel, the American law officer who served as Sheriff of Broward County, Florida until he was suspended (see Table 7.6). This is followed by a reference to the South Korean boy band #Got7 (n = 7718), #CNNtownhall (n = 7370), a CNN-hosted political show that provides a televised live platform for presidential candidates to talk about their policies, and #Iheartawards (n = 4579), the famous iHeartRadio Music Award. Upon examining the remaining top 20 hashtags, we can conclude that there are no unified topics in the set, since they range from politics to music, sports, and celebrity. In other words, there is no overwhelming theme among the top hashtags.

In terms of references to elite MSM outlets and journalists, the *New York Times* and CNN are the only news organization included in the top 20 words, but other outlets are found in the data set, including Fox News (n = 14 116), MSNBC (n = 7019), and the BBC (n = 3486). However, this elite media ranking needs to be complemented by examining the most mentioned Twitter users, especially in relation to elite news organizations. Here, Table 7.7 shows that the *New York Times* is the most mentioned news outlet (n = 24 043), followed by Fox News (n = 13 409), Fox News host Sean Hannity (n = 8231), and the *Jerusalem Post* (n = 7699).

Table 7.5 Top 10 most recurrent phrases in the Twitter data set.

No.	Phrase	Frequency
1)	President Trump	107 172
2)	Cows are Kissing this Dog	76 726
3)	Donald Trump	58 114
4)	Raided By FBI	56 598
5)	South Korea	54 230
6)	White House	51 234
7)	North and South Korea	40 756
8)	Puerto Rico	38 207
9)	Trump Administration	37 349
10)	Teacher Fired	36 833

Table 7.6 Top 20 most recurrent hashtags in the Twitter data set.

No.	Hashtag	Frequency
1)	#Breakingnews	116 217
2)	#Breaking	31 559
3)	#News	22 607
4)	#Resignsheriffisrael	7796
5)	#Got7	7718
6)	#CNNtownhall	7370
7)	#Iheartawards	4579
8)	#Football	3909
9)	#Soccer	3616
10)	#Premierleague	3601
11)	#92newshdplus	3542
12)	#Footballnews	3527
13)	#Trump	3389
14)	#MAGA	3370
15)	#Eyesonyou	3284
16)	#Indilens	3157
17)	#ICO	3143
18)	#Bestfanarmy	3125
19)	#Amjoy	2780
20)	#Sridevi	2598

Regarding the nature of the top users and their likelihood of being bots, the majority of the most active 100 users are journalistic actors (59%), including 27% that seem to be alternative media outlets that mostly exist on social media and whose goal is to disseminate breaking news stories taken from different sources (Figure 7.2). As mentioned, these journalistic actors are a mixture of MSM organizations and journalists as well as alternative news outlets and other self-proclaimed citizen journalists. Additionally, 26% of the top users were non-journalistic actors who either retweeted news that mentioned breaking news or who appropriated the term or its hashtag to attract attention. Finally, 15% of the top users' accounts were suspended or deleted. Table 7.8 lists the top 20 Twitter users, which include a mixture of ordinary citizens, journalists, and news organizations. It is interesting to note that some of the news outlets that periodically use the term "breaking news" are based in non-Western countries like Bangladesh @bdnews24 (n = 24 947), Pakistan @atvpakistan (n = 16 852), and Indonesia @BNewsCoID (n = 11 652).

Table 7.7 Top 20 most mentioned Twitter users in the data set.

No.	User	Frequency
1)	@Btsarmyna	38 359
2)	@Nytimes	24 043
3)	@Sethabramson	16 099
4)	@Stangotbangtan	15 731
5)	@W_Terrence	15 466
6)	@Foxnews	13 409
7)	@YouTube	11 829
8)	@Jeremy_Hunt	11 815
9)	@Kalenminaj	11 704
10)	@Enca	11 003
11)	@Keepnhspublic	10 788
12)	@Seanhannity	8231
13)	@Jerusalem_Post	7699
14)	@Bts_Army_Int	6417
15)	@Saracarterdc	6285
16)	@Logic_Triumphs	6104
17)	@TES	5845
18)	@Got7official	5726
19)	@Arianagrande	5684
20)	@Troyesivan	5684

In order to understand the likelihood of users being bots, we examined the top 20 users and found that three were suspended, probably due to violating Twitter rules on automation. The average bot score was 2.7/5 (where 0 is human and 5 is a bot), which means that the majority of the top users seem to be humans (Table 7.8; Botometer n.d.). We then expanded the assessment to the top 2000 users using a Python code, because the remaining users that had not been included in the bot detection tool were not as active as the chosen sample. The automated examination excluded 294 accounts that had been suspended, mostly due to violating Twitter automation rules. Figure 7.3 shows the distribution of the bot scores. The average is 2.0, which again means that the majority of the top users seem to be actual humans rather than bots. However, 529 (31%) that scored around 3 and above are likely to be bots or cyborgs (semi-automated accounts). This remains difficult to judge with certainty, because some human users can be

Top Twitter Users

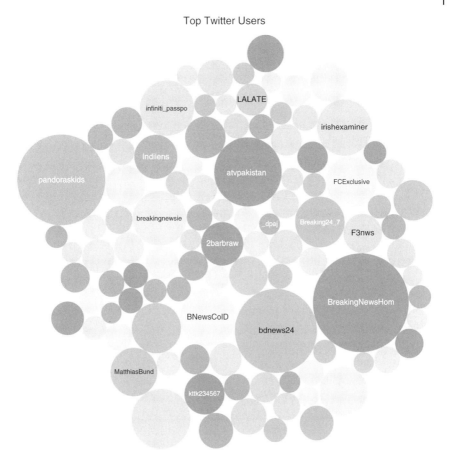

Figure 7.2 Top 100 Twitter users based on the frequency of their tweets.

active at certain times (Botometer n.d.). In comparison to the total number of users (over 2.7 million), this is regarded as a very small fraction. Since these suspended users, who were possibly bots, are not available online anymore, it was not possible to examine whether they were journalistic or non-journalistic actors.

In conclusion, examination of a large data set indicates that ordinary people, whether unintentional journalists (Spyksma 2019) or non-journalistic actors (Carlson 2015), are fiercely competing with journalistic actors to dominate breaking news discourses on Twitter. Similar to the way citizen journalists try to reverse the hierarchy of access to MSM channels in their coverage of issues (Hackett 1985; Atton 2010), these non-journalistic actors, who do not enjoy the same privileges as MSM journalists, attempt to become more visible online through use of the term "breaking news" or the hashtag #breakingnews. In this regard, Chris Atton (2002),

Table 7.8 Top 20 most active Twitter users in the data set.

No.	User	Frequency	Bot score
1)	BreakingNewsHom	34 376	3.5
2)	pandoraskids	29 058	2.6
3)	bdnews24	24 947	1.5
4)	atvpakistan	16 852	1.5
5)	N_BreakingNEWS	12 805	4.7
6)	BNewsCoID	11 652	2.6
7)	irishexaminer	11 238	0.3
8)	infiniti_passpo	10 914	3.2
9)	breakingnewsie	10 676	—
10)	FCExclusive	9572	—
11)	Breaking24_7	9195	2.6
12)	Family_General1	8961	3.8
13)	robinsnewswire	8530	3.3
14)	MatthiasBund	8288	4.3
15)	Indilens	6841	1.8
16)	2barbraw	6721	3.9
17)	DJROMANROXFORD	6211	3.2
18)	kttk234567	6086	—
19)	ImprobableColla	5958	0.4
20)	newstodayhot	5907	3.1

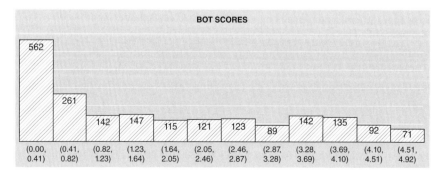

Figure 7.3 Bot likelihood of the top 2000 Twitter users.

in his discussion of alterative media, mentions that readers and writers often exchange information and publish content on the same platforms, making them appear equal. This provides a "challenge to intellectual discourse as well as the opportunity to discuss the ideas in that discourse to an extent unknown in the mainstream media. Such a strategy not only introduces new forms of knowledge from a much wider writing base ... it also introduces many more social actors, and offers them the same empowerment as it offers the intellectual: an equal platform for their ideas" (Atton 2002, p. 111). The same argument applies to the case study examined here, since non-journalistic and journalistic actors are both striving to attract the attention of online audiences on the same platform. In this sense, Twitter itself can be regarded as an alternative journalism platform (Poell and Borra 2012) or a non-journalistic site that can empower its users.

The main challenging outcome, however, is the possible confusion among Twitter users regarding the distinction between what is actually news or newsworthy and what is clickbait, whose sole purpose is to maximize visibility with sensational headlines. Added to the fact that we are currently bombarded with the breaking news label on different channels, I argue that in the long run this confusion of our new, diffuse news ecosystem may undermine trust in what breaking news is, and ultimately the credibility of the news itself on social media.

In conclusion, while journalists and news organizations constitute the majority of top active users (59%), who are mostly humans, non-journalistic actors make up the majority of sources in relation to the most retweeted posts (52%). Regarding the major topics that Twitter audiences engage with most, the study indicates that politics, celebrity, and human interest stories are the most prevalent; this is partly confirmed by the examination of the most recurrent words and phrases. In other words, audiences mostly prefer to consume soft news characterized by positivity, since these identified topics are different from the hard news items that MSM periodically highlights or tags as breaking news (Lewis and Cushion 2009). In terms of theory, I argue that there is a need to expand the concept of metajournalistic discourses since the productions of non-journalistic actors are not part of the original framework even though they constitute an important alternative means of dissemination of breaking news discourses on social media.

Finally, this chapter is limited in a few ways. It is important to conduct interviews with journalists in order to better understand how they define breaking news and its use on social media. Also, some news organizations may use specific terms for breaking news, such as #brknews, or not use a term at all, which means that the data set examined here is not comprehensive. Other search terms could be used to capture more data from social media. It is also important to examine the topics of breaking news stories from a cross-national comparative perspective, especially since numerous non-Western news organizations are actively using the term "breaking news."

References

Allan, S. (2006). *Online News: Journalism and the Internet*. London: McGraw-Hill Education.

Allan, S. and Thorsen, E. (2009). Introduction. In: *Citizen Journalism: Global Perspectives* (eds. S. Allan and E. Thorsen), 1–16. New York: Peter Lang.

Al-Rawi, A., Groshek, J., and Zhang, L. (2019). What the fake? Assessing the extent of networked political spamming and bots in the propagation of #fakenews on Twitter. *Online Information Review* 43 (1): 53–71.

Atton, C. (2002). *Alternative Media*. Thousand Oaks, CA: Sage.

Atton, C. (2010). Alternative media theory and journalism practice. In: *Digital Media and Democracy: Tactics in Hard Times* (ed. M. Boler), 213–228. Boston, MA: MIT Press.

Bastos, M. (2016). Digital journalism and tabloid journalism. In: *The Routledge Companion to Digital Journalism Studies* (eds. B. Franklin and S. Eldridge II). London: Routledge.

Bell, C. (2009). Hard versus soft news. In: *Encyclopedia of Journalism* (ed. C.H. Sterling), 687–690. Thousand Oaks, CA: Sage.

Botometer (n.d.). FAQ. Available from: https://botometer.iuni.iu.edu/#!/faq (accessed November 28, 2019).

Bruns, A., Highfield, T., and Lind, R.A. (2012). Blogs, Twitter, and breaking news: the produsage of citizen journalism. In: *Produsing Theory in a Digital World: The Intersection of Audiences and Production in Contemporary Theory* (ed. R.A. Lind), 15–32. New York: Peter Lang.

Caplan, R. and Boyd, D. (2016). Who controls the public sphere in an era of algorithms? *Data & Society*. Available from: https://datasociety.net/events/who-controls-public-sphere/ (accessed November 28, 2019).

Carlson, M. (2015). Metajournalistic discourse and the meanings of journalism: definitional control, boundary work, and legitimation. *Communication Theory* 26 (4): 349–368.

De Maeyer, J. and Le Cam, F. (2015). The material traces of journalism: a socio-historical approach to online journalism. *Digital Journalism* 3 (1): 85–100.

Deuze, M. (2005). What is journalism? Professional identity and ideology of journalists reconsidered. *Journalism* 6 (4): 442–464.

Deuze, M. (2008). The changing context of news work: liquid journalism for a monitorial citizenry. *International Journal of Communication* 2 (18): 848–865.

Facebook (2018). Removing trending from Facebook. Available from: https://newsroom.fb.com/news/2018/06/removing-trending (accessed November 28, 2019).

Fallows, J.M. (1997). *Breaking the News: How the Media Undermine American Democracy*. New York: Vintage.

Ferrara, E. (2017). Disinformation and social bot operations in the run up to the 2017 French presidential election. *First Monday* 22 (8).

Ferrucci, P. (2018). Mo "meta" blues: how popular culture can act as metajournalistic discourse. *International Journal of Communication* 12: 4821–4838.

Galtung, J. and Ruge, M.H. (1965). The structure of foreign news: the presentation of the Congo, Cuba and Cyprus crises in four Norwegian newspapers. *Journal of Peace Research* 2 (1): 64–90.

Guest, G., MacQueen, K.M., and Namey, E.E. (2011). *Applied Thematic Analysis*. Thousand Oaks, CA: Sage.

Gupta, A. and Kumaraguru, P. (2012). @Twitter credibility ranking of tweets on events #breakingnews. Available from: https://repository.iiitd.edu.in/jspui/handle/123456789/12 (accessed November 28, 2019).

Hackett, R.A. (1985). A hierarchy of access: aspects of source bias in Canadian TV news. *Journalism Quarterly* 62 (2): 256–277.

Harcup, T. (2014). *A Dictionary of Journalism*. Oxford: Oxford University Press.

Harcup, T. and O'Neill, D. (2001). What is news? Galtung and Ruge revisited. *Journalism Studies* 2 (2): 261–280.

Imran, M., Meier, P., and Boersma, K. (2017). The use of social media for crisis management. In: *Big Data, Surveillance and Crisis Management* (eds. K. Boersma and C. Fonio). New York: Routledge.

Johnston, J. and Wallace, A. (2017). Who is a journalist? Changing legal definitions in a de-territorialised media space. *Digital Journalism* 5 (7): 850–867.

Kantola, A. (2016). Liquid journalism. In: *The SAGE Handbook of Digital Journalism* (eds. T. Witschge, C. Anderson, D. Domingo and A. Hermida), 424–442. Thousand Oaks, CA: Sage.

Kwak, H., Lee, C., Park, H., and Moon, S. (2010). What is Twitter, a social network or a news media? In: *Proceedings of the 19th International Conference on World Wide Web*. ACM, pp. 591–600.

Lewis, J. and Cushion, S. (2009). The thirst to be first: an analysis of breaking news stories and their impact on the quality of 24-hour news coverage in the UK. *Journalism Practice* 3 (3): 304–318.

Luchsinger, A. and Barnett, B. (2019). Breaking or spot news. In: *The International Encyclopedia of Journalism Studies* (eds. T.P. Vos and F. Hanusch). New York: Wiley-Blackwell.

Miller, A. and Leshner, G. (2007). How viewers process live, breaking, and emotional television news. *Media Psychology* 10 (1): 1–18.

OED (2019). Break, v. Available from: www.oed.com (accessed November 28, 2019).

Osborne, M. and Dredze, M. (2014). Facebook, Twitter and Google Plus for breaking news: is there a winner? In: *Proceedings of the International AAAI Conference on Web and Social Media*.

Petrovic, S., Osborne, M., McCreadie, R., Macdonald, C., Ounis, I., and Shrimpton, L. (2013). Can Twitter replace newswire for breaking news? In: *Seventh International AAAI Conference on Weblogs and Social Media.*

Phuvipadawat, S. and Murata, T. (2010). Breaking news detection and tracking in Twitter. In: *2010 IEEE/WIC/ACM International Conference on Web Intelligence and Intelligent Agent Technology.* IEEE, Vol. 3, pp. 120–123.

Poell, T. and Borra, E. (2012). Twitter, YouTube, and Flickr as platforms of alternative journalism: the social media account of the 2010 Toronto G20 protests. *Journalism* 13 (6): 695–713.

Ramisa, A., Yan, F., Moreno-Noguer, F., and Mikolajczyk, K. (2017). BreakingNews: article annotation by image and text processing. *IEEE Transactions on Pattern Analysis and Machine Intelligence* 40 (5): 1072–1085.

Rusbridger, A. (2018). Alan Rusbridger: who broke the news? *Guardian.* Available from: https://www.theguardian.com/news/2018/aug/31/alan-rusbridger-who-broke-the-news (accessed November 28, 2019).

Sen, K. and Hill, D. (eds.) (2010). *Politics and the Media in Twenty-First Century Indonesia: Decade of Democracy.* London: Routledge.

Shadwell, C. (1720). *The Hasty Wedding; or, Intriguing Squire. A Comedy.* Dublin: Joseph Leathly and Patrick Dugan.

Shoemaker, P.J. and Cohen, A.A. (2012). *News Around the World: Content, Practitioners, and the Public.* London: Routledge.

Small, T. (2011). What the hashtag? A content analysis of Canadian politics on Twitter. *Information, Communication & Society* 4 (6): 872–895.

Spyksma, H. (2019). Unintentional journalists: the role of advocacy group 350 in filling a news gap for reporting from the Pacific region. *Journalism Studies* 20 (1): 1–21.

Strauss, A. and Corbin, J. (1998). *Basics of Qualitative Research: Techniques and Procedures for Developing Grounded Theory.* Thousand Oaks, CA: Sage.

Tenenboim-Weinblatt, K. (2009). Jester, fake journalist, or the new Walter Lippmann? Recognition processes of Jon Stewart by the US journalistic community. *International Journal of Communication* 3: 416–439.

Twitter (n.d.). Twitter: live news, sports, and chat. Available from: https://itunes. apple.com/ca/app/twitter/id333903271?mt=8 (accessed November 28, 2019).

Usher, N. (2018). Breaking news production processes in US metropolitan newspapers: immediacy and journalistic authority. *Journalism* 19 (1): 21–36.

Vis, F. (2013). Twitter as a reporting tool for breaking news: journalists tweeting the 2011 UK riots. *Digital Journalism* 1 (1): 27–47.

Wahl-Jorgensen, K. (2016). Emotion and journalism. In: *The SAGE Handbook of Digital Journalism* (eds. T. Witschge, C. Anderson, D. Domingo and A. Hermida), 128–143. Thousand Oaks, CA: Sage.

Weigel, D. (2012). How "breaking news" broke the news. *Slate*. Available from: http://www.slate.com/articles/news_and_politics/politics/2012/04/cable_tv_and_ the_internet_have_destroyed_the_meaning_of_breaking_news_.html (accessed November 28, 2019).

Wimmer, R. and Dominick, J. (2013). *Mass Media Research: An Introduction*. Boston, MA: Wadsworth, Cengage Learning.

Zubiaga, A., Spina, D., Martínez, R., and Fresno, V. (2015). Real-time classification of Twitter trends. *Journal of the Association for Information Science and Technology* 66 (3): 462–473.

Part IV

Mobile News

8

Mobile News Apps as Ethnic Mediascapes

Introduction

This chapter examines the use of mobile news apps by transnational audiences in five English majority-speaking countries. It offers a unique theoretical insight into this aspect of audience news consumption by building on Arjun Appadurai's (1990, 1996) theory of reterritorialized transnationals and mediascapes. It argues that non-English mobile news apps offer a site for cultural consumption and a lively platform for connection and engagement, allowing immigrants to maintain the link with their original homelands and enhance their collective ethnic identity. Similar to social media, mobile news apps provide their audiences with opportunities to interact among themselves and with journalists, like a news comment section. Indeed, there are a few studies that have focused on mobile news apps in relation to transnational ethnic communities, though aggregate data taken from these apps has not been used in this context before. As Oscar Westlund recommends, more research on mobile news is needed in terms of "mixed approaches and methods, preferably aiming for cross-cultural comparisons rather than national studies" (2013, p. 22), and this chapter aims to fill the gap.

In general, news consumption today has become a highly networked, personalized, and individualized experience due to the prevalence of new technologies in "most parts of the world" (Ling and Horst 2011, p. 363). Aside from consuming news using computers, an increasing number of people access it via mobile devices like tablets and smartphones. According to a 2017 report by the Pew Research Center, over "eight-in-ten US adults now get news on a mobile device

---

This chapter was previously published as Al-Rawi, A. (2019). Mobile news apps as sites of transnational ethnic mediascapes. *Journal of International Communication*, 1 (19), available at: http://doi.org/10.1080/13216597.2019.1678506

News 2.0: Journalists, Audiences, and News on Social Media, First Edition. Ahmed Al-Rawi.
© 2020 John Wiley & Sons, Inc. Published 2020 by John Wiley & Sons, Inc.

(85%), compared with 72% just a year ago and slightly more than half in 2013 (54%)" (Lu 2017). In fact, older people aged above 65 years consume more news on mobile devices than any other age group (Bialik and Matsa 2017). Mobile devices seem to provide affordances and flexibility in the way news is consumed, with many people finding them appealing because they allow access to news anywhere and at multiple times a day (Wolf and Schnauber 2015; Molyneux 2018). Many people living in the global south do not have the financial means to subscribe to telephone landlines, so "the mobile phone has quietly provided people at the bottom of the income pyramid access to electronically mediated communication; often for the first time" (Ling and Horst 2011, p. 364). Though there are still differences between the global north and south in terms of using mobile technologies, we find a clear increasing rate of mobile use in the latter, according to public data retrieved from the International Telecommunication Union website (2018) (Figure 8.1). China, for instance, has "the world's largest number of mobile phone users" (Thussu 2007, p. 26).

To examine more evidence on mobile usage, I used Facebook Ads Manager to identify a number of mobile news consumption patterns. Out of 2.1 billion total Facebook users, 1.7 billion primarily access the platform using mobile devices. Meanwhile, 98.4% of the news consumed on Facebook along three selected categories (interests in newspaper, broadcasting, and magazine news) is accessed via mobile.[1] This clearly shows the popularity of mobile devices in news consumption around the world.

Theoretical Framework

Globalization and the convergence of new technologies are believed to bring people together. Indeed, "new information technologies ... enable the development of new forms of rapid social coordination and collective mobility" (Grieco and Urry 2011, p. 1). In this context, the term "globalization" has become an ambivalent concept due to its different and often opposing interpretations (Siapera 2012,

---

1 I made the following selections: Location – Worldwide; Interests – Entertainment – Reading (i) "Newspaper" and (ii) "Broadcasting News" and (iii) "News Magazine". The total number of audiences on Facebook who expressed interest in these subjects was 630 million users aged 18–65 years old. Then, I selected the following regarding audience behaviors: mobile device user – all mobile devices (620 million users). To look into some of the smaller details, I selected the following devices: tablets (100 million users), feature phones that are older than smartphones (2.7 million users), and new smartphones and tablets (40 million users). However, Facebook Ads Manager does not provide figures on the use of older smartphones, so it is not clear what the number of users is. Finally, the news selection shows that of 340 million news users, 54.8% are men and 45.1% are women.

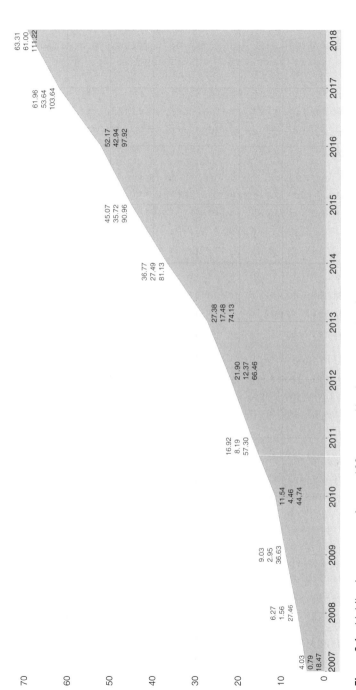

Figure 8.1 Mobile phone penetration per 100 persons. Numbers arranged as follows: bottom, developed countries; middle, developing countries; top, world. Ahmed Al-Rawi (2019) Mobile news apps as sites of transnational ethnic mediascapes, The Journal of International Communication, DOI: - 0.1080/13216597.2019.1678506. © Macquarie University reprinted by permission of Taylor & Francis Ltd, http://www.tandfonline.com on behalf of Macquarie University.

p. 24; Hesmondhalgh 2013, p. 273), but I define it here as the compression of the world and its ongoing global interconnectedness (Giddens 1990; Robertson 1992), which can be linked to the concept of cultural convergence and the increased sharing and exchange of knowledge and information. Regarding the influence of globalization, many scholars like Herbert Schiller (1975), Cees Hamelink (1983), and Sreberny-Mohammadi (1997) cite the concept of cultural imperialism to refer to the hegemonic Western cultural domination over peripheral countries and sub-cultures in the way cultural products such as news production, homogenization, and cultural synchronization are implemented and imposed, including the destruction of indigenous cultural values. These are some of the typical ways in which globalization from above functions, but new to the mix are Western-made social media platforms and mobile apps like Facebook, Twitter, WhatsApp, and Instagram that have become integral to peoples' lives across the globe. These cultural practices and products reflect the homogenization of the world as people everywhere seem to be consuming similar apps, websites, and other mass media outlets.

The rise of transnational immigration and the rapid use of new technologies, with their convergence and their affordances, have also assisted in what is known as globalization from below (Falk 2014), with transnational communities playing active roles in their countries of origin. In this regard, transnationalism is defined in the field of anthropology as "the processes by which immigrants forge and sustain multi-stranded social relations that link together their societies of origin and settlement. We call these processes transnationalism to emphasize that many immigrants today build social fields that cross geographic, cultural, and political borders ... An essential element is the multiplicity of involvements that transmigrants sustain in both home and host societies" (Basch et al. 1994, p. 6). Here, there are different pull-and-push cultural forces that shape the lives of transnationals, so there is divergence as well as convergence, which is linked to the processes of globalization from above and from below. In other words, local and global cultures are becoming equally influential in creating meaning for transnationals (Kearney 1995; Levitt 2003), leading to what is known as glocalization (Robertson 1997) or translocality ("being identified with more than one location," Oakes and Schein 2006, p. xiii). Glocalization refers to the varying influences of global and local cultures, whose cultural processes are greatly enhanced and intensified due to the "technological improvements in communications and transportation" (Portes 1997). There is obvious convergence in the way people are globally using the same mobile devices and sometimes the same apps, but there is obvious divergence as well, with people using these technologies in different ways to serve different needs, and with some apps being unique to certain transnational and ethnic communities.

Regarding international news flows, Lisbeth Clausen contends that they are "both affected by globalisation trends and [are themselves] an agent of their ideological influence" (2010, p. 134). Daya Thussu notes that there are both global and contra-flows (which include local and regional ones), and argues that the "media and communication contra-flows can shape cultural identities, energise disempowered groups, and help create political coalitions and new transnational private and public spheres" (2007, p. 3). These contra-flows often originate from the "peripheries of global media industries, designated 'subaltern flows'" (Thussu 2007, p. 4). The same argument applies to non-Western mobile news apps, because they assist in globalization from below by disseminating news from peripheral countries. This is regarded as contra-news flows, which mostly provide different narratives than what is routinely found in the global news flow. However, there is little literature on news flows on mobile apps since "news consumption via mobile devices is still a relatively restricted phenomenon" due to the interpersonal and private aspect of mobile phone use (Jansson and Lindell 2015, p. 85).

In this regard, Arjun Appadurai (1990) asserts that the global configuration of technoscape "moves at high speeds across various kinds of previously impervious boundaries" because it is not confined to one territory alone. Globalization from below is also reflected in the increasing popularity of ethnic food, music, fashion, and media consumption habits in most Western countries. As Appadurai (1996) emphasizes, transmigrants create "mediascapes" or "global ethnoscapes," making their users "transnations" that are reterritorialized through the use of media, including mobile communication technologies. An ethnoscape is defined here as a "landscape of persons who constitute the shifting world in which we live" (Appadurai 1990, p. 297), while mediascapes refer to the:

> distribution of the electronic capabilities to produce and disseminate information ... which are now available to a growing number of private and public interests throughout the world; and to the images of the world created by these media. These images of the world involve many complicated inflections, depending on their mode (documentary or entertainment), their hardware (electronic or pre-electronic), their audiences (local, national or transnational) and the interests of those who own and control them. What is most important about these mediascapes is that they provide (especially in their television, film and cassette forms) large and complex repertoires of images, narratives and "ethnoscapes" to viewers throughout the world, in which the world of commodities and the world of "news" and politics are profoundly mixed.
>
> (Appadurai 1990, pp. 298–299)

Appadurai's account was written about three decades ago, so it is relevant now to include mobile news apps as part of these mediascapes, whose software is designed, produced, and used by many people in non-Western countries. As users of ethnic news media apps, such people can interact on these mediascapes or digital cultural platforms wherever they go (Goggin 2011), making them transnationals and shifting the main node from the centralized English-language Western world and its hegemonic control into the global and wider network (Appadurai 1996). These news apps also empower transnationals because they tie them to their ancestral roots and assist in maintaining their collective cultural identity. Many peripheral countries like India, Brazil, and Singapore are presently producing several important apps in different sectors, though they are still placed in the "informal economies" sector since they are not as regulated as those made in the Western world (Goggin 2012, p. 308; Kshetri 2017). In this regard, Jonathan Donner (2015, pp. 162–166) refers to the challenges app developers in the global south face and lists several factors that limit or restrain their productivity, including infrastructural issues (Sheller 2015); still, many producers succeed in driving profit and making their apps prosper.

Here, Appadurai (1996) stresses that the Western world is no longer the focal point, but merely another node in the wider transnational network. This is especially true given the increasing popularity of mobile news apps, which are readily available for anyone anywhere in the world who owns a smartphone and has an Internet connection. Though these transnationals, or what Karim Karim (2018) calls diasporic transnational nomads, do not reside in their original territorial borders, they still occupy them indirectly via their use of mass media outlets including mobile apps, which allow them to maintain their cultural roots and assert their collective ethnic identity. In this sense, the apps become sites of collective cultural expression and practice that resist the hegemonic Western culture, forming the nucleus of globalization from below. Transnationals often seek "cultural sites" (Olwig 1997) to express themselves and compensate for the lack of physical contact with their original homelands. As Homi Bhabha (1994) suggests, these diasporic sites are considered a third space, following the first and second spaces represented by the home and original countries. To borrow Benedict Anderson's (1983) imagined communities concept, I argue here that even if these spaces and communities are imaginary ones, they remain important in many aspects, mainly because of their impact on ethnic and collective identity. In this regard, Oiarzabal and Reips (2012) emphasize that the study of diaspora and communication in the age of social media and mobile Internet requires continuous revision because of the rapid changes occurring in that space. If one takes into account the continuous production of new mobile apps, this rings even more true. John Urry (2012, p. 75) asserts that new technologies allow "virtual travel" or mobility in order to maintain bonds with and proximity to one's ethnic community and original homeland, especially as various new communication tools "can in different ways substitute for physical transportation" (Urry 2002, p. 256).

Mobile News Apps as Cultural Sites

There is no doubt there is a great lack of literature on mobile app use among immigrant, racial, and minority groups (Marchi 2017, p. 192). In the United States, for example, minority youth are "engaged with mobile devices and social media, with Hispanic, Black, and Asian youth spending significantly more time on mobile devices than White youth" (Marchi 2017, p. 191). Further, studies on ethnic media in different Western countries are generally limited to traditional media (Black and Leithner 1988b; Ojo 2006) and are almost exclusively ethnographic or theoretical in nature. Dalia Abdelhady (2011), for instance, conducted interviews with Lebanese immigrants living in the diaspora, including in Montreal, New York, and Paris, to better understand how Lebanese immigrants defined their identities and kept the link with Lebanon. However, she does not mention mobile apps except in a few references to the role of social media in maintaining the connection. Hang Yin, furthermore, studied the Chinese diaspora in New Zealand and makes a passing reference to mobile apps in a footnote, stating: "Chinese immigrants around the world can now access the digital version of all the major newspapers in China … through CNTV's (China Network Television) desktop application and mobile apps … in real time" (2015, p. 570). Also, Regina Marchi (2017) interviewed 30 poor Latino immigrant youth in Boston, examining the way they use mobile devices for newsgathering and analysis. She mentions that these youth had more up-to-date and diverse news than their parents, calling them "news translators" because they identified, critiqued, and posted online content, giving them greater civic engagement roles than older immigrant generations. Finally, Kyong Yoon (2018) examined the digital media habits of 22 young Korean-Canadians living in Toronto and found that many of them used the Korean-made messaging app KakaoTalk for socialization with other Korean-Canadians in Canada rather than consuming news. Here, the app functions like a private cultural site for communication. As one respondent affirmed: "I like the name; it's really cute. I like that it's Korean made. I know for sure if I want to talk to Koreans, they mostly have it. It's exclusive, but it's mostly inclusive to Koreans. So, I like that" (Yoon 2018, p. 155). To sum up, there are only a few ethnographic studies that focus on transnational ethnic communities' use of mobile apps, since the majority are related to traditional media outlets.

In this context, one needs to examine the existing literature on the consumption of traditional ethnic media, because non-English mobile news apps can be categorized as a form of ethnic media though they are often transnational in nature. Ethnic media are generally defined as ethnic-language media produced by an ethnic group that reside in a receiving country to serve their information needs (Johnson 2000; Georgiou 2001; Shi 2009). However, this is not a fixed definition, because there is also ethnic media produced in English (Yu 2018), and many outlets are regional or transnational in scope due to the affordances of new media technologies. In reference to Korean immigrants, Youan Kim mentions the importance of these outlets since "the mediated networks established through the Internet and the transnational ethnic media ... allow dispersed yet networked migrants to maintain transnationally their home-based relationships and to regulate a dialectical sense of belonging in host countries" (2017, p. 279). In general, ethnic media offer the following services: (i) provide basic information that is vital to civic engagement; (ii) preserve ethnic culture; (iii) unite and strengthen the sense of ethnic community; and (iv) offer an alternative voice. Indeed, the relevant literature can be summed up in two main trends: the integrative approach, which stipulates that ethnic media can help in integrating ethnic and minority groups into the mainstream culture by fostering social cohesion and cultural maintenance (Black and Leithner 1988a; Riggins 1992; Melkote and Liu 2000; Fleras and Lock Kunz 2001; Matsaganis et al. 2011; Ramasubramanian 2016) or in enhancing the public sphere due to their role in encouraging debates on different issues that are relevant to these ethnic groups (Husband 2005); and the non-integrative approach, which claims that ethnic media can have a divisive role by leading to further alienation of minority groups from the mainstream culture (Deuze 2006; Wilson et al. 2012). As already mentioned, the problem is that this definition of "ethnic media" is static because it assumes such media are produced only in a receiving country, which ignores the new reality, in which apps can be in English as well as an ethnic language (see Table 8.1) and are often regional or transnational in scope; this diffusion of news is often missing in the literature.

Non-English Mobile News Apps

There is a lack of available data on mobile news apps, since news organizations do not offer data on their audience's engagement with their apps. This has created a blind spot for academic researchers. Further, app stores provide a ranking of the top free and paid apps based on different categories like games, entertainment, and news for the country where a user is situated; hence, it is not possible to have an overview of the top apps in other countries. As a result, I had to find alternative sources of data, which is why I chose to use SimilarWeb, which provides updated statistics on the use of mobile devices on the Google Play and Apple Stores (see Table 8.1). Based on their usage rank, the algorithm takes into account "current installs" and "active users" in a selected country, category (in our case, mobile news apps), and leader board for the last 28 days. Apps whose names are written in non-English languages were selected, while English-language non-Western apps like the Chinese CCTV-Global edition, Sputnik, and Al Jazeera English were not included, except for a few exceptions that clearly indicate the language or

Table 8.1 Selection of the top 100 news apps used in five majority English-speaking countries.

USA – PS	USA – AS	UK – PS	UK – AS	Australia – PS	Australia – AS	Canada – PS	Canada – AS	New Zealand – PS	New Zealand – AS
Yahoo! JAPAN ニュースにスポーツ、検索、天気まで。地震や大雨などの災害・防災情報も	今日头条	Apple Daily 蘋果動新聞	彭博商業周刊繁體中文版 Bloomberg Businessweek	News by The Times of India Newspaper – Latest News	今日头条	Apple Daily 蘋果動新聞	今日头条	腾讯新闻	今日头条
Apple Daily 蘋果動新聞	腾讯新闻-事实派的热点资讯娱乐短视频软件	Polish Express News	今日头条	Yahoo! JAPAN ニュースにスポーツ、検索、天気まで。地震や大雨などの災害・防災情報も	今日澳洲-华人生活服务信息类 app	网易新闻	腾讯新闻-事实派的热点资讯娱乐短视频软件	無綫新聞	腾讯新闻-事实资讯派的热点资讯娱乐短视频软件
	NewsPicks（ニュースピックス）	Onet – wiadomości, pogoda, sport	EL PAÍS	NDTV News – India	腾讯新闻-事实派的热点资讯娱乐短视频软件	東網 – 東方日報	UC浏览器 - 免流头条新闻资讯的浏览器	头条视频	新浪新闻-热门新闻头条抢先看
		NDTV News – India	腾讯新闻-事实资讯的热点娱乐短视频软件	腾讯新闻	UC浏览器 - 免流量看头条新闻资讯的浏览器	文学城 - Wenxuecity.com	星島新聞 (加拿大版)		凤凰新闻-有料的热点资讯、娱乐短视频
		Gazeta.pl LIVE Wiadomości	らぶっ!	detikcom – Berita Terbaru & Terlengkap	新浪财经-股市股票金融头条新闻	加国无忧	新浪新闻热门新闻头条抢先看		ブログまとめニュース速報 for ユニクロ (UNIQLO)

(Continued)

Table 8.1 (Continued)

USA – PS	USA – AS	UK – PS	UK – AS	Australia – PS	Australia – AS	Canada – PS	Canada – AS	New Zealand – PS	New Zealand – AS
		Jagbani Punjabi App	Le Monde, l'info en continu	The Hindu: English News Today, Current Latest News	BÁO MỚI: Đọc Báo, Tin Mới 24h	星島新聞 (加拿大版)	趣头条 - 头条新闻热点资讯阅读平台		無綫新聞
		NAIJ – Nigeria Latest News & Popular News Free App	RTÉ News Now	Apple Daily 蘋果動新聞	网易新闻 - 热点新闻报道 头条资讯概览	今日头条(新闻阅读)	华尔街见闻-财经资讯头条新闻		中国新闻 - 合成最新消息
		Delfi.lt	ARY NEWS URDU	知乎日报 每日提供高质量新闻资讯	SydneyThai ซิดนีย์ไทย	Yahoo 新聞 – 香港即時焦點	NewsPicks (ニュースピックス)		地震予測プラス
		Interia – Fakty, Pogoda, Sport	Nabd نبض الأخبار العالم، عاجل	Gujarati News/ Samachar – Divya Bhaskar	mtv Al Lubhaniya	Gujarati News/ Samachar – Divya Bhaskar	新浪财经-股市股票金融头条新闻		新闻大连
		腾讯新闻		明報新聞	华尔街见闻-财经资讯头条新闻	NDTV News – India	天天快报 -腾讯兴趣阅读平台		ولایات و اردو
		الجزيرة		South China Morning Post	凤凰新闻-有料的热点资讯、娱乐短视频	台灣蘋果日報			UC浏览器–免流量看头条新闻资讯的浏览器
		网易新闻		今日悉尼	蘋果動新聞	天天快报·年度成长最快的个性阅读智能推荐资讯软件			趣头条 - 头条新闻热点资讯阅读平台
				Jagbani Punjabi App	凤凰视频·精选全球头条新闻的短视频平台	Yahoo! JAPAN ニュースにスポーツ、検索、天気まで。地震や大雨などの災害・防災情報も			

USA – PS	USA – AS	UK – PS	UK – AS	Australia – PS	Australia – AS	Canada – PS	Canada – AS	New Zealand – PS	New Zealand – AS
				Yahoo 新聞 – 香港即時焦點	和讯财经-22年财经新闻软件	新浪新闻			
				ZAKER-扎客新聞	澳洲悠悠网	Jagbani Punjabi App			
				今日头条(新闻阅读)	新浪新闻-热门新闻头条抢先看	ZAKER-扎客新聞 الاخبار			
				文学城 – Wenxuecity.com	NDTV				
					外交部12308	腾讯新闻			
					趣头条 - 头条新闻热点资讯阅读平台	壹週刊			
					الاخبار	Hespress هسبريس			
					1688澳洲-澳洲留学租房工作第一资讯	頭條日報			
					BBS澳洲	Now 新聞 - 24小時直播			
						Aaj Tak Live TV News – Latest			
						Hindi News India			
						Ajit			

Data collected on October 15, 2018. PS, Google Play Store; AS, Apple Store.

Ahmed Al-Rawi (2019) Mobile news apps as sites of transnational ethnic mediascapes, The Journal of International Communication, DOI: 10.1080/13216597.2019.1678506. © Macquarie University reprinted by permission of Taylor & Francis Ltd, http://www.tandfonline.com on behalf of Macquarie University national scope, such as Ary News Urdu and Polish Express News. This was done because non-transnational communities might also consume the same news outlets.

The five majority English-speaking countries selected were the United States, United Kingdom, New Zealand, Canada, and Australia. According to figures provided by the International Organization of Migration (IOM) in 2018, these countries have welcomed many immigrants from around the world. For instance, between 2000 and 2016, the United States, Canada, Australia, and the United Kingdom were the top four countries in the world in terms of admitting and resettling refugees (IOM 2018, p. 35), as well as skilled immigrants coming from diverse places. As of 2015, the majority of immigrants in Australia, for example, come from China, India, Vietnam, and the Philippines (IOM 2018, p. 90). Another important indication is the number of foreign-born people living in these countries. In this regard, the United States has the highest number of foreign-born people in the world, increasing from "less than 12 million in 1970, to 46.6 million in 2015" (IOM 2018, p. 18). About 28% of Australians and 23% of New Zealanders are foreign-born as of the end of June 2016 (IOM 2018, pp. 90 and 87), while Canada has the seventh-largest number of foreign-born residents at just over 20% as of 2015 (IOM 2018, p. 83).

Table 8.1 shows the popularity of different mobile apps in the five selected countries. Australia seems to be ahead of the others along Play and Android non-English news apps, while Canada comes second in terms of Play Store apps. The United States has the lowest number of non-English news apps among the top 100 in comparison to the other selected countries. The top languages used include Chinese, Japanese, Arabic, Vietnamese, Indonesian, Polish, French, Thai, Lithuanian, Punjabi, Gujarati, and Hindi. In addition, a couple of apps are categorized as news, though they offer other services like information on jobs in Arabic (وظائف - أي وظيفة) and earthquake predictions in Japanese (地震予測プラス). This is expected, as a number of social media apps, like Twitter, are also classified as news apps. Generally speaking, the most popular language in all the top news apps among the five selected countries is Chinese. According to IOM's 2015 figures, "Chinese-born international migrants were the fourth largest foreign-born population in the world after Indians, Mexicans and Russians, with nearly 10 million Chinese migrants living outside of China" (2018, pp. 59–60). In addition, Chinese and Indian students are the top two groups of international student migrants in the world (IOM 2018, p. 321). These immigration figures provide an explanation for the popularity of Chinese news apps in the five countries examined. Following Chinese, a number of Indian/Pakistani languages and Japanese come second and third due to the high number of immigrants from these countries.

As suggested by Light et al., I partly followed the apps walkthrough method, which examines, among many other aspects, an app's "embedded cultural meanings and implied ideal users and uses" and provides some "interpretative aspects" that are "underpinned by specific theoretical frameworks" (2018, pp. 881 and 882). Since many apps were identified in the first stage of the study, and due to a lack of space, only the top ones from each country are examined here. I used Google Translate, installed as part of the Chrome browser, for any non-English news app.

In this regard, the top news app on the Apple Store in the United States, Australia, Canada, and New Zealand is a Chinese one called 今日头条 (www. toutiao.com), which exclusively provides national Chinese news reports and updates, with sections on educational, financial, and technology news updates. As for the United Kingdom, the top news app is another Chinese one called 彭博商業周刊繁體中文版 (www.bbwhk.com), or Bloomberg BusinessWeek, which is linked to the American *Bloomberg* magazine and is described as "an international business magazine tailored for the Greater China business elite."

There are a few variations found in the top apps in the Google Play Store. For example, the top app in the United States is ュースにスポーツ、検索、天気まで。地震や大雨などの災害・防災情報も or Yahoo! Japan, which includes news updates on a variety of Japanese events, especially breaking news on "disaster information and disaster prevention information," including "earthquakes, tsunamis, [and] typhoons." In the United Kingdom and Canada, the top app is a Hong Kong-based Chinese news platform called 蘋果動新聞 or Apple Daily (hk.video. appledaily.com), which provides updated news mostly on Hong Kong, while the top app in Australia is the English-language Times of India (www.timesofindia. indiatimes.com), which exclusively offers news on India, including politics, sports, and entertainment. Lastly, the top news app in New Zealand is a Chinese one called 腾讯新闻 (www.news.qq.com), which is connected to the famous Chinese instant messaging app QQ. Again, it provides exclusive news on mainland China, mostly regarding politics. In brief, all of the top apps mentioned here provide national and local updated news from non-Western countries, constituting contra-flows of news disseminated from peripheral regions in the world. They present alternative narratives to the coverage of global news channels.

The accounts just given have deeper theoretical implications in relation to the cultural practices of transmigrants, whether they be first-, second-, or subsequent-generation immigrants. As previously stated, mobile news apps are sites of cultural expression (Olwig 1997) and venues for connection and possible interaction with immigrants' original homelands, showing the need to maintain older cultural roots. Also, these transnationals' mediascapes function as deterritorialized third spaces (Appadurai 1990; Bhabha 1994), for space and physical presence are secondary, while consumption of mobile news apps becomes the primary bridge and a means of "virtual travel" (Urry 2002) toward the transnationals' original homelands. Here, news consumption is a reflection of globalization from below and a way of expressing resistance against the hegemony of Western mainstream media (MSM) and culture, which routinely practices globalization from above. There are different information flows taking place at the same time, and Youna Kim rightly observes that "the rise in multi-directional flows of digital media, information, and communication technologies ... parallel[s] people's transnational mobility for creating new conditions of identity formation in digital diaspora" (2016, p. 69). In addition, the consumption of these mobile news apps offers opportunities for socialization with like-minded people and with transmigrants from the same community.

Conclusion

Whether integrative or not, it is important to study transnational ethnic media because of their vital role in cultural maintenance and societal impact. Chinese ethnic media outlets in Australia, for example, have been exploited by a number of political parties especially during election times, as they "have been particularly sensitive to multicultural and multiracial policy debates, especially on topics and issues that potentially threaten the Chinese community's own political and economic interests, or challenge their cultural values and traditions" (Sun 2007, pp. 55–56). There is no doubt that transnational ethnic media can be a form of alternative media that is complementary to MSM since they are part of the convergence culture in what Annabelle Sreberny-Mohammadi (2005) calls "not only, but also." In other words, alternative media provide a complementary perspective to what is already covered in MSM. Transnational ethnic media, or alternative journalism, attempt to change the hierarchy of access to news (Philo 2014) by focusing on the ethnic group rather than those who are powerful. This is achieved in the way different media platforms provide an outlet to highlight the important issues relevant to specific ethnic groups (Franklin and Murphy 1998), which aim at reterritorializing and re-embedding their identities by consuming transnational ethnic media. As Karim Karim mentions, "Displaced from their homelands, [transmigarants] find ethnicity as the necessary place or space from which they can speak and counteract dominant discourses" (2007, p. 102).

In brief, globalization from above is manifested in a variety of ways, including the homogenization of the world and its convergence in terms of news production and consumption (Schiller 1975; Hamelink 1983; Sreberny-Mohammadi 1997); however, there is also divergence as the increasing number of transnational immigrants in Western countries and elsewhere participate in the process of globalization from below, partly due to the way these immigrant communities use new technologies to stay connected and maintain their cultural links to their original homelands. These transmigrants shape reterritorialized mediascapes, whereby mobile news apps become cultural sites that remind them of their ancestral roots and help them in enhancing their collective ethnic identity. Unlike previous studies on news flows, which focus on traditional media like TV, newspaper, and radio channels, this chapter proposes that ethnic mobile news apps have become part of a contra-flow of news that often resists the hegemonic control and dominance of Western news media, or what is known as the global news flow. I argue that due to the general characteristics of news apps, they can even be more effective than traditional ethnic media, for several reasons. First, mobile devices are personalized and customized based on the user's individual preferences, so they can become more engaging. Second, news can be easily viewed anytime, as long as there is an Internet connection, especially now that devices can be carried anywhere, making mobile news far more accessible than traditional media. Third, news is often more affordable than with traditional media, which mostly requires paid subscriptions. In addition, mobile news can provide faster updates than news from traditional newspapers, especially in relation to updates on natural disasters. Finally, mobile news is often interactive and is mostly packaged in appealing ways, including multimedia formats like video, colored images, and text that can be easily adjusted, unlike traditional media. In other words, mobile news can be more engaging than traditional news, and can be beneficial in creating a vigorous public sphere. As Matthew Hindman puts it, "being boring can be nearly as damaging to the goal of an informed public as being wrong" (2017, p. 190).

In terms of future research on mobile news apps, ethnographic research is still paramount, and it is important to empirically examine transnationals' news consumption habits by conducting cross-national surveys to investigate how engaged they are and how often they consume mobile news, as well as their news sources. The overall objective here is to understand the influence of global and contra news flows on these transnationals' lives. Other quantitative approaches involving big data and computational social sciences are also urgently needed. Yet, most mobile apps cannot be accessed by researchers with modest knowledge in data science due to technical difficulties, financial constraints, privacy issues, and mobile companies' interests in protecting their metadata. It is not easy, for example, to access the BBC and CNN's news apps and retrieve metadata as one can with their websites (Dylko et al. 2012; Larsson 2013). Some news organizations offer data science and digital journalism researchers access to their mobile app data, but not all scholars have such access due to lack of connection or geographical distance, something that Arjun Appadurai calls the "academic digital divide" (2016, p. 8). In other words, there are many difficulties facing digital journalism and media scholars, especially those living in poor countries in the third world, because of the lack of access to these news organizations and their mobile platforms. This is unfortunate, as many researchers in these regions have local insights that are invaluable to the study of transnational communities and their mobile news app use. Also, Facebook's Ads Manager remains an interesting and under-researched means of studying Facebook audiences, because it allows one to identify minute details regarding their behaviors, interests, educational background, habits, and types of mobile device and operating system, among other things. It is important to conduct cross-national comparative studies on the ways transmigrants use mobile news apps and whether these apps assist in cultural integration in the receiving countries or whether they even exert any political or democratic influence in their original homelands.

References

Abdelhady, D. (2011). *The Lebanese Diaspora: The Arab Immigrant Experience in Montreal*. New York: NYU Press.

Anderson, B. (1983). *Imagined Communities: Reflections on the Origin and Spread of Nationalism*. London: Verso.

Appadurai, A. (1990). Disjuncture and difference in the global cultural economy. *Theory, Culture & Society* 7 (2–3): 295–310.

Appadurai, A. (1996). *Modernity at Large: Cultural Dimensions of Globalization*. Minneapolis, MN: University of Minnesota Press.

Appadurai, A. (2016). The academic digital divide and uneven global development. In: *The 2015 PARGC Distinguished Lecture in Global Communication*. Available from: https://www.asc.upenn.edu/sites/default/files/documents/0106_15_PARGC_Paper4_FINAL.pdf (accessed November 28, 2019).

Basch, L.G., Glick Schilier, N., and Blanc-Szanton, C. (1994). *Nations Unbound: Transnational Projects, Post-colonial Predicaments, and De-terrirorialized Nation-States*. Langhorne, PA: Gordon and Breach.

Bhabha, H. (1994). The postcolonial and the postmodern. In: H. Bhabha, ed. *The Location of Culture*. London: Routledge, p. 172.

Bialik, K. and Matsa, K.E. (2017). Key trends in social and digital news media. *Pew Research Center*. Available from: http://www.pewresearch.org/fact-tank/2017/10/04/key-trends-in-social-and-digital-news-media (accessed November 28, 2019).

Black, J.H. and Leithner, C. (1988a). Immigrants and political involvement in Canada: the role of the ethnic media. *Canadian Ethnic Studies/Etudes Ethniques au Canada* 20 (1).

Black, J.H. and Leithner, C. (1988b). Patterns of ethnic media consumption: a comparative examination of ethnic groupings in Toronto. *Canadian Ethnic Studies/Etudeséthniques au Canada* 19 (1): 21–39.

Clausen, L. (2010). International news flow. In: *The Routledge Companion to News and Journalism* (ed. A. Stuart), 127–136. London: Routledge.

Deuze, M. (2006). Ethnic media, community media and participatory culture. *Journalism* 7 (3): 262–280.

Donner, J. (2015). *After Access: Inclusion, Development, and a More Mobile Internet*. Cambridge, MA: MIT Press.

Dylko, I.B., Beam, M.A., Landreville, K.D., and Geidner, N. (2012). Filtering 2008 US presidential election news on YouTube by elites and nonelites: an examination of the democratizing potential of the internet. *New Media & Society* 14 (5): 832–849.

Falk, R. (2014). Globalization-from-below: an innovative politics of resistance. In: *Civilizing Globalization, Revised and Expanded Edition: A Survival Guide* (eds. R. Sandbrook and A. Güven), 151–172. New York: Suny Press.

Fleras, A. and Lock Kunz, J. (2001). *Media and Minorities: Representing Diversity in a Multicultural Canada*. Toronto, ON: Thompson Educational.

Franklin, B. and Murphy, D. (1998). *Making the Local News: Local Journalism in Context*. London: Psychology Press.

Georgiou, M. (2001). Crossing the boundaries of the ethnic home. *International Communication Gazette* 63 (4): 311–329.

Giddens, A. (1990). *The Consequences of Modernity*. Stanford, CA: Stanford University Press.

Goggin, G. (2011). Ubiquitous apps: politics of openness in global mobile cultures. *Digital Creativity* 22 (3): 148–159.

Goggin, G. (2012). Driving the internet: mobile internets, cars, and the social. *Future Internet* 4 (1): 306–321.

Grieco, M. and Urry, J. (2011). Introduction: introducing the mobilities turn. In: *Mobilities: New Perspectives on Transport and Society* (eds. M. Grieco and J. Urry), 1–2. London: Routledge.

Hamelink, C. (1983). *Cultural Autonomy in Global Communications*. London: Longman.

Hesmondhalgh, D. (2013). *The Cultural Industries*. Thousand Oaks, CA: Sage.

Hindman, M. (2017). Journalism ethics and digital audience data. In: *Remaking the News: Essays on the Future of Journalism Scholarship in the Digital Age* (eds. P.J. Boczkowski and C.W. Anderson). Cambridge, MA: MIT Press.

Husband, C. (2005). Minority ethnic media as communities of practice: professionalism and identity politics in interaction. *Journal of Ethnic and Migration Studies* 31 (3): 461–479.

International Telecommunication Union (2018). Statistics. Available from: https://www.itu.int/en/ITU-D/Statistics/Documents/statistics/2018/ITU_Key_2005-2018_ICT_data_with%20LDCs_rev27Nov2018.xls (accessed November 28, 2019).

IOM (2018). World Migration Report 2018. Available from: https://publications.iom.int/system/files/pdf/wmr_2018_en.pdf (accessed November 28, 2019).

Jansson, A. and Lindell, J. (2015). News media consumption in the transmedia age: amalgamations, orientations and geo-social structuration. *Journalism Studies* 16 (1): 79–96.

Johnson, M. (2000). How ethnic are US ethnic media: the case of Latina magazines. *Mass Communication and Society* 3 (2–3): 229–248.

Karim, K. (2007). Nation and diaspora: rethinking multiculturalism in a transnational context. *International Journal of Media & Cultural Politics* 2 (3): 267–282.

Karim, K. (2018). Migration, diaspora and communication. In: *Diaspora and Media in Europe* (eds. K. Karim and A. Al-Rawi), 1–23. London: Palgrave Macmillan.

Kearney, M. (1995). The local and the global: the anthropology of globalization and transnationalism. *Annual Review of Anthropology* 24: 547–565.

Kim, Y. (2016). Digital diaspora, mobility, and home. In: *Routledge Handbook of East Asian Popular Culture* (eds. K. Iwabuchi, E. Tsai and C. Berry), 69–80. London: Routledge.

Kim, Y. (2017). The Korean Wave: Korean popular culture in a digital cosmopolitan world. In: *Routledge Handbook of Korean Culture and Society* (ed. Y. Kim), 269–282. London: Routledge.

Kshetri, N. (2017). The economics of the Internet of Things in the global south. *Third World Quarterly* 38 (2): 311–339.

Larsson, A. (2013). Staying in or going out? Assessing the linking practices of Swedish online newspapers. *Journalism Practice* 7 (6): 738–754.

Levitt, P. (2003). Keeping feet in both worlds: transnational practices and immigrant incorporation. In: *Integrating Immigrants in Liberal Nation-States: From Post-Nationals to Transnational* (eds. E. Joppke and E. Morawska), 177–194. London: Palgrave-Macmillan.

Light, B., Burgess, J., and Duguay, S. (2018). The walkthrough method: an approach to the study of apps. *New Media & Society* 20 (3): 881–900.

Ling, R. and Horst, H.A. (2011). Mobile communication in the global south. *New Media & Society* 13: 363–374.

Lu, K. (2017). Growth in mobile news use driven by older adults. Pew Research Center. Available from: http://www.pewresearch.org/fact-tank/2017/06/12/growth-in-mobile-news-use-driven-by-older-adults (accessed November 28, 2019).

Marchi, R. (2017). News translators: Latino immigrant youth, social media, and citizenship training. *Journalism & Mass Communication Quarterly* 94 (1): 189–212.

Matsaganis, M.D., Katz, V.S., and Ball-Rokeach, S.J. (2011). *Understanding Ethnic Media: Producers, Consumers, and Societies*. Thousand Oaks, CA: Sage.

Melkote, S. and Liu, D. (2000). The role of the Internet in forging a pluralistic integration: a study of Chinese intellectuals in the United States. *Gazette* 62 (6): 495–504.

Molyneux, L. (2018). Mobile news consumption: a habit of snacking. *Digital Journalism* 6 (5): 634–650.

Oakes, T. and Schein, L. (2006). Preface. In: *Translocal China: Linkages, Identities, and the Reimaging of Space* (eds. T. Oakes and L. Schein), xii–xiii. London: Routledge.

Oiarzabal, P.J. and Reips, U.-D. (2012). Migration and diaspora in the age of information and communication technologies. *Journal of Ethnic and Migration Studies* 38 (9): 1333–1338.

Ojo, T. (2006). Ethnic print media in the multicultural nation of Canada. *Journalism* 7 (3): 343–361.

Olwig, K. (1997). Cultural sites: sustaining a home in a deterritorialized world. In: *Siting Culture: The Shifting Anthropological Object* (eds. K. Olwig and K. Hastrup), 17–38. London: Routledge.

Philo, G. (2014). *The Glasgow Media Group Reader, Vol. II: Industry, Economy, War and Politics*. London: Routledge.

Portes, A. (1997). Globalization from Below: The Rise of Transnational Communities. Oxford: ESRC Transnational Communities Working Paper WPTC-98-01.

Ramasubramanian, S. (2016). Racial/ethnic identity, community-oriented media initiatives, and transmedia storytelling. *The Information Society* 32 (5): 333–342.

Riggins, S. (ed.) (1992). *Ethnic Minority Media: An International Perspective*, vol. 13. Thousand Oaks, CA: Sage.

Robertson, R. (1992). *Globalization: Social Theory and Global Culture*, vol. 16. Thousand Oaks, CA: Sage.

Robertson, R. (1997). Glocalization: time–space and homogeneity–heterogeneity. In: *Global Modernities* (eds. M. Featherstone, S. Lash and R. Robertson), 25–43. Thousand Oaks, CA: Sage.

Siapera, E. (2012). *Understanding New Media*. Thousand Oaks, CA: Sage.

Schiller, H. (1975). Communication and cultural domination. *International Journal of Politics* 5 (4): 1–127.

Sheller, M. (2015). News now: interface, ambience, flow, and the disruptive spatio-temporalities of mobile news media. *Journalism Studies* 16 (1): 12–26.

Shi, Y. (2009). Re-evaluating the "alternative" role of ethnic media in the US: the case of Chinese language press and working-class women readers. *Media, Culture & Society* 31 (4): 597–616.

Sreberny, A. (2005). "Not only, but also": mixedness and media. *Journal of Ethnic and Migration Studies* 31 (3): 443–459.

Sreberny-Mohammadi, A. (1997). The many cultural faces of imperialism. In: *Beyond Cultural Imperialism Globalization, Communication and the New International Order* (eds. P. Golding and P. Harris), 49–68. Thousand Oaks, CA: Sage.

Sun, W. (2007). Chinese-Language Media in Australia: Developments, Challenges and Opportunities. The Australia–China Relations Institute (ACRI). Available from: https://opus.lib.uts.edu.au/bitstream/10453/100651/1/1609%20Australia-China%20Relations%20Institute%20Publication%20-%20Chinese-language%20

media%20in%20Australia%20Developments,%20challenges%20and%20
opportunities.pdf (accessed November 28, 2019).

Thussu, D. (2007). Mapping global media flow and contra-flow. In: *Media on the Move: Mapping Global Flow and Contra-Flow* (ed. D. Thussu), 10–29. London: Routledge.

Urry, J. (2002). Mobility and proximity. *Sociology* 36 (2): 255–274.

Urry, J. (2012). *Sociology Beyond Societies: Mobilities for the Twenty-First Century*. London: Routledge.

Westlund, O. (2013). Mobile news: a review and model of journalism in an age of mobile media. *Digital Journalism* 1 (1): 6–26.

Wilson, C.C. II, Gutierrez, F., and Chao, L. (2012). *Racism, Sexism, and the Media: Multicultural Issues into the New Communications Age*. London: Sage.

Wolf, C. and Schnauber, A. (2015). News consumption in the mobile era: the role of mobile devices and traditional journalism's content within the user's information repertoire. *Digital Journalism* 3 (5): 759–776.

Yin, H. (2015). Chinese-language cyberspace, homeland media and ethnic media: a contested space for being Chinese. *New Media & Society* 17 (4): 556–572.

Yoon, K. (2018). Multicultural digital media practices of 1.5-generation Korean immigrants in Canada. *Asian and Pacific Migration Journal* 27 (2): 148–165.

Yu, S. (2018). Multi-ethnic public sphere and accessible ethnic media: mapping online English-language ethnic media. *Journal of Ethnic and Migration Studies* 44 (11): 1976–1993.

Index

News 2.0: Journalists, Audiences, and News on Social Media, First Edition. Ahmed Al-Rawi.
© 2020 John Wiley & Sons, Inc. Published 2020 by John Wiley & Sons, Inc.